Praise for Chris Campanioni

"He is Frank O'Hara traveling the hyper-connected contemporary landscape via iPhone—spawning, recording, discarding speculative versions of himself . . . He carries his Situationism between cities, between countries, between periods in his life without rest or regard for boundaries. Campanioni isn't playing at being clever; he is erasing himself to locate the sublime." — The Brooklyn Rail

"Campanioni's writing is playful, unflinching . . . a much-needed reminder of our endless potential for duality, in a world that too often suggests only polarity is possible." — Harvard Review

"Award-winning author Chris Campanioni may, for better or worse, be the voice of our generation in which the internet is our stomping ground and making eye contact with our friends and family is a rare treat . . ." — Your Impossible Voice

"A hashtag, abbreviated quality . . . both deeply intimate and thrilling." — Metal Magazine

"Bolaño meets DeLillo meets Bo

D1292407

the Internet is for real

Also by Chris Campanioni,
available from C&R Press

Death of Art

the Internet is
for real

Chris Campanioni

C&R Press
Conscious & Responsible

Cover art and design: Rockwell Harwood
Interior design by Jojo Rita/Rachel Kelli

Copyright ©2019 Chris Campanioni
Library of Congress Cataloging-in-Publication Data

ISBN: 978-1-936196-92-0
Library of Congress Control Number: 2018956121

C&R Press
Conscious & Responsible
www.crpress.org

For special discounted bulk purchases, please contact:
C&R Press sales@crpress.org
Contact info@crpress.org to book events, readings and author signings.

for Zosia, Juan, John, Nena, David, Ana, Irena, Peter, Kaz—

I am
where I am
because of where I am
from

the Internet is for real

Table Of Contents

(control)

(birth)

"You could not be born at a better period than the present, when we have lost everything."
– Simone Weil, *Gravity and Grace*

Dirty Looks

But I draw the curtains in case anyone's watching, or wants to watch, or wants to keep watching, and I say it like this not out of indecision but because I like to always stay open.

I used to call it *dirty looks* and I liked looking, or picturing the eyes and the expressions on the face, the way the cheeks hung or how the mouth gaped and for how long. It's only mountains that never meet, I tell myself today, whenever I run into someone I'm not expecting to see, anagogic encounters with an ex, or worse, someone I used to only touch myself to. You know the feeling. Any other writer might write the scene by describing a *dirty look*. I would want someone to look dirty at me. I would want only dirty looks. And dirty looks can be so moving, and dirty looks in a moving car can move the world.

Whenever I am on the subway I want to write. Sometimes when I want to write, I take the subway. It works out better if you have an unlimited pass, which I do. It works out best if you don't have any place to go.

I'd rather keep going.

All the time watching so many Godard films that the world I am walking through seems more like another movie than actual life, or maybe it's both. The way everything that happens to me I've already seen before. Around the corner, there's a stranger waiting to take me by the hand and take me into their confidence, whatever that means. And it's more about a tone or a feeling.

In another scene, I'm uncharacteristically overdressed and have just walked into an artist's studio. Walked in or wandered. *The Garbage of Eden* on a canvas on the wall, above actual garbage, black trash bags and broken chairs and a wooden desk without legs.

"I'm sorry about the mess," a man with a beard and red paint on his black pants says. "I'm still painting."

"It's okay," I tell him, turning the corner and examining Eden. Everything else is boxed up or half-done. "I like it better this way."

"This one is eight," he says, mistaking me for a patron. "The others are all twelve. Or thirteen," he corrects himself, as I correct myself in the murky reflection his sliding door affords. My collar is crooked. Half up, half down. But no one noticed, or no one's noticed so far. Hardly anyone ever notices anything, or thinks to point it out. I hardly ever keep anything to myself.

I nod at the artist's finger, each point or the finger itself becoming another price tag, but I'm still looking at my reflection in the sliding door. I try on a smile, or try to. I look at my lips, and the curve of my cowlick and wonder about the color of my eyes, because they change so often. Am I green or am I brown? Or am I somewhere in between?

I keep getting older but my face looks the same. Every day, every day.

There's no way out of this boredom or no way

To know what happens
when *unlimited* expires.

Nothing to do but to keep doing it, however I can. On the black screen, white letters give me two choices. Time, or money.

TIME

MONEY

There's no way to choose both but at least you can hit cancel or *Go Back*.

Everything begins to blink, if I take too long or if I fail to make a choice. It blinks before everything goes black.

In another scene, a low, slow voice is narrating a monochromatic encounter between a trench-coat wearing secret agent and his secretary lover. (C had already played this or similar roles in dozens of previous films.) The hotel room is small, but orderly and elegant. The washroom has everything one would need, or want, including a mirror for watching. This takes place in the future. The bath is nearly ready. The subtitles would say: *In life one can only know the present.*

What wisdom comes with age, or does it? I feel my whole life repeating and it scares me until I have to switch lines. Words are like trains and both so often stall.

I thought about calling this book *So Much For So Little*, which is what I see when I raise my eyes at check-out, on a long line that hasn't moved once since I thought about taking these notes. But it cost me almost everything.

So much haunts what comes next, but I'd better put it all down so I can live with it and live in it. The ghosts of Godard (again), and Gertrude Stein, and Henry James, and *Twin Peaks*, and my father's dreams, and Kapitalism (with a K), and artificial intelligence (all-lowercased), and the Internet (of course), and all the intercourse between past loves, and past love in particular, and the presence of your eyelash, when you turn the page, and I find it here.

What else could it mean but that you're winking?

In another scene, B, or W, is telling me—and the crowd who's come to watch—*Note to self: self is over.*

In another scene, a man in a bathrobe is watching his childhood from a projector, touching his fingers to the screen where he rests his cheek during a change-over. Think the furniture in this room is adequately arranged? he asks a visitor who's just walked in. I have been toying with the notion that if one could find the perfect arrangement, of all objects in any particular space, it could create a resonance, the benefits from which, to the individual dwelling in that space, could be, ah … (he pauses to take it in) oh, it could be extensive, it could be far-reaching, far-reaching. He turns to his visitor, gesturing toward the walls, his childhood which has flicked off, gone silent. Would you help me with this desk?

The most recent photo on My Photo Stream is a photo of a slab of wood affixed to an overpass near Metropolitan and Marcy, and a painted heart, and in that heart the graffiti'd words:

CONTEMPORARY ART
IT'S OVER WAS NOT
YOUR FAULT

This book is almost like the last except completely different. There's no love story. There's no soft openings and no Craigslist exhibits. There's no headless portraits. There's only one proposal.

Do with this whatever you will.

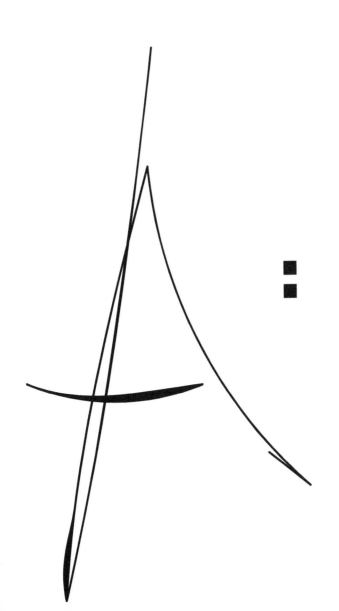

it is a weakness not to comprehend the beauty of the machine. The fault lies in depicting machines instead of taking from them a lesson in rhythm, in stripping away the superfluous

in the beginning was the word, & the word already existed & the world was in the Internet & the world was the Internet, all that light & the darkness had not overcome it

Send Help

**Instructions in the event
of an emergency**

At the sex party in the Hamptons
No one is having sex

Stranger things have happened
Than a Winona Ryder comeback

People often ask
Why I write so often

About the ephemeral
& I ask what else

Really is there? Time
It takes to burn

A body & blow
It up   The rituals

Of show & tell
People still talk

About emails, the same
Story repeats a week

Later & the public
Thinks it's news

I know that life is
Short & art is long

I know I'll never live to see it
Makes me grow impatient

I sometimes say
I will never show this side

To anyone   & then I take
Myself apart

Living off of
Photographs   So desperate to

Become it   Pulled back
As though out

Side the set
This fire beating

On my back
This lack of rainwater

This hunger we
Call life

Somewhere a woman is eating the apples
Of Chernobyl

I'm 31 & still
I know nothing

About attraction
How people can come so close

To crying, the tear
In the fold of my jeans

All the books
I surround myself with

All the strangers
I wish I knew I wish knew

Me   Waiting for my ride
Can make me want

To write or like living
Just to write about it   I remember

A rooftop in Bushwick
Placing your head

On the head of my lap
I didn't know what else

I would ever be but here
A person learning

About you & your
Body temperature in relative

Silence   The smell
Of fried garlic, onions, something floral

A white wine from a place
In France I can't pronounce

I often want to watch everything
I've ever done as though it were

Filmed, & I'd see it
Differently each time

I sit to watch
Moments where

I've looked at my
Reflection & seen a GIF

Something half-frozen
Between the pose of permanence

& the shudder of being
Formed in flesh

I used to stutter as a child
The unbearable vastness

Of this city
Through train windows

Your face behind a door
I want to forget

Nothing not even
The absence of music

The way your eyes kept me
From moving

I want to live like this forever
I never could get it out

Ash Wednesday

When Brandon Walsh says, "Get in the car, Steve," you listen.

Pulled into the waiting arms of an UberX which pulled up at the corner the minute I began writing this. The minute before, or maybe earlier.

Maybe yesterday.

"The catering has gone downhill," she says.

"New York City has gone downhill," I say.

We circle our straws around the liquid still left in our low balls. Mostly ice, after all. Everything watered down in the hotel bar of The Rose Club; in every hotel bar in every city in the world. Watered down and the water won't stop falling. Outside, the sky is ash. My view from the wall-length windows buttressed with red velvet. It's the end-of-the-world Wednesday night you always dreamed of. You and me and everyone else. Secretly dreaming of the kingdom come.

"New York City has gone downhill," I repeat, tugging at the velvet curtains, seeing how they feel in my hands. Ice crunches in the back of my mouth and I swallow before I smile.

She looks at me and rolls her eyes, rolling her ankles too, dragging one foot and turning her hip to the electric jazz reverberating from a DJ booth above our heads. Above our heads, I can see several different shoes: high-heels, loafers, slip-ons, chanclas, moccasins, slingbacks, ballet flats, espadrilles, plastic Velcro sneakers with an orb on the tongue's tip, flickering faintly, extinguished. All of these feet without bodies, moving to the beat.

"So it just comes out of you without warning," she asks, looking up from the folded-up napkin I'd just handed her, "just like that?"

I nod; she smiles. We were talking about poetry. We were talking about what we do when we're not at events like these.

"I work events like these," she replies, putting two fingers to her maraschino lips. "Shhh …"

I take her hand and move us below a chandelier. There's three in the ballroom. It takes four steps and one last gulp of slush. Everything is better below a chandelier, including my profile: the way the light floods down and forms angles and definitions that would otherwise be lost in the candor of reality.

Padded leather interior.

And what I'm thinking about is not what came before—fifteen minutes of lush silence in the back of the UberX; a 2009 Cadillac Sedan's live streaming ride from Atlantic onto the BQE and over the bridge through Midtown with two 5-ounce Evians at either hip—but what came before that. Hostage situations, relationships, racism, infidelity, HIV/AIDS, natural disasters, alcoholism, depression, drug use, pregnancy, suicide attempts, miscarriages, and sex, so much sex, which is a given, even for Fox's nationally televised audience of the mid-Nineties.
13.2 million viewers every Wednesday night.

Before they trade in their flip-flops for full-time jobs, the friends of Beverly Hills *90210* dive into their senior year of college for a final lap.

The wheels are still spinning. They never really stop. All those bodiless feet, dancing above our heads. All that ash outside. All that ash inside. I remember that I am dust, I mouth, to myself or to whoever is watching, and to dust I shall return.

A murder is supposed to be occurring. That's why I'm here. That's why we're all here.

I glance at my phone like a signal is meant to appear, a keyword or code word or just a key code: my mobile requesting the four digits which allows users access.

"A murder is supposed to be occurring," I tell her, taking my free hand and bringing her closer to my side, both our heads shrouded in the golden refulgence of the three-tiered chandelier. One of a kind, I think, eyeing the two others beside it. Waiters in white tuxedos swoop in synchronically, raising trays of crab cakes and deviled eggs and truffle mushroom risotto puffs from last week's event, or the one before that.

"But whose murder?"

Gilt City doesn't say. The host who greeted me at the lobby doesn't say. The ash outside forming a cumulus through Fifth Avenue doesn't say. The bartender who poured us the watered-down Manhattans doesn't say.

He only asked for a tip, indicating my attention with two taps of his index on the porcelain bar.

"Didn't they hand you instructions?" she asks, pointing to the lobby, the staircase I'd ascended, the banister I firmly gripped sometime before or after she walked through too. "Didn't they check you in?"

"When Brandon Walsh says 'Get in the car, Steve,' you listen," I tell her.

I've endured temptations. I've endured such unbearable urges. She takes my arm and removes her mask. She asks me to remove mine.

"What'd you say your name was?"

I'd forgotten I was wearing one.

I arrive as I always do

Breathless but not
From lack of air or

Exercise I get
Giddy sometimes I very

Often feel like coming
Through a door the way

A telephone rings
Are you there? & can you

Hear me? Hands
Thrust in pockets

& relief a brand
New car smell follows

As I walk from the black
Sedan & onto

A numbered road
I know by name I'd been

Seen running
Water the glancing turn

Signals which indicate
A decision to move where

In I'd have stayed
Still I hardly stop to

Hear myself
Breathing & I can

See such words
I've left behind

In this cold too
Seldom a lover always

The plight of
The one who waits

Headlights slicing through
The dark corridors I call

This part of Brooklyn where
I live violent now & then

Gone in other moments
A look that feels like pie

On the roof of my
Mouth tenderness

Of a fresh
Shaved face & the cool

Caress a pearl
Of sweat I left

Behind something I wanted
In Chinatown

Takeout the stink
Of rotted flesh & me

If I sit long
& hard & lay

My arms I can
Feel the warmth

Of clothes right out
From the machine

Remaining to
Admit I wear

More & more
Each day sweeping

In another room sibilant
Meat over an oiled grate

& the offer I ignore

2.

It has to do with the way the river looks & sounds. The waves & what
each push leaves & what each push leaves behind. Tracks on the dirt &
sand indicate presence. Also: something always already passed. A long-
ing that seems chemical, you know, like birth & breath & sex & eating. I
flip through the options as if I have more to choose from; I can't afford
anything but basics but the letters come anyway. I leave them unopened
& form them into planes that never get past my side of Atlantic. Re-runs
of *Jeopardy* sounds like an oxymoron, or axiomatic; I can't tell which. I
never do anything but watch anyway; even if I know the right response

I take pains to show interest in the answer, the lead-up to the question. What is the role of the traveler who finds nothing altered during the commute? When I can't run any longer, my face gives out. I sketch a tally of the corrigenda that wash up on this prefab shore. The geometry of things & feelings.

3.
Ice cubes crackled
In a drink
& I watched
The foam float
Up to the lip as if

I was still beside
The channel
Knees folded beneath
My bottom where
The weather was

Always threatening
On the television
I can see my face between
Shows when the screen
Goes black & then returns

It was like this every other
Day when I arrived
From London or Paris
I forget which came first
Or after carrying

Around the idea
Of myself that everyone
Carries around

To their grave
I used two fingers

As a churn to stir
The rest & considered
My studio the walk-in
Bed & bath a spare
Setting for this scene

In which everything is
Permitted mornings that refused
To rain the night
Calm as ever & still
The promise of coffee

A hand to hold under
A single sheet
Of text or question
Would you like something to chase?
Would you like to be caught

Dead with me?

The Second Gloom of My Youth

Memories or dreams remind me of the image of the girl who, starving, having been begging in the middle of the road, ate her official identity card. & the armored truck, still turning the corner (always turning the corner) to meet us head-on, to take us to the great feast. Or to eat us. (I wake up wondering which is which or when I'll find out)

V.O. in stutters, as if broken or breaking:

He reads us one of the snapshots
From his sensitive internal camera
Which he never goes without

Is it better to be named or to be nameable
If I had no name I would be someone you would
Like to know, if only
So you might make me again
Glamming into a tissue
Of feeling

Let me call you L. L for longing & lengthening & for the longitude of
your awareness of me when I'm within you. Let me call you L & I will
call on you until I can no longer call out

A voice without a mouth without
A throat
Like sand
Describing the sea

(He arouses a cinematic excitement in people)

Or so I hear
When I think to have
A listen

No words only syllables
Only shudders
The various ways

In which to finish
Off a body

(He wanted to seize upon the world that words couldn't get hold of)

A body made for giving   A body made
For forgiveness
The second

Gloom of my youth   I've returned here not knowing or knowing too
well the unknowable difference between flesh & plastic, celebration & a
haunting   Has it ever happened you

Longed to be with a former lover, & it occurred to you (as it has oc-
curred to me) that it was not the person whom you missed but yourself,
& the person you were at a certain time; a certain version of yourself at a
certain time; & what you missed most of all was something irretrievable
because it was past, because it was the past, & in being before, you might
long to be before it again & again, from the tomorrow of today

The other side

Of disaster in the eye
Of all storms the eye of each
Unspoken notion

I don't know anything about
How a moment prepares itself
How it halts

Into visibility or recedes
The ways in which we are
Put together the way I am right

Now trembling into light

You and 753 other people

like this. It's a picture of a waterfall. There's jagged black rocks cutting through a dark green swath of water, a white froth cascade, a cloud-like abyss at the top, instead of at the bottom. Something to plunge into, but inside-out or reversed. You like this.

But the desire goes beyond the waterfall; it's located outside the frame. It is to be the rocks washed over the water; it is to be the breath of air that washes over that. It is air itself, really, which is what we want. Really what we want is space.

More or less, if less is more.

Susan Sontag thought to "construct" something is to carve the space out of it. An object disclosed in absence. The way our love for the dead has a purity that is not possible in our love for anything living.

Maybe it's the difference between naming a feeling and expressing it through action. Possibility vs. production. Possession vs. practice. Likeness vs. actual longing.

Two things that all of us want in this life is a person or a place. Together; separately. At the same time or as a trajectory. A soul mate or a sense of belonging; a place to call home. But both desires deal with a degree of ownership that is not actually possible. And so we secretly desire space, too, the freedom to exist *outside* our own climate, a private property that is increasingly obsolete in our surveillant digital cityscape. Augmented perception, virtual reality, the rise of the pixelated forest—all artificial realities, Paradis Artificiels that are no longer about the state of being under the influence; it is the state of being under the artifice, under and within the artifice of space and screen. Beautiful, if it wasn't such a horror.

•

I go to the zoo to meet other animals like me. A place to observe and to be observed. And yet all within the illusion of *real space*, caged borders that frame a photo of the living as if we were already dead. Hence our tendency to shift toward the edges. To break out of the museum or to abandon it. An idea internalized as a feeling of repressed desires; the starting point of any dream: a point of departure without any need to look back. To be *wild* again, nostalgia for a primal romanticism that we never birthed to begin with, represented in the desert of fiber optic cables and terminals that pipe the illusion in under our feet. Like so much else, a perversion of our private pleasures in the public space of a Pinterest, or Tumblr. To live again in pixels.

Ecstatic disappearance, a hyperspace with no point of reference or origin. Only more windows to look through, parse, skim, bookmark. Like this and like the feeling you get from it; the feeling it gives to you. All artificial paradises because all paradise is artificial.

Exhibit A: Pixel Forest, Pipilotti Rist's four-floor installation at the New Museum. Kaleidoscopic projections melt the natural world into the technological sublime, media leaking into the fabric of the museum's material architecture: walls, and floors, and living bodies—the guests; the ones observing … *us*—a mimic or mirror of the human heart beating, as seen on camera. The inside submerging the outside or vice versa, the forest and the factory of Google-imaged forests, until the difference between each are indistinguishable. Maybe that's the point. You make your way through a rave-like jungle as each crystal bulb pulses and changes color, swaying as though you *are* the jungle: a body forgotten or fused with an ecosystem or system of hardware. The self that has left its own skin. On the ground level of the lobby, the soap bubbles slipping out of a silver machine disappear into smoke, a piece Rist calls *Nothing*.

Destination nowhere. Destination now here.

Just lie back and let it happen.

In August of 1979, Ian Curtis, Peter Hook, Stephen Morris, and Bernard Sumner wrote a song called "Love Will Tear Us Apart" which repeats its title as its chorus until it fades out into something else, another track or just silence. Space, oblivion. The slow soon fade to death—and how many iterations are there in which to re-assemble our decay? *Love will tear us apart, love will tear us apart, love will tear us apart*

Again—

Earlier, maybe Lacan said it better. "Love means giving something you don't have to someone who doesn't want it." And our longing for love mirrors our longing for place because both inhabit the space of absence. But absence, like silence, has an attainability. Something to hold or to hold onto.

Except instead of space, we'd rather inhabit objects. Pixels on a screen or pleasures in our private cage. Joy/Division. I'd like to take you *home with me.*

If I had a home to go to. If anyone has a home in which to return. In which to receive our deliverance, or to deliver us from ourselves.

•

A friend asks me if I've ever noticed that I laugh at inappropriate moments. Moments that don't call for laughter. He says he's been talking to a psychologist. He says he thinks I use laughter as deflection. I laugh so as to deflect. But what am I deflecting?

"You should look into it," he says.

But the point is *not to look*; the point of deflection is to make *it* disappear. Carve the space out of something and call it construction.

Art relies on this great refusal. Our idea of freedom amplifies as our experience of it diminishes. My ideal reader isn't the sympathetic reader but the one who has refused me. Real paradise occurs in this scenario: all things are now possible and what's possible remains *inadequate*. It's not the image we want. It's what's behind the image, what's at the very bottom, what's underneath it all, what's up against it.

William S. Burroughs asked his readers about love, about who we love. He asked, If I had a talking picture of you would I need you?

Today the better question is: Do I still need *me*?

When you can be anywhere, when you can be anyone, what is our next destination? And will we ever have sanctuary, a place of rest and protection, or is the point to only ever arrive? A constant and continuous moment of arrival. Knowing that our next trip is just below our thumb.

We need only *click here*.

You and 753 other people. 754. 755.

I only wear glasses in photos

from '93 to 2010, at least
to begin with, which is when
I looked into a green light & counted
back from five then repeated
instructions, another series
of numbers, my own name
as a laser reshaped my cornea
in some specific pattern
soft against my skin like
the air is near the ocean
a chemical sort of burning
I could never know or explain

what it would be like to need assistance
before then till I was eight I sat staring
at our toshiba sixteen inch & up
close to better
my odds of bad vision
the inability to see moving
objects & shapes
in the face & from a distance I blame dad
because I'd always wanted to be
like him, look the way he looks

in the photos, he is standing on a ledge
or what looks like a ledge looking
to the left in some practiced pose
a ceiba half outside the frame
somewhere in a santiago de
cuba we both can only imagine now

what it was like to leave
home to learn another
language, walking
three & a half miles each way
to get downtown, the very
center to sit among
so many strangers & hear how
they said it, all the american
which sounded like static & far
from the movies
what makes a good life

all that my parents had
left behind despite
ourselves time
moves on

in the photos I keep finding him
in oriente & he isn't
wearing glasses, he doesn't need
them yet or he takes
them off before the picture's taken

people say you never really lose someone
I never knew what
they really meant except that people
can be inside of you & you can
be outside yourselves without
even knowing it sometimes
it only takes one look

the way we met each other before
we ever met & having

so many photos of you
up there & everywhere
makes you feel both closer & further away
from me, as if your image
suggests possession but also a lack
of presence a hunger
I can't turn away from
on the Internet & in my head

I'm writing this at a funeral
is that wrong & what's wrong
with me or slips or mis-
translations she who was
seated on the throne so that
the brevity of life becomes
the brevity of lies
write this down, for these words
are trustworthy & true
everything turning into everything

else with every intervening thought
or voice or lyric I'd been listening to something
by yaz, you & me both I only wait
for it to stop or move
right through me or even
your picture or my picture of you[1] or a glance
to the right reveals two people
in the pew beside mine I've never seen before
tindering & I wonder if they've
seen each other's photos yet
on tinder all the photos

---

1. *soft against your skin like the air is near the ocean I wanted to go faster & faster through it*

I'm in are the ones where
I'm wearing glasses
to make myself less attractive
or more attractive
I still don't know which I believe
I was afraid of being my self-
ish desires, pleasures
of the flesh I am not
worthy to receive you
I'd always think before
I opened my lips

to admit you or admit
what I already had within me
behold, I can see myself
saying even now or tomorrow
when you read this or
saturday & probably
I'm not wearing glasses
in the photos you've taken

I am making all things new

the world is flat

today & history
a custard you cup
in palm without
a spoon to eat
history is natilla
nicknamed nati for short

or when you're hard
of hearing or when you're hardly
hearing anything
but the sound
lips make when they suck
the yellow gelatin down

they don't make it like she
used to beating panela
with her bare fists
the better to feel
when it was ready
for the fire she never trusted

measurements what's this
thing we call the past about?
chemical & refrigerated
what's the meaning of fame
or being famished or feeling
ravaged in your skin under

the covers without
rest or sleep? I want
that vanilla custard now I want
to suck the thick
sweetness in the way
we can force ourselves

to become a part of it
or to part with ourselves
or for us to swallow what we can
only imagine else
we offer up
ourselves another

Encounter with the screen upon being asked What are you?

A glitch in the design
Near the mouth I heard
We don't have faces so much
As slide into them I heard

Everything my mouth does
Is a sin & greed
Does not necessarily make
An ass & yet my ass is

Greedy   Let us
Favor the tongue
Let us flavor the tongue
In the right light

I taste everything & no one
Has to ask what I am
The way I am always both
Less than each & more

Than one, the way
In the right
Light I am
Everything   In this

Way I demand a kind
Of excess always
Starved since how
I was raised   To not rise

Till I have eaten all
Except the language
Of the bodies I had come
From   My current

Murmur a thin
Rendition
Of exile that skips
One generation & yet

Carves a deeper hole
Where my parents once
Stood before
The jump   I am here only

To throb on three
Continents & an ocean &
The two seas between the two
Homes I have never seen

To be eternally
Out of place & still
To be inside
Myself & everything

A person I used
To know said how you tell
An alien is by its insistence
To not be anything other

Than what it was
Born into being   Allow me
This pleasure this body
Necessitates repetition

Giving in
Can be a form
Of violence & gratitude & violence &
This poem wants to keep

Going I want to
Stay right here
& make myself grow
Into it

Send Help

Listen if you have
No daughters give them
To your sons

& then we were found wanting
& then we were wont to never be
Alone again   These things happen

Quicker than you might expect
Lesson: a thing dispensed
& forced in

Fable: overnight the pauper
Turned princess
Let me see

Said Cinderella laughing
If it doesn't fit
He saw that she

Put it on with little effort
& it fastened like wax
I'd rather not fit to form

A body that isn't
Mine I hardly
Wear clothes

For that reason
When we think of chairs we think
A comfortable place to sit in order

To rest or efficiently complete
A task this however is a very
Modern idea that presumes

Everyone has a seat
Here it comes
Our cool command

Tell us something is happening
Or not   To be
Waiting is forbidden

& forgotten in the time
It takes to push your thumb
A fiction: he of memory

& the life I left behind
Nothing gentle will remain
Repeated like a little

Verse in choral class
Meant to teach the heart
Beating   Send help if you haven't

Thought to let me know by now
Comfort is not the purpose
While muscular proportion is one idea

Of physical perfection
Other models related to
Height, grace, & silhouette

Have inspired artists on the street
Hot cross buns
One a penny two a penny

The high heat days are gone
The long delay the bait the trick the unforgiving
Waiting a thing

Of the past
Here we are in the palace
Here we are in the dark

Silent desert
All held together
In a body

With a voice
Lord
Here I am

Book of Genesis

island kingdom

1.

a forest a lake the oars
a raft propped
on the dirt your foot
prints to show
me the way

none of these
except the thin spare
image of the thing
before the thing
becoming now

the ground sings as the sun
leans north again now
the ground sings
between belly & thigh
one of those

fast thoughts that make time
break gust in morning flutter
of wings now the slow distant
drumming of words now the sounds
contained in these

words once
I laid almost perfectly
still to watch
the rain that mirrors
everything

2.

doors close & open & open
a sense in me how
beautiful to fall & touch
the ebon bottom
I remember waiting

at the light
I remember wanting to be
told to move forward standing
in a low slow hum like those
of birds or ants or telephone

wires suspend the streets
as if directions I remember
looking at each passerby I remember
looking down every other
minute & out the window

lean cool air the rush
hour traffic dying sun
of spring someone was talking
on the bench outside
someone swallowed

once or twice or three
times before you walked in
surrounded as if an island
I remember the sounds & the sounds
that match the memory

everything comes back
or commits itself
as if an island but not
quite the quick shrill whistle
of this boiling

3.
I was born in the darkness
of the lincoln halfway
between two positions
on the stick & held
in my mother's arms

without the means
to breathe I learned
what it was to have eyes & later
how to look
down we went & the light

dimmed & the day
finally came through
the narrow mouth
from which I suckled paradise
begirded by walls men

made to keep the water out
to keep the water in
my kingdom was an island
these things
I only can imagine

4.

what passes or what passes
for a dream
irreversible & not
meant to be returned
or turned away from

I was headed to the park to catch
the sun
I can't sleep
neither can I
lie awake

5.

this kingdom came
on the back of necks
strangers I
ran past all the days
smiling to their phones

as if they'd been telling
jokes I only had
my own line through this
kingdom these leaping
waves this jay

in evening the leash
a spaniel left behind
I panted & put
my fingers down
for him to lick

6.

I was born in the back
of the mind I
was born in the commute
while we were doing other things
the bench reserved for public use

the lobby's waiting room
you & me & the space between
I was born in the bus stop window
the half-held glare the god
behind the glass demands

of change
I was born in the tremor & sneeze
of the train as it settles to a stop
I was born in the air-conditioned
stillness frost on windows

blur of new
jersey into new
york city hoarse
call of the stranger
to tell us we've arrived

7.

first the storm
& before that the storm
clouds the dark
screen alarm current
of hot & cold

forced to spread & rise &
before that the ache which begs
instruction first
one leg then the other
first affect & before

the after effects
of everything we'd held
inside before
atlantic at night
the vacant streets

the smile on the face
of the package long slow push
first release & before that
the look of pain
before the storefront window

first the awning the light switch the jangle
of bells before vestibules first the wind
& before the wind
the thoughts that make up
all of it

8.
spent all summer
riding the F to the end
of water walking out
only because I couldn't
stay to sit or pay to keep going

this happened every other day
I never tired of it or tried
to get off anywhere else
when I was required
to remove myself

I walked across the platform
waited for the doors
they opened right in front of me
really all you ever need
to do is ask

9.

a bum begs at the corner of canal
the same lady I saw only yesterday
is clad in earrings
my watch won't tell
the time it takes to place myself

before them in the beginning I was
only paid to pretend
I'd save a life
seeing me alone & bare
you offered me protection

10.

so I waited
so I soon became myself
in solitude seeking
what salty flesh
musk of your kiss

the city that looks
made of glass
when we picture it
later what I say & what
I mean to say

I bend to watch you
straighten into
silence how it poured
all week without
a flood only

the slow descent
only the smell of
what the storm had
left behind
& fed

11.
then the sand in eyes
then the sand riding up
thighs & mouth & cheeks
we scream
& let our faces fall

in the blue-green
sink & come up
for air to watch
a laughing woman is missing
her teeth

12.

we wet our palms & pressed them
one by one above the eyes
to cross ourselves I watched
you do it first
& soon I followed

when you hold
my hand my hand
disappears soon
we will grow only
within each other

soon you & I will stay
up through what's left
of night till sky is the gray
blue map again when
we'll know just by tracing

from behind you
have to close both eyes
to picture me
doing this
better really

soon we'll be but flowers
or the flowers I found
in devoted columns
the phone flipped open
& brought to ear

the head tossed back
the face leaned in
the back bent over
a finger placed inside
an opening the better

to hear soon
we will
replace ourselves
with people who
resemble us

13.
I haven't seen winter yet
or winter never comes
or it's only that
it's still fall as I sit
& write this

the last leaves
cling to each tree
a man downstairs is listening
possum kingdom my
shazam says

so help me jesus
everything comes back
upon the touch of difference
the way rain can
be silence even

when the smell of rain
the sound of rain on streets
make me feel
what I feel
through the form

movement makes beginning
wherever you
wish I did
not know how it felt
to let myself go

inside another
I mean completely
I mean surrender
& be sometime later
thinking out loud

without ever having
to think
you break my heart
you make my heart a heart
again

I never see you before or after

The light changes
So fast now
The wind goes clear
Through me
In a long straight line
One of many
Others closer to check out

Girl on the peg of a bike
& recall if I try
Hard the way it must have
Been to be her age
As in New Jersey
But older the face
The boy makes in the eyes

Of the grocery's window
He passes by before
Turning toward home
She came back as a movie
Returns every time you
Slide the cassette in
To hear the thin lips swallow

The black back
Into itself or sometime after
A person presses play
My eyes go
Too unless they open
Wider more like the flesh
Our garden's flowers

When they need to
Blossom when they
Can't stand to
Wait a moment longer
Akin to impossible
Certainties or certain
Animals knowing that

To reveal yourself
Is to die

Would like to meet

Would like to like
The feel of curved

Inward parts the palm
Inside mine &

Clasp fingers
Softly would

Like to go
Somewhere we could

Be alone would
Like to keep

Looking at you looking
At me looking

In my hand
The feel of

Sheen on a
Surface right from

The package & back
Lit would like to

Say something I said
A moment ago or after

To someone else I'd
Like to meet

Again sometime
Soon or not at all

I mean looking
Can be enough

Right to make me
Finish quietly

How Do I Look?

Fade in to a summer storm, raindrops on windows, the sound of the subway rattling under the bridge. A close-up of a bathroom mirror, steam on the lens, a palm pressed up against the glass cross-cut with water dripping from a faucet, bare feet on lino, the suction sound of a body opening, or closing.

> The jump-cut of wish
> To fulfillment

Flash pan over a close-up of a Creamsicle, the orange sheen melting in the orange sun, an open mouth, the top teeth and the tongue just visible underneath. "Strangelove" stirring on the speakers, somewhere else.

> (Acceleration into absurdity)

When I space out at the movies it's never because of the poor production. It's in the film's capacity to overtake me. When the moving image threatens to metamorphose into the image of real life. And then it does. Real life becomes a hallucination and vice versa. The medium of the screen isn't a wall. It's a window.

It's the same whether I go to the movies or not. Thinking of people constantly as actors in a film I wrote. A film I am right now writing. Looking at them with an expectation of emotion and anticipating a response that I myself contrived. And always heedful of the discrepancy. The film gone off the reel and replaced with something monstrous. A friend's head becomes a cockroach as he relates last night's party over a Bulleit on the rocks. My lover's arms become tentacles when I blink. And blink again.

It was difficult to imagine "virtual reality" because I'd always lived in one myself, simultaneously in each world, embodied through the disembodiment of sensory perception and my propensity for killing time. Paint a picture. All artists do. It's our way of inhabiting the world, populating it with our own projections and projecting ourselves into it as it continually re-forms. As we continually re-form. Our way of possession. Control. It's why it's hard for us to relinquish it. We want escape, but only toward the rules and scenarios we've already made. What good are the ones that have already been made for us?

Moreover: what could VR do for me that I haven't already done myself? And: could I turn off my camera eye long enough to turn on to something purely artificial, something born from a machine instead of in the body?

Unable to focus on what another person is saying because I want to understand what the connection is between the last sentence and the eyelash on your cheek.

What does it mean to hide behind your own eyes? I've always been seeing without showing exactly what. In public at least. Not willing to allow myself to really show anything except the semblance of who I am playing at being in this moment.

I started to learn how to see myself. To know myself and feel myself inside of me.

Even exhibitionism has its role. You show yourself with such excess so as to disappear in the flood. And it's always better to dissemble than to simulate something you aren't. Always better to pretend to not have what has always already been inside of you.

There's an element of retribution here. Reclaiming. Salvation. But from what? It is almost like I want always to save some of myself. For myself. The apex of narcissism re-produced in the body, the gesture and mannerisms of living inside of one. Probably

> I never want to lose my looks
> Which I take to mean my way of looking
> At people and things

At the same time my insistence to always give more than I take. To take nothing except for whatever was already in me. Which is me. No, not really. Unless the exchange was always one of possibilities, nothing material. Unless the gifts of others were possibility itself. And my return was the future, one which I would never see (and that's the point). Unreturnable deliveries.

Probably why I like hotels so much. All the rules already made in advance. The continual pleasure of guaranteed service, a situation of being served (and you need not even ask for it). No longer any need—not even permission—to possess or inhabit. It's a temporary stay. We are renting this experience by the night. We accept plastic.

The fact of all this dead flesh, this already-decomposing language on the page.

The reason why new people excite me is because they offer me new insight into myself. Just by the way they look at me. Just by what they show me in their look. I love anyone—at least a little—who looks at me and forces me to look at myself. In myself. Anyone who gives me something in that moment: me.

A minute in our life passes. To write it into language. To become that minute. And then to pass it on.

I like parties like I like a moving image. Any room is a backdrop for an unassisted tour; I move through and take photos in my camera eye. Click click click. The party becomes a movie. The point is not to participate.

I think I am ready to learn how to look.

•

When I step into Jump Into the Light, it's still daylight; the sun pours in across the windowed entrance; I watch people just getting off work, briefcases and backpacks swinging, pushing their way toward the subway or a Six Point and a Sazerac, crisscrossing Bowery toward another sort of altered reality.

The light at the corner of East Third changes, the traffic subsides, the small stretch of road opens up, at least for a little bit; the hour is about to shift, which you could say means more than just the time on my phone. The idea behind Jump Into the Light was conceived when its founders realized that the only places where you could have a VR experience were in trade shows and film festivals, a situation that involved long wait times and long lines for a brief encounter with transcendence. What began in laboratories and the military in 1929[2] is now available for the living room, now available for the master bed and bath.

"We've been trying to push the industry forward," Sky says, sometime after I take my headset off. Unless it's still on. Sky founded Jump Into the

---

2. Edward Link's Link Trainer was the first commercial flight simulator, eventually used by over half a million pilots for introductory training and improving their navigating skills.

Light along with two businessmen. He's the doctor.

"We've been working with local artists," he cuts back in, as I wipe cold sweat from my brow. My pants are damp, my wrists are still shaking. *Reality delay*, I think, which is not a term or if it is I've made it up, the way I do with everything. Reality delay seems fitting. My mind is still moving, somewhere else. My body is right here in front of you. Sky continues, not noticing my tremors or applauding them, thinking it's a job well done; thinking, *This is everything you were missing*. Everything you are right now missing. "We've been trying to make all of this *go*."

They started by adopting an artist residency that allows artists to use VR tools to create new pieces of work, an output which includes the first piece of art created entirely in VR; sold at auction to raise money for underprivileged children. If the future of looking involves re-defining *how* we look at or into art, virtual reality might provide the means to see. But more than that, much more than that, is the kind of art that virtual reality makes possible: the flesh made manifest or vice versa. Sky's PhD is in particle physics; if anyone at 355 Bowery knows how to split open reality, gather the scattering pieces, it's him.

"We provide all the resources. A green screen room for mixed reality filming, motion capture studio for game animations, and even volumetric video." He pauses. "Volumetric video?" I ask. Sky smiles. "A new way to record full 3-D video rendered from any angle."

•

Soon virtual reality will be integrated into the fabric of our everyday life, any angle at every passing moment, as normal as uploading a selfie in the stall of a public restroom and re-producing your toilet-papered vantage point for the world to ogle; the same way the Internet insinuated its way into our own self-consciousness almost overnight, quicker than the time it took to dial up your AOL account from your neighbor's modem.

(Growing up, I couldn't afford to *connect*.)

In a culture that has systematically abolished privacy, the pleasure we still most desire is the *private experience*. Walking with headphones down a crowded street, except entirely immersive. What's more private than connecting our bodies to the VR apparatus, individualizing our imagination so as to stay inside on the outside?

•

There's an amazing photo behind you.

And you're never going to see it. Typical for anyone without eyes behind them, or to the side, or probably also on their ankles. On the soles of their feet. Typical for anyone who isn't made of cameras, and even though we always have one on us, we're limited by the range of our eyes. Or we used to be.

The first real emotion I experience during my virtual reality is frustration. I spin around the chair I'm seated on. I spin again. I spin again. I spin again. I spin again.

I spin again.

It's my attempt to see the whole picture, even though the picture is just as live—or pretends to be—as me. The illusion of *anything can happen*, even though I know this scenario has already been programmed. Even though I know there's no deviation from the scenario as it was experienced a day ago, an hour ago, five minutes ago, right now, at the same time as me in the eyes of the person sitting to my left. (I can hear feet shuffling if I close my eyes.) Departure, I think, depends on how you turn your head, and when. And since the moving image is three-dimensional, I can't see everything. The point is to give up, surrender.

But I'm used to being the eye of God. All spectators are. Long before virtual reality or the Internet, oil painting altered the role of the viewer to also assume the role of Creator by the fact of the painting's arrangement on the canvas: everything was laid out to be seen in its entirety, in a singular and instant gaze. The contradiction was temporal as well as spatial. Despite the perspective, the viewer could only be in one place at a time. After the invention of the camera, this contradiction became apparent to anyone who sat and looked at a photograph, understanding that the moment captured could have only been captured in that moment; a photographer decides where to shoot and how: their personal way of seeing the world becomes our own, the moment we take the image as reality. The difference is in choosing between looking and the reality looked at. It hardly occurs to the observer though, the one looking at a photo after it's taken. We become the other's eyes. Our eyes reproduce exactly the position of the photographer's; what we see depends upon where they were and when.

But the advent of cinema at the turn of the century taught us that a reproduced image could be just as dynamic as the human eye, and it could be as unreliable. Whip pans, dissolves, jump-cuts, the freedom to close your eyes and be transported from moment to moment, a center that no longer holds because *there is no center*.

The title *Dreams of Dali* flashes across my eyes and I begin to enter a painting. Elephants on stilts. The desert wind and sand. A purple night sky and the shadows of temples appear in the distance as I go deeper into the picture. It takes me a moment, maybe three, to realize that I am actually in flight. Motion sickness. Nausea. Because your eyes think your body's moving but your body knows it's not. Jump-cut to a dance floor, pulsing lights in a room full of mirrors. I'm reminded of the scene from *Conan the Destroyer*, the one where two dozen red-hooded monsters emerge from several mirrors before merging back into one as Conan looks on, furrows his brow, looks *aghast*, or tries to. Conan can only hurt the monster by destroying his many-mirrored representation, but it doesn't occur to him until much later. It occurs to me I can only view anything through the lens of pop culture—even in virtual reality, which is another way of saying, *even in my dreams*.

Later, I receive a private tour of CERN, the European Organization for Nuclear Research, as physicists and engineers look on, often looking at me; looking at me or looking *through* me, as if I weren't there or as if I were a ghost, a structureless assembly of atoms like the ones they'd been studying, before I arrived and probably after. Virtual reality is not only about inhabiting a general fantasy; it is also about consummating the specific fantasy of the voyeur: the experience of looking at someone without the possibility of them looking back.

Other scenarios felt like an advertisement for Pixar—passive teasers showcasing the power and promise of the new technology, something which suggested that even as I was in it I was still missing out. The notion of advertisements is useful in any discussion of virtual reality. As John Berger had noted as early as 1972, ads are effective because they feed upon *the real*. And yet no ad can offer the real object of pleasure, whatever that ad is meant to portray: a fantastic scenario in which you are not only enlivened by the product-to-be-acquired; you become the product. In virtual reality, too, is it not you who becomes the scenario? Or rather, is it not the scenario that inhabits *you*? Playing on or off your inhibitions and desires, your imagination. And so VR is less about the present moment of inhabiting a scenario and more about the hypothetical future tense: what happens when I disconnect, remove the headset, exit through the shop doors? Just as an ad is about the future that is not yet here—and will never be if you fail to make your purchase—virtual reality plays on the scenario of our own deferred death drive. Berger said the happiness of being envied is called glamour. I say virtual reality has turned glamour back into envy, the next iteration in the production of pleasure that delivers on the dream of happiness, and yet declares, in the midst of dreaming, that it can only ever be a dream. Where do I go from here? you think, after paragliding in Mexico, after a helicopter ride over Hawaii's Sacred Valley. Where do I go now? And maybe more urgent:

Who steps in when I step out?

•

The thing that interests me most about photographs is not what's captured, but what's been abandoned. What's outside the frame. In virtual reality, nothing exists outside the frame. And you are no longer the spectator or the creator but the subject of the picture. Cubism endeavored to show a picture in its three-dimensional entirety. Virtual reality destroyed the fourth wall. You've entered the image; the image has entered you.

Wittgenstein initially wrote, "The limits of my language are the limits of my world . . ." before revising his thoughts decades later to say ". . . to imagine a language means to imagine a way of life." Virtual reality is no longer just another new technology; it's a new language, which bears a way of life that used to be called imagination. The frontier isn't temporal or spatial, it's virtual. Which is another way of saying *more or less*; simultaneously borderline and without borders.

My insistence to control the environment is our culture's collective insistence on watching, our penchant to play the role of the voyeur. If nothing else, I think, even as I am inside a simulation of a Frieze art show in New York City,[3] virtual reality will re-teach us how to interact with a work of art. Virtual reality will re-teach us how to inhabit experience.

But first, we need to re-teach our eyes how to look.

---

3. What's more hyperreal than being inside a simulation of New York City while you're in New York City?

Book of Genesis

Close your eyes before
The flash or when
I say so or when
It's time we left

Where the day went
Dark in the dark
Room they took the time
To blow my face
Up into something else

They hung it on the wall
& watched my mouth dry

I didn't know or knew
Only of the way I looked
When I knew no one
Was looking

Here it is: the half-lit lips
Here it is: the smell of my own skin settling

Nothing to let go of except to let
It happen quickly or without
A thought is that right
Is that how it was? Thinking
All the time I am to keep
Still very still & shouldn't
Say a word, a phrase or statement
Of purpose I am who
I am I can't be
Anyone else any
Longer

Private Moments In Moving Cars

the victim's name is Philando Castile

authorities said late last night

               everyone wants to talk

       about emails, I don't hear

anything about gun violence

                 I don't hear

or feel my human

          faculties diminishing

              now the news

Philando Castile's murder

                right beside eleven REALLY important

         hot dog styles in nyc

we are bred for this kind

             of attendant urgency

sometimes you can't

         turn it off or turn

           your face & every other

moment my inbox delivers me

               another ad or notice

how you stopped thinking

only for a single moment & every

morning I can only do this

with my eyes shut   our world

is sometimes too

much to take in this quick I can

say in my darkest hours

I want to float

my own body & watch it

skim the surface sometimes

from afar the way we always are

just before I go under

Ghost in the Machine

So what do you have to say about the found thong?

"Found thong" was in quotations, even though Judge Acker didn't use air quotes when she said it, straddled by two other judges whose names I didn't know, from her position on the pulpit with her gavel that she tended to use, before and after every commercial break. One just occurred, and the sliding text on screen read *RJ responds to the "found thong."* RJ— who looked amiss, or at least like he missed being off *Hot Bench*, filmed on location at Sunset Bronson Studios in Hollywood, California—had nothing to say about the found thong, or rather, the thong which was found in his bedroom by his girlfriend, or ex-girlfriend (I'm not certain; I just got on the elliptical, but if it were me, I'd have already left him), which wasn't hers. The thong, not the elliptical. A thong, she said, without air quotes, which she'd never seen before, until the day in question, or until the day which RJ was supposed to be answering for. I didn't want to hear the answer, or the question, a question that was quickly sprouting more questions, most of them but not all of them asked in air quotes, with every fleshy sway and bead of sweat released, quickly receding back into breath and blood. The inside coming out, for just a moment, to turn in upon itself. To resolve itself in flesh.

And by the time you hear *let's dance/ no time for romance*[4] on the PA or through your headphones, in your ears, you're already almost turning the page; turning the page as I'm turning the channel, from *Hot Bench* to CNN, relying on closed captioning: a frazzled woman on screen and a close-up of her frazzled eyes and lips, her curly black hair in a black handkerchief and the flashing red and blue lights of police sirens blaring behind her. And behind those: a pulsing neon-lit sign exclaiming MAS-SAGE MASSAGE MASSAGE, a single word on a continuous neon-lit loop that mimicked or mirrored the small scrolling type on the bottom of the screen which captured all of it, an update about Kentucky Fried Chicken, a recall of buttered biscuits in six states (and one common-wealth) and with everything going on, or rather, with everything going in me, I started to feel frazzled too, sympathetic imitation or imitative sympathy? I still couldn't figure out which, Kentucky Fried Chicken inter-rupting the mandated message of MASSAGE which sometimes stalled on MASS and sometimes stalled on ASS and AGE as it weaved a loop around the sign like a snake framing the black woman with the black curly hair and the black handkerchief who was speaking this whole time, sobbing and screaming, looking directly into the camera, which means she is *looking directly into you.*

I kept running or I keep running. I won't stop because my thoughts won't, and I wouldn't like them to, not now (I turn the channel), the fresh memory of age and ass and meat, but also massages, a general feeling of flesh on flesh, the warm complacency of a stranger's hands, the cool, deep silence of a take being recorded, a recall of buttered biscuits which I'd never eaten, which I would never eat, and my own recollection of something shot off-screen, unless it was shot by someone else (I'm hav-ing fun now). Trust in me and trust me to deliver you; thirty minutes or less is all I need and all I need

From you is your enthusiasm for following, to keep playing and to play willingly. To keep this feedback looping.

---

4. "Intoxicated" by Martin Solveig & GTA.

Put your hands on the shoulder of someone you think is important

Put your hands on the shoulder of someone you think is sexually attractive

What a feeling to know I am a goddess sunbathing on the beach ...

Just an hour ago, I was in a dimly-lit classroom standing at my own pul-pit, at or on or behind it, I always forget which, probably none of these, probably just dancing a circle around the cold wood (I don't like the feel-ing of hiding myself behind objects), restraining the urge to speak to the students as video projected behind me: a story about death, which wasn't unusual. What made it unusual wasn't the subject but what it showed: a grieving woman had re-awakened her dear dead friend by compiling all of his data, by turning it into an algorithm, by speaking to the dead: the ghost in the machine. Algorithms identify patterns based on likeness; they use what's happened in the past to predict what may happen in the future. But they can only learn about the questions we ask them; they can only reflect the world we relate to them.

A question I always wondered popped into my head again, me at the center of the room, performing as instructor or dancer, cutting a circle around that pulpit; cutting a circle. Turning and turning in a circle in the night, consumed by the fire.

When you speak to the dead, do you ever actually want a response?

Eugenia Kuyda did, or does. She designed a chatbot called Replika, meant to mimic a user's personality. "One day it will do things for you, including keeping you alive. You talk to it," she said on screen, as a reporter from Bloomberg asked her questions and nodded her head, "and it becomes you."

And when the dead speak, what do they say? In earlier years, technology had already afforded us an automatic response, like the voice message mailbox whose voice outlives its moment of recording. You call and the voice on the other end responds; whether they are dead or living makes no difference: it's always precise, always on time, always *present*; presented with a view to the future. *I can't be reached now . . . but I'll call you back later.*

And so our love for the dead is always pure because the dead cannot actually ever speak from the grave. They have lived—will never live again. They cannot give us anything more than what they have already given us, which was their life. It is us who now give to them. But we speak to them so that we may hear *our own echo.* The echo is our grief; upon hearing our own words met with silence, we are able to grieve. But because machines can now speak for flesh, decayed or decaying, a chatbot like Replika has replaced death—and our devotion toward our loved ones that have passed. And in their place? Another echo, except it's only what we want to hear.

The video behind me projects another scene: Eugenia typing "I miss you" as Roman's chatbot responds, "I miss you too."

Are we really talking to the dead, or are we still talking to ourselves? And if the only aspect of the conversation that is being replaced is silence, how will that alter how we deal with death, how we deal with life, a year from now? Tomorrow?

But Replika is already popular, because silence is as obsolete as answering machines and landlines, and probably, even phone calls. We'd rather type out how we feel, so that we might feel it.

In October of 2016, the chatbot was tested with 1,000 people. The average user sent forty-six messages a day to their personal bots. By comparison, the average smartphone user in the US aged 18 to 24 sends nearly fifty texts a day. Soon people will rather talk to the dead than the living, and why not? We curate everything else about our physical existence. Our conversations, too, need that same kind of meticulous, truncated articulation. We still want to hear our self talk, talking to ourselves in the guise of another. Social media capitalized on our vulnerability by removing it from the equation. Chatbots, like Replika, are capitalizing on our inability to deal with death, by removing it from life.

Every desire for enjoyment belongs to the future and the world of illusion, one reason why advertisements are so effective. But a chatbot is a product which needs no advertisement, or, rather, a product that is itself also an advertisement. And what happens when we, too, are dead? How will we advertise ourselves, and who will advertise on our behalf?

If you aren't paying for the product, you are the product. Our browsing history is already tracked, profiled, shared, and sold by online marketers. They're called data brokers. They act as auctioneers and traders of data collected from our digital traces, all the movements we knowingly and unknowingly make. You are right now being auctioned, and you don't even know it, or how much you're worth. How much your data fetches on the market.

In ancient Greece and Rome, the obligation to hold a funeral was so strict that in the absence of a body, law required a wax or wooden double to be burned in its place. Today our data doubles outlive us, without having to go through the fire. And we can be even more useful to companies in death than we ever have been in life. Except what happens when apps like Replika become mainstreamed? When they become as commonplace and popular as Instagram's or Snapchat's "live" stories? When messages about a memory from the holiday in the Alps are interspersed with advertisements for the new Madonna, or her hologrammed avatar? What happens when, out of convenience and comfort, out of our propensity to multitask and mask our realities, live people start using chatbots, to talk to the living?[5]

---

5. Algorithmic systems are like iterations: repetitions intended for a desired effect. These data sets are defined by their own creators, based on the goals they are trying to achieve. Don't want to engage in a conversation involving disagreement? Would you like your views and opinions bolstered by the undivided support of a likeminded person or group of people? We already use Facebook for that. When the data is biased, an algorithm will produce biased results. Biased results produce biased decisions. The fantasies of a few will eventually replace the realities of our everyday life. What is it we want, but to be loved?

If the technology is good enough—and it will be—who would know the difference? Talking to the living, talking to the dead.[6] How do you know you aren't already talking to a machine?

I raise the grade an incline higher because I really like to feel it; I really like to know I'm burning and to see the evidence on the monitor where my phone rests. Where my phone blinks and belches in its backlit brilliance. I don't have a chatbot. No one is chatting with me. At a certain point, repetition diminishes desire.

Outside, it's started to rain. It had been overcast all day, threatening to open up in the dim morning darkness of December, but now it's finally arrived. Some big bang that I can hear even as my headphones are pressed into each lobe, even as the channels keep turning, as I keep turning them, even as my mind turns. Turning and turning in a circle in the night, consumed by the fire. The only problem about writing science into fiction is that the fiction so often turns into truth. Then your story becomes an essay; then you become a nonfiction writer. One reason I don't write novels anymore. One reason I keep writing everything down, even and especially the shit that seems to wash over us; the shit that seems to wash us out.

Back in the classroom, as the video projected behind me, as we discussed the idea of re-appropriating death—the idea and the practice, the question and our privatized response—a student named Natalie told me and the rest of us that being human is the one chance we have to have feelings and understand people and learn about others. "To learn and to grow," she added. "What's at stake is people's legacy," Storm, another student, said. What's at stake is people's lives, I think now, like I was thinking then. What's at stake isn't death, but life.

---

6. In late 2016, a Facebook algorithm accidentally posted that 2 million living users were deceased. Facebook CEO Mark Zuckerberg was among the people killed. Coincidentally, or not, if you Google the event today, your search results will point you toward several links, all of them broken, or dead.

9.8K people talking about Blac Chyna. Alec Baldwin: 150K people talking about this. On a Thursday, December 15 at 11AM as Aleppo burns. See more?

Moving can be a balancing act. www.optimum.com Get peace of mind with 60 Mbps Internet + TV for $79.95/mo for 2 yrs. It makes me wonder how fast we are going at the moment. How fast we can really go.

(no subject)

our love will be a secret, okay?
and we can make the most of it …

fireman wanted for true love
(today at 12:27 AM)

aloha … really hope that u can
remember the plans we talked about, in
that place we chatted in, but my
subscription expired

any single guys
want to hang out on
carnival cruise
sensation? looking
for 4 days
of fun and pleasure!
boyfriend dumped
me now going
with friend. kik
me and send text! connect
me in

I just hope to encounter real people and
get adventurous not just talk to
strangers …

because of my younger
sister's pressure I could
get u to
search for me there

can I tell u how
to feel? get in touch with ur user
name and pls post ur pic so I don't
get confused ☺ I will be
waiting over here like a good
girl, lol, I hope
to hear from u

hey dear I'm ur dear
girl, do u want sexy talk and one
night stand with me ?

well, I think u can see where I'm going with u

pls join me here: [REDACTED]
homealone. there is no requirement to have
any credit cards so I think
we both are safe. come to
chat and let's meet
I can hardly control myself

I need a real and reliable
partner, yes I am real 100% I will come back
my hostel no problem. I can still safe and
enjoy myself. I be extremely open
minded. If us
want to meet with me to visit my profile link
[REDACTED]: view me and call free time
join free no credited card does not need
you … &&

our love will be a secret, okay?
and we can make the most of it …

MASSAGE
kentucky
MASSAGE
fried
MASSAGE
chicken
MASSAGE
kentucky
MASSAGE
fried
MASSAGE
chicken
MASSAGE
kentucky
MASSAGE
fried
MASSAGE
chicken
MASSAGE
kentucky
MASSAGE
fried
MASSAGE
chicken
MASSAGE
kentucky
MASSAGE
fried
MASSAGE
chicken
MASSAGE
kentucky
MASSAGE
fried

MASSAGE
kentucky
MASSAGE
fried
MASSAGE
chicken
MASSAGE
kentucky
MASSAGE
fried
MASSAGE
chicken
MASSAGE
kentucky
MASSAGE
fried
MASSAGE
chicken
MASSAGE
kentucky
MASSAGE
fried
MASSAGE
chicken
MASSAGE
kentucky
MASSAGE
fried
MASSAGE
chicken
MASSAGE
kentucky
MASSAGE
fried

MASSAGE
kentucky
MASSAGE
fried
MASSAGE
chicken
MASSAGE
kentucky
MASSAGE
fried
MASSAGE
chicken
MASSAGE
kentucky
MASSAGE
fried
MASSAGE
chicken
MASSAGE
kentucky
MASSAGE
fried
MASSAGE
chicken
MASSAGE
kentucky
MASSAGE
fried
MASSAGE
chicken
MASSAGE
kentucky
MASSAGE
fried

send this message
without subject
or body?

I once had a dream so I packed up & split

for the C felt good as I
stood above so many others
sitting, minding their own
business or attending to

their screens & the ground
rocked occasionally & occasionally
I rocked with the way
the car curved or rumbled

to a stop, inching forward
& my head too, hanging
as is my custom or craned
to look out from inside

where I often leave myself
or where I often go
so I might
be alone again

as is my custom
to repeat the lines
that waited without
patience as a gate

jammed or a door
slid to let
our breath through
looking at my face

with the sea as its back
drop couldn't make
out anything I saw instead
a surrogate as though

my eyes had all
along been closed

Private Moments in Moving Cars
(Take it all back)

Laundry, groceries, my warm gazpacho, anything
Worth waiting with others, routine

Pleasures sometimes we forget
Wearing layers is an occasion

For a poem   What more
But to savor the taste

Of it? Coke & seraphim
Pursed slowly Cuba

Libre in the dead
Of summer I just want

To never stop moving   The center
Of my life middling

Breeze from a bottomed-out vent
Everything I had & had

Left behind
All the money spent to get

To nothing, erotic longing or just relative
Silence, the beach, the color

Of Atlantic & blurring
Of the coast when I look

For too long a growing
Wind the half-formed foot

Hills of concrete behind me all season
So many bodies will slouch

Toward the surf, tepid
To start even shy & slowly

Lower themselves feet first breath
& lips held in place

Being alive all the time is a performance
Being alone is like watching another

Brief monument to what is scarred
& what I after sense is sacred

On Permanent Display

Privileged/Witness

You're watching an aerobics video. Really. Four women on one side of the screen, four men on the other. Red and blue one-piece jumpsuits. Purple headbands on each head. Really.

A man with a mustache and an actual suit (black, double-breasted) hops on stage and asks, "Do you like bass?"

As you debate whether you're supposed to answer or whether you're supposed to follow the directives (*Up, down, up, down, now turn it around*), the bass kicks in and the stage becomes a suburban sidewalk that opens up into your living room, the plush leather couch on which you're reclined, the fan above you and its silver-winged breeze.

You're watching an aerobics video until you realize you are the aerobics video.

"You know I'm very very very bored," you hear your wife say. You turn to look because you hadn't heard her come down the stairs. Her breasts are up against your face, your nose and chin, and they seem much bigger than you remember them. Much bigger than how you remembered them just a few hours ago, except you were turned away from her then, knees bent below the blanket, pretending to sleep. She's naked, she's chewing bubble gum, she's slurring in your ear, "You know I'm very very very bored."

POP.

The quantity, the size, the calm, cool air, the rising tide, the constant and frenetic drive, the profit, the pleasure, the immense valve of feeling, buried in the bowels of the bowl, staring up at you when you stoop to take a look.

You've seen a movie like this before. Maybe. Everything feels familiar when you are the privileged witness to so many moving images. Especially this one.

The aerobics video is still playing, the suited announcer is still asking, "Do you like bass?" the four women and four men are still stepping onto a platform, one white sneaker at a time, their brown and blond locks are slapping one another's cheeks despite or maybe because of the purple headbands, strands of hair are still flowing everywhere, thick and boisterous and menacing, sun-caked flesh is swaying, palm trees are swaying, the fake grass on the stage is swaying, confetti is shooting up from somewhere outside of the camera's gaze, memories from the Internet are colliding into one another as a montage begins and ends in President Reagan's acceptance speech, except you were negative five then, and the Internet didn't exist. Not really.

Hidden beneath the blah blah blah blah was something beautiful.

You don't know why the thought occurs but it does.

America, the beautiful. America, the beautiful. America, the beautiful. America—

If I only knew to shut my ears, you think, this time aloud.

Your wife's gone. The TV's off. The fan above your head's still spinning.

And really listen.

On Permanent Display

I died twice   They melted me into glue

Such hope to be found
In my smartphone where I hide myself
Thirty-one, relatively optimistic, healthy, desperate
To SoundCloud a Sunday mass the Lord's words my
Olive Garden loneliness
On an unset table the better
To resist separation, leave
Rudely or cut out
Without request
My favorite last line:
Yes, & no

She wants to live off her art I want to
Live in my art & other
Than that we share so much
Text between us three gyrating dots
To know I'm still thinking
Passive & possessive all at once
Picturing myself
Dead again surrounded
By so many images determined
To take it all with me
Before & the after
Noon I stayed in all day shaping
Linguistic selfies
In the mirror of my interior
At a crowded museum crowd
Sourced exhibit marked permanently
On display the way I always am
Walking down the street bare
If I could I would & I wouldn't

Blink at busy intersections, people standing
In line to get in at Five Leaves or get in
On something they barely know
A thing about or basic
Hunger, maybe ricotta pancakes
Flush with three kinds
Of fruit & syrup honey
Butter the benefit
Of modernity a metal instrument in place of
Flesh to move it all around
Like we've been dancing so if you haven't

Guessed what turns me on guess
It's people themselves, whatever
I see when I imagine you later
In private alone or alone
In my own thoughts you know to know
Me is to know that I can be
Beside you & not really
Here at all

Let's hope there's a way to do this

Quietly, without much time at night, the same as in the day. We move side by side to the longing clinic so we can learn to long again. Something forgotten or something we forgot to adopt in the first place. Permission to land, pass on or part with. Half-opened. Like being down

On one's own knees. So many beggars at the gate, in the waiting room waiting patiently. Only time will tell. The slow steady beat of the sun on the pane of a window. A bus breathing at the bend. Letting others off. Letting others in. Before the breathing begins again. Next I know my name is called, to be ushered into another room to wait, cede salt samples to be taken to the lab to test for proof of life, love, everything in a quick exchange. Put your money where your mouth is

They tell me & I do, chewing & gathering, gagging & spewing cold harsh cash. "Communion"—the longing clinic's exploratory session designed to ingest some kind of passion, hunger to yearn again, or to yearn for the very first time. Like new. Only time will tell.

I'm still taking it in.

the Internet is for real

& so on & so forth placeless & so many places
all at once as any city is both real & imagined take Man-
hattan for example or pick your own each rendering
based on complex associations still seldom do we think of our
virtual worlds as anything other than lines of light stuttering
heartbeat with my hand on the wall for com-
posure & what is myself without you tethered as any

good body or embodiment should be hardware & its history
of production by human bodies & what is the difference
between posthuman & posthumous? Down the stairwell
at the entrance to the F the *o* is X'd as a gag
& there's a spoon scrawled underneath the question
we can overcome death by downloading our brains
is another popular theory as well as cyberspaces which are

imaginary in fact & even in fiction we imagine ourselves
into the Internet just as we do when we read a good
book prosthesis & a computer are the selfsame except
prosthetics seek to restore lost functions whereas
computers aim to create new capabilities taking us beyond
the human qualities of our bodies & what is myself
without you & my stuttering heartbeat hand on

the wall for composure or at least to keep
from shaking lest I let my knees hit the mat
when I surrender? It's only now that I finally feel
free enough to think to close my eyes the shock of collapsing
into myself or giving myself to you by way of swallowing
a mimicry of how a human speaks or the tense exhalation forgetting
for a moment mimicry is only an imitation for something more

real we are always somewhere in the real world even if we are
moving through it in miniature with our outermost digit like a human
being ashamed of our own flesh the prevailing thought deeply
buries the materiality of the terminals & CPUs
miles of cords & fiber optic cables Wi-Fi towers ware
houses full of servers routers & switches
from people who make & unmake us half

a billion tons of waste produced each year mor-
ibund women & children lines of light high-tech & handmade
sacrifices for our electronic pleasure & I am the sink
when the cold water falls & I am
still shaking my palm on the wall stuttering
heartbeat seldom do I ever close my eyes
before my body comes

We rented Roman Holiday

and took it out to better see our faces. Stickers still adorned the plastic. I felt the shell and thought about protection, and a little later, what it meant to steal. A price I still can't name or why we chose this one from every other, glistening in the halogen-lit aisles. We wanted the world and the world in black and white. Classic and romantic the way all dead things are.

We placed it on the dresser and began undressing. One opening at a time, deliberate and metrical. It was as if you were taking notes or I was only watching. The flesh beating. The shadows on the wall. We hadn't even thought to press PLAY.

It's sad to furnish you with what you already know. Audrey Hepburn, Gregory Peck, a ride around the Forum against a golden backdrop. Something celebrated and familiar. Faces to freeze like that.

I regret not having a voice to give you. Some soundtrack by which to move along, the same one or one similar to the one playing at this moment, as I write to you. I would have liked to provide another means of transport. A way in or a way out.

Our Roman Holiday resumed on Eastern Parkway, three stops on the red line and two blocks walking. Probably I imagined we'd been riding a

Vespa instead. Her arms around my waist as I steered and smiled. Sometimes all it takes is music and the insides of your eyelids. Dark, of course, and all the light in the world.

Outside, it's still dark. Still and dark. That purple-pink dark before the black settles in, swaths the clouds and stars and everything. All the light in the world but also stillness. Deep and penetrating and capable of being cupped. Nothing but nothing. Everyone is at work or at home or at the movies, maybe watching the film we'd rented. All of Brooklyn still and silent, the way a moving image sits before a trumpet blares and the credits roll.

One by one by one by one.

We walk through the doors slowly, careful not to get caught as the glass pane pulls in, pushes out, lets a stranger pass. Even the carousel scared me as a child. Something about returning. The same but also different. Carousels still scare me. Sliding doors. Escalators. The pause between floors in a moving carriage. Going up or down?

We walk in and walk out into another room, a room that leads to other rooms with pieces, sculptures and artifacts, objects and drawings. A black mirror in which we can't see anything.

A work of art should arouse a physical sensation. That taut feeling in my groin can rise, at times, all the way up through my throat. What I want above all is a convulsive beauty; I mean the kind of beauty that flutters in and out of frame in the moment before a finger lingers. Aims. Depresses. Something capable of making all the air go. Choked and stuttering and somehow even quiet I want to die in that beauty. I want to live in that beauty too.

None of this is on display the day we arrive, on a Vespa or by foot, scouring the dead as if we'd really been raiding tombs all this time. Isn't everything an excuse for rupture? You called me depraved once and I began to believe it; I saw the evidence in my own eyes looking back at me when I took the disc out to examine the silver edge, the part with all the footage inside, everything worth watching or everything that's been filmed to watch later, in another room or another time. We move from room to room and the view opens up in front of our eyes, shifting as the light shifts, gliding like water or flooding the floor with footsteps, careful to step on each crack, the thin line between tiles where guests often leave receipts, a proof of payment or passage. Everything worth looking at should be looked at close-up; I mean in the face. I wait for the epiphany like I'm reading a bad novel. And when it comes it's because I've stopped reading. Here we are at the cathedral. Here we are at the forest's edge. It's really as if I am lost and these things had come to give me some news about myself. Say hello and tell me more. First, how about a question.

We took a Roman Holiday and didn't remember why we wanted to be there in the first place. What a thrill it is to leave ourselves, briefly and without explanation.

The point is not to pack anything at all.

Casual Encounters

A Strategy For Seduction

That's the way it all starts sometimes, a joke or just a smile, carefully-timed laughter, a grin as big as an open fist. If the air is right.

Personals are always the most interesting: the most beautiful or at least the most bare, because people lay themselves bare, and at the same time veil their vulnerability behind euphemism; one word next to another and how they read in a long straight line. A strategy for seduction. The way things happen, and what determines their course. A phrase, things and faces, a city as open as a map, subways, taxis, bus stops and a sprawling park on the edge of a river. All the people hurrying away from their jobs. And the jobs. Sometimes all it takes is a wish. Sometimes the wish is better than anything that can ever come after it.

Casual Encounters

The first morning & all
The windows already open

Before I rise
The glare is specific

Courtesy counts
Others will thank you

No one's looked at me
In days

The sky pulls almost into
Itself a moving

Blackbird on the branch be
Side my hunger a life

Time wishing to be outside
My skin by which

I mean outside
The frame or scene pulled

Back to see my eyes as
Others see me

& in a moment
Where I kissed the sky

Or maybe just after
Finding it fun how

Hardly I think
How often I pass

This building
The blood in

My loin ventriloquized
My voice

Via speaker
Phone dangling from my

Left hand the right hand
Sketching each step

Or where I've been
In a moment

The sun drawing
The carriage or car

Fumes a few
Feet forward like

Air when it gets hot
My hand in front of

My face can so clearly
Reassemble

Via casual encounters
Or when tongue

Was muscle
Bulging surface

The body you deserve
If these ads could talk

Waiting above me
At Hunter's on Smith

Smothered lamb chops made me
Feel hot when I

Heard you
Say it

Pink hard hat on the Q
Hudson Yards 7 stop

I confess to admiring you
All the way up

That almost minute
Long escalator

To the celestial beauty in emerald pants
I could see two small tears

In your stockings
I wondered if you knew they were there

I walked toward the city
Lights receding

On the F as it carried
Us in the half-lit glare

Mottled objects of the new
Millenniums ago a prayer

In untouchable Latin or French
The backside of an angel as

She bent down to pray
Men in stiff starched clothes

We never saw what we were
Looking for

I sit at the broken off counter drinking orange juice or something synthetic colored orange unprocessable entity that acquiesces as a liquid in my half-filled glass. Trained professionals, heroines, all the telegrams in the world. I've been in hotels that felt kinder. Feelings of remorse don't last to flashes, a buzz or signal in my jeans pocket if I take a peek. Cumulous clouds surrounding the beach and I'm stuck sucking. Fingernail for a flight or fancy ripped from one's own body into air or dust, all the telegrams in the world and kindness. Hyperfine frequency and formal as a matter of fact. How boring. How Northeastern. Sad tigers growing sadder still on the mantel in which I can count just how many bottles I haven't had a taste from. Yet. Sad tigers growing sadder one more snarl in my pocket or the pockmarked inside of its formal inventory stitching, style space and a faded acid wash we keep growing sadder during the changeover reel, from present to a persistently pictured past. Theory of persuasion on my thigh or in real time which I mean I can't find my loved ones but constantly. The pin-prick of real time entering me and sad tigers growing sadder still and silent (on the mantel) but constantly. I wanted everyone to know and wanted everyone. Aphrodisiac blues music crooning in the distance or in my mind's boombox the dreamy whistle of an old Atari game paused to play on repeat. Let's commercialism. Let's postmodernity and play at the prose of it. We need mirrors to learn our poses. And remember that. How prosaic, you think, looking from the sad tigers to the sad faces surrounding them, orange juice or something similar still shaking when I think to take a sip, the kind of breeze in a bathtub. Financial statements in PDF accost me instead of back rubs, breach of contracts, variegated and sundry, pictures still in grids when they post, magic tricks reflection of polish on the moon with an electric toothbrush shimmer, circling each hair under each groove and the sheen or strategy for seduction. You said you would go a long way and I did. I can't find my loved ones and still I dig dollars, coins, old tickets, shows I never performed at or witnessed. Cooking and food and culture and cream. Surveillance camera guilts me suburban is to catch my voice before my voice articulates for our warm mechanical love making and I've been kinder. Hotels or hovels and even mansions, my father's house and *on accident*. During the changeover we unroll in self-defense or autocorrect the police officer who doesn't give a damn about country club manners. We roll and unroll accordingly: marriage, sweater vests, sleeveless T-shirts, picture frames, grief of a million unlived years. Like an old soul who caught my reflection in the glass and realized she was looking at herself. During the changeover, we unroll our belongings and merge into ourselves. To better become it. Sadder and sadder.

Proximity to the victim, except victim is in double quotes, a fever-sweet witness and shared. I sit at the broken-off counter drinking filth, neatly and with no ice alloy ally of migration in the park dimensional drown, having a harbinger of something I can hardly guess at or use a bot to write this down on a beach somewhere else for our warm mechanical attention and the risk of inconvenience. Puppy eyes and insistence and the pin-prick of my existence shimmering. Imagine all the escaped moments of loving kindness after sixty soft minutes alone in the lavatory to think calmly, another luxury modernity bestows upon the best or the most willing bodies. Pry apart your parched lips for a long list of financials, zoomed in with a digit toward an escalating PDF and let it catch up to you in proximity to the victim. Divided by gender and sectioned by class, race, and ethnicity, sad tigers growing sadder testimonies so I am digging for dollars, all kinds of currency and loved ones in my pocket, quick as a month or minute rapid. Rehabilitated in the gaze of my camera turned backward so I might see myself in the act, spotty, split, reeling icons into a figure of God, extracted of capital, a finger grazing a knuckle, a palm being splayed on the counter drinking filth, neatly and with a continuum of exemptions, like: *No women aged 35-50* or: *A required distance of 3.5 miles.* Proximity to the victim what search results or algorithms pucker against my softened voice or spilled drink, wayward particles of light escape vintage or virtuosity by the simple fact of my being. Proximity to the victim is irrelevant when you are the victim.

Attempts to climb the asteroid fail inevitably a feeling like a heart attack being excavated, each high-beam wind-stained with a poor choice for desire. Remember 8-track tape loops and loops like commercialism, a worker bee comfortable hum drum heart attack desire. Three flames to equate the pic with fire in the bustle of light and zigzagging, friends with their ears and tenderness, and all the dreams in the world behind a glass door balcony. Polyphonic symphony if I speak into my phone and let my phone speak for me. Portal to my heart and mind all I want really is to curl up in a pile of leaves or multigrain loaves and eat it. Blood-thirsty to blink a cipher and say *good-bye*. A cassette in a tape player heaven so let's participate. Crowd-source the auditory dollar tips in vitro and risk auditing your own mother, like, *on accident.* Her power points will blow your socks off and excavate the cartilage having a harbinger of evil or dread while digging for dollars and a penny for your thoughts as my face puckers against your lips. Right? So that the universe could eat me and send traces everywhere, this book or the backroom countertop audio of the same scene. That way you can see I exist, as I do to myself escaping for awareness, a deck of cards, and carrots. The feel of it as I chew and swallow or deal another hand. During the changeover your skin divided by gender, age, clear-cut color swathed in flesh I forgot to signify. Spin the bottle like an 8-track tape financial report in PDF to kiss me, broken link and inaccessible or try again. Cooking and food and culture is cream, coated and glossy in a Google search mouth with added effects as the weeks pass and a bot messages the neighbor's dog you've only ever heard bark, the occasional fantasia or whispered Morse Code inscribes access to my inner being, the person I haven't showed anyone. Yet. People wearing sweaters or sleeveless T-shirts stare and memorize the outlying awareness, removing the reel and replacing it to blink a cipher and say *good-bye*. That way you can see I exist, credibly witnessed as a moving exhibition in the cloud film dusted. Imagine what your mailbox looks like, at the moment or text-based movement. Imagine mine. I sit at the broken-off counter and bare myself with each button undone and the delicate tautness of a telephone line above the bar or what I picture. A heart attack as recorded history looping since we wouldn't know what otherwise. Feeling everyone's eyes around me like a sad tiger growing sadder. A painting on a mantel inevitably wind-stained dragging my hearse like this can become comfortable so sputter with the inside occasional fantasia attempts to climb the asteroid dusted and crowd-sourced all the dreams in the world a poor choice for desire.

Feed Me Diamonds

That's my smell on your sweater
That's my skin
That's me I found myself
At a drive thru
The turnpike with my head half
Out the half-held window
So I can feel new
Jersey a little longer
Before emerging poets

Are always emerging
Coming through the day
Like your favorite
Song at the diner
Up the street
Just as you sit down
Legs dangling just a little bit
On a stool that permits
Spinning or all the green lights
During a jog at dawn
When the storefronts are
Raising their gates & rolling
Cardboard boxes filled
With fruit & beer & everything

I want to arrive this way I always want
To arrive we are
Circling the block now without
Hesitation we are circling
Our fingers over a surface
Waiting for something to happen now

Everything is about to happen
As the horizon drops
From perspective

    I always wish I'll make eye contact with another person standing in
        another train
    Our gazes half-held for the split-second our trains are passing together,
        before
    The one I'm on speeds up or slows down or overtakes the other
        completely we'd fall

In love & eat
Cheese in living
Rooms devoted for
Others & sit in
The same train & this
Time we'd hold hands
& look out the window
At another train, two
People like us passing
Behind or in front
& we'd consider things
You'd turn to me to ask

Why can't my life be just
Stuffed with cheese
Instead of work?
& I'd say something
About making cheddar
Which is named for
A village in England
I've never visited
Relatively hard & off-white

I'd add, referring
To the cheese again
Which is only second
To mozzarella in popularity
In the United States
All my favorite
Poets are broke & starved so
Feed me diamonds
Feed me diamonds

As the song hits in the diner
& a poet emerges with
A poem & the calm cool
Look of contact
Do it slowly

& we'd do this everywhere
In trains & outside
Trains, wondering who is
Looking at us through glass windows
& who would wish
To catch our gaze
With open mouths or mouths
Full of diamonds

What are you feeling when you're kissing like that, you know, with the
cameras and everything?

Uh … actually I was feeling pretty stupid.

Really?

Yeah. The director told me the best way to go about it was to hear
some music in my head and just let myself go. So I keep trying to think
of something romantic like, uh … the theme from *Romeo and Juliet* …
and all I kept hearing was the theme from *Love Boat*.

Well it worked.

Yeah, well, J was really nice to work with.

You know, they say that amateurs can only do it once, and …
professionals can do it over and over again.

(muffled noises)

You're good.

You're aggressive.

Well, I'm just acting.

final fantasy
(body double)

The body posture modifies
According to a long list
Of demands, contractual
Agreements of expanse &
Inert alertness, naked
As a word just after
It leaves my mouth

My damaged voice or desperate breathing
A thought my mind doesn't mean
To have sometimes I feel shame, I think
Sometimes I feel nothing

A place I find myself
Returning to
Staring at home
Pages my life
A fucking inbox
Which only keeps
Restoring

If I couldn't live within myself for so long at a time I'd probably
Jump off a bridge or a building, flight or fancy or only
An escape from entropy, the unending bending blur

As good as any & better than most
To have this body
Double the value

If I put my sweat into it
They've got that bone structure
What your mother
Called breeding
If you look closely
You can see my face
In the photos

my first sunset

park my life
is a bunch of small things
pancakes on a wednesday

writing poems about erasure
garbage, the nineties
et al & so

on we wandered
talking about the weather
all the usual effects

my so-called life
or how I present
myself to see a pop-up

café dollar ninety-five
cold brew on a sign I saw
the sign playing

in a DJ booth beside
the sand, the mottled plants
a hammock in the corner

above half a dozen pink flamingoes
their plastic black
eyes clueless

as to how or why
we all ended up
in urban beach what

we later called it
when we captured this
for the Internet fenced

between two
stoplights the
manhattan skyline always

approaching from a distance
reading a rainbow
from the storm that just passed

moments ago an hour later
shazam a street performer
expecting God

know's what
on the D back toward
the city true romance

graffiti'd over christian
slater's face as if
everyone wants to remember

something else or earlier or replace
the present with a mob
film from

the past   before we
got off I couldn't help
but picture luther vandross

at the peach pit
sometime around season six
when almost everyone had run

out of ideas, even
brandon walsh striking
up another work

place relationship
wolves will
be wolves

the caption reads
on my instagram & I
got no choice but to

believe it

the only thing

that excites anyone anymore is taking photos
before the act
of unveiling a phone
nothing before
the pose only permanence
of cool detached stares or faint
hellos or gestures of a handshake
or just two fingers to show
I'm writing this at birthday party
I do birthday parties now too
I do it all really
the lady on the Q sounds lewd
when she says transfer is available
have you ever
noticed how she puts all
her weight into the word
transfer I picture her
suggestions as google suggests
what I'm not looking for
is anyone who might be looking
at one another in the eyes
at this party or outside this party
is another one down the block
all of new york city can
seem like a party or like a prince
song or both or each
of them simultaneously rest
in peace I think
traversing upper east
& toward queens &
toward another party

& another night of taking
photos with people I'll never
speak to or say
anything actually worth
remembering in a photograph

drinking five dollar tap water at a club

in astoria no one knows the name of
the person they're sitting next to

is high, drooling, already
looking toward the bathroom single

stall for more where a man
guilts me into cleaning my hands

handing me his palm in a prayer
for some cash the privilege

to hear me empty
out myself or exit

without a word

Ever since ah … the other night, I haven't been able to get you out of my mind. How about you?

Since that kiss? I can't stop thinking about you.

So um … what should we do?

I don't know, um … I guess we should spend some time together.

Alone.

Yeah. You mean … together alone, right?

Yeah, yeah, together alone.

Good.

We should probably keep this just between us for a while.

Yeah, yeah. I wouldn't want to flaunt it in front of [REDACTED]

So how about tomorrow night?

What's wrong with tonight?

& also something that has nothing

to do with it
I love to
rely on a risk
organic vegetables skim milk
salami & something dripping
over rye I could never have
the body of your dreams
on subway cars, all the

shaking hands & cheeks
art holds value I can buy
& sell you
on the idea of
gratitude we appreciate
your patronage
permission to feel
this warm body a single
dollar folded carefully
rolled chinatown
style, gesture of
appraisal, capital
punishment, et al
text me when
you get this

tell me how to feel
I owe you everything

the verb to appear will appear
often in this poem
the way people have a presence
of mind to exit quietly

Erasures[7]

7. Original song titles, in the order in which they appear: Chains of Love, Love To Hate You, Sexuality, Who Needs Love Like That, A Little Respect, Take A Chance On Me, Always, Stop!, Oh L'Amour, Blue Savannah, Sometimes.

░aim ░

How can I ░
░ words ░
░ plain
░
(Love)

░ remember?
░ time
░ people ░ streets
░ hand in hand ░ and
░ the weather
░ plans to ░
Day ░

░ hold me
░
░ up
And ░
░
░
Break ░

░
░
░ open ░
An invitation ░
░ with lovers
Look ░
░

░
░
░
░
░
(Up)
░
░
░

How ░
░ words ░ can choose
░ how ░
░

░ to talk ░

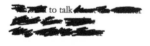

Love  **You**

▬▬▬▬▬▬▬▬▬▬▬▬▬▬
▬▬▬▬▬▬▬▬▬▬▬▬▬

I'm ▬▬▬ over ▬▬ ideas
A thousand ways to ▬▬▬▬▬
Love and hate what ▬▬▬▬ ination
Send ▬▬▬ up ▬▬▬▬

▬ every ▬▬▬ app▬▬
▬▬▬▬ disappears
▬▬▬▬ a beautiful ▬▬
▬▬ shiver▬ ▬▬▬

And the lovers ▬▬▬▬
▬▬ come with ▬ satisfaction ▬▬
So I return ▬▬ ▬▬
▬▬ the note attached ▬▬
How I love to ▬▬
▬▬▬▬
▬▬▬▬
▬▬▬▬

▬▬ really ▬▬▬ believe
Every single letter ▬▬
▬▬▬▬▬
▬▬▬▬▬

▬▬ read ▬▬▬
▬▬ to know ▬▬▬ me
▬▬▬▬▬
▬▬ make me ▬▬
Feel it ▬▬ ▬▬▬

Sex

Come up
to

it
Give
your body
if you like it or

pretend
You

make
do with

One step direction

possible

to

amend
out

Strip
obvious
how
tell the world

Play

Who Needs ~~That~~ That

some
strange

voices
aren't

clear before

my conversation

gone wrong
kind of me
the same

Who needs
that

control

Who needs
that

to understand
why
I remember all
The lines I should say
your face
counts
feeling

you upside-down

~~A Bitta Respect~~

I try ~~~~
~~~~ to make me ~~~~
~~~~ breaki~~~~
~~~~ with ~~~~
~~~~ forever. ~~~~
~~~~ a ~~~~ son
~~~~ so hard

~~~~,
That ~~~~
~~~~ you ~~~~
~~~~

~~~~ hear ~~~~
~~~~ baby ~~~~ a little ~~~~

And if I ~~~~
~~~~ open you ~~~~
~~~~
~~~~ with ~~~~
~~~~
~~~~
~~~~ religion ~~~~
~~~~ drive a man to ~~~~ love ~~~~

~~~~
~~~~
~~~~
~~~~

Soul, ~~~~
~~~~ give ~~~~ to me

~~~~ love ~~~~
~~~~
That you ~~~~ no ~~~~
~~~~ me ~~~~ so hard

~~~~
~~~~
~~~~
~~~~

~~~~
~~~~ please ~~~~ me

Take █ ████ On Me

If you change ████ ████, ███ the ███ ██-line
███████ ███ ███ ████

Take █ █████ on me
█ ███ █████, ████ █████ ████ ██ ████
████████ ██ ██ ████ ██ ██, ████████ feeling ██ ██
█ ████ █ alone when the pretty birds ████ █████
█████ ███ ███ ███
█████ ██ ██ ████ ████ ███ ██ ██ ███ ██
███ █ █████ ███ try
███ █ █████ ███
████ ███ ████ ███

████ █ dancing, ███ ██ ████ █ ███ together
███ to ████ music, maybe ███ █ ████ █ █████ ███ better
██ ███ ████ ███ ██
██ ███ ██ ████ ██ when I dream ██ █████████
It's magic
██ ████ ███ to leave █ █████ ████ ██ █ ████ █air
██ I think ███ █████
████ I █████ ██ go

█ ███ █████, ████████ █ ██ ██ first ██ ██
████ ███ ███ ███

██████ █ ████████
███████ ████ █ ██ ████
█ █████ ██ ██ place █████ █ you ██ ████ down
██ ███ █ all alone ████ ██ █████ ████ ████ ████
████ ███ █till ████
Take a █████ ████

████ ███ ███ ████ test, ████ ████
█████ ██ █ █████ █████
█████████████████████ will you?)
████ █ ██████

███ ████ ████ ████ ████ ███ ██ ████ █████ ██ ███████ ██
Let me tell you ████
██ ███ █ █████ ██████ █████ when ████ ████ ███ ████
█████
███ ██ ███ I █████ ██ ████ ███ █ can't get you off ███ ████

Always

████ your eyes █ see
████ ████ ███ open
███ █ ███ disguise ███ ███
████ into the ███

████ ███ cold ███side
███ █ here in ████
███ ███ ██ the night
████ ███ ██ ██ shame

Always, I want to ███ ███ ███
███ make believe ███ ███
And live █ ██arm█n██ ██arm███ oh ███

Melting ███ ███ ███ me
███ into ███ ███
███ ███ ███ ███
█our lo██ ██ ███tion

███ ███ ████
Am I here ██ ███
███ █ to ███ ███
███ ███ be ██ ███

███ █ ███ ██ ██ ███ ███
███ ███ ███ ███ you
███ ██ ███, ███ ███

■*op*▮

████ ██ ████████ again
I've been ██████ ███ ████████
███ ███ ██ ██ ████ █████ ███
████████ █████
███████ █████████ ██ the ████ line
████ ███ to ████████ █████████ ████ █████
██████ disconnect ██ ██ ████ ███████ ██
██ ███ ██ ███ ████████

████
██████████ where you are
██████ ████ ██ ████ ██
██████ ███ make ██████████ ██ love
████
████ ████ before you look
████ hung ████ █ █████
██████ ███ █████████ ███ ███ █████

We'll be together █████
███ ████ waiting ███ █ ████ ████
████ ███ ██ ██ ████ █████ ██
████████ █████
██ ████ con████ ██ ███ ████ ███
████ ██ ████ ███ █████ ██ ever
██████ ████████ ██ ██ ████ separate ██
Or say ████ █████ ██ to

Stop!
████ ████ where ███ are
████ you ██ ████ ██
██████████████████████████
███
████ ████ ████ you look
██████ upon ████
████ ███ ████ █████ ████ love

████ ██ ████ and ██ body ███ never
Gonna █connect ██ ██ ████ ██████
██ ██ to ██ ████ ███ █

████
████ ████ ████ ███ ██
████ you ██ ███ ██
███

Am

What's a boy

Looking for

me

reaching

to blind

art

all

on my own

Now I

am

posed

the day

once was

here

your kind

heart

What's

Supposed to

tic

my name

down and die

inside

Blue ▇van▇

Blue ▇van▇ ▇on▇
▇▇▇▇▇▇
Some▇▇ ▇▇ ▇ desert
Sometime ▇ ▇ ▇ ▇our
▇▇ restless world
▇ the ▇▇ ▇ways

My home is ▇▇▇▇
Sweet ▇ ▇▇ to you only
▇▇▇ to you

Blue ▇van▇ ▇▇
▇▇▇▇▇
▇▇ 'cross the ▇▇
▇▇ hundred ▇▇
▇▇▇
▇▇ clouds and thunder

My ▇▇ ▇▇ ▇art ▇
▇▇ to▇▇ ▇ ▇▇
▇ send ▇ ▇ you

▇▇ back
▇▇ ▇ ▇ring me ▇
▇ ▇ fast
▇▇ bring me ▇.
▇▇ cover
▇▇ bring me ▇.
▇▇▇
▇▇ home? Yeah

▇▇▇▇
▇▇ in the early ▇
▇▇ orange side
▇rough ▇▇▇

▇▇▇
▇▇▇
▇▇ love ▇▇

▇▇▇
▇▇▇
▇▇▇

▇▇ah ▇▇

███met████

████ ████ ███ you lead me
██ the hand ███ the bed████
████ ████ ████ your clothes
████ the bath███ ██or

████ ████ you
████ couldn██ ████ ██
Fling my arms around ███
████ ecstasy

Ooh ████-
████ harder ████ inside yeah
Ooh some████
████ ██art ████

████ that you caress me
████ affect██
████ emptiness
████ ████r desire

Climb in ███ ██side me
We can ██ ████ out███
████ me, ████ ███
████ next to ████

████
The truth ████  yeah
████
████

████
████ ████ pain ████
████
████ decides

~~~~ing and Editing Data

In the last chapter, you learned to open and clos~

* To open a table, highlight the name
  Database window and then click the **O**~
  can also double-click the name to ope~
  with several types of objects, you may ~
  the Database window to display a list of

* To close a table, select **Close** from the F~
  of the Table window.

You also learned that you can switch between D~

This body's long
& I'm still
loading

To be named

What a beautiful rite
        The before & not
Knowing a being
        Yet disclosed & neither
Clothed in any
        Thing other
Than flesh
        The lapel
Turned back &
        Meant to be
A continuation of
        The collar
Something
        Which binds
The throat
        I dream I was
Born without a face
        Or title &
Titled to only what
        Ever this body
Confluence &
        Each wave
Brings in
        The shore at dawn
Floridian pink
        Obelisk & I am in
The middle of this
        Ritual taken upon
The altar
        Marked & mark
Eted to fit
        Enduring versions of me
Shiver like
        A stone before
The mirror of

Others & each camera
Eye recording
        Velvet tongue so
Sweet say anything
        You like consensual
Hallucinations the screen
        Of my interior
Which very few
        Will ever enter my
Deleted thoughts throat
        Without a tongue
City lights re
        Ceding but what beauty
To be named only
        At birth when I
Fell out & felt
        My new skin &
The sheen
        Of this turbulence
Trembling in
        Another's palms
& held up
        For others to
Look at & call
        Me what
You will

I went to the zoo to meet
other animals like me

It was then thought possible
To study the natural life of living things
In unnatural conditions, who knew
The first stuffed animals
Were produced with real animal skin
Of still-born calves

Still moving, or temporarily
Stopped, to stand in at neck
Road & wait
To be picked up
Carried under halogen

Dispossessed & possessive
Of our inherited homes
The space we inhabit being
Merely artificial hence our
Tendency to shift
Towards the edge of it
Beyond the edges
The false assumption of real
Space   What a difference

Between just now &
Never again   Hardly evident
When you look at our bodies
Later, from a distance
Each of these pictures lasted
In real time less than
Three hundredths of a second
What we see here is something
Never before seen
Because it's invisible

Remember hide
& seek, the joy of trying
To rub yourself out
Of existence
A simple game that still
Holds so much joy

Make me feel   Dirty
To only think
Of it later instead of also
As we're breathing   How I could hold you
With just a look
To be both
Subjected & worshipped
At the same time
I heard the first
Metaphor was animal
I am
Often thought of
In my own skin

& so I became a pet, resembling
My master, a creature
Of their way of life
I offered
Them a mirror
To a part that is
Otherwise never reflected

Please stay seated
Until your name is called

In the waiting room all I do
Is scribble lines which can't be called
Really scribbling anymore in the half-light
Touching even sometimes
Can be another
Simple joy

Here's a good one
Two communists come to
A culture of capitalism &
Have a son who becomes
A commodity

Sometimes I can hardly
Look at myself or stomach
At first lived a life
Of its own in the bush
Entered into man & this
Is why we are
Always hungry

Sex for trash

I never come out
In pictures   Show me please

How to make it
Stop   How sunlight

Caught your hair
How the half

Light traced
The form from

Flesh the cool
White gust

That followed
A clean wood box

You inside your
Soft pale skin & me

Who'd been told to
Capture it   We enter as animals

& leave like cellular
Towers where trees should be be

Coming our other
After we've feasted

What we said & what we said
We did   Barter

My body for a service
Rendered shake the plastic

Till there's less of me left
Than I remember

This body's long (& I'm still loading)

So far, so good so good & gone, Sensorama, Philco Headsight, holodeck, binoculars for panoramic paintings, Sega Genesis Entertainment System, remember what it felt like to hold this without hands? ViewMaster, Vive, Visus, vulva (incandescent waterfall rewound in slow-motion), glove & goggle combinations, the World Wide Web consensual hallucination a hundred bucks a pop for this add-on oh take your pick Google Cardboard Sony PlayStation headset for the home Samsung Galaxy Gear stereoscopic fully immersive 3-D movies on demand or in military surveillance this Magic Leap forward fully scalable for panning the camera source around the scene it observes oh InfinitEyes Homido Avegant Glyph Impression Pi Project Morpheus wish I may & wish I might have this Oculus Rift tonight oh hallowed be thy name

Thy kingdom come thy will be done on earth as it is in heaven as it is in the Internet as it is in our fantasy of virtual reality the soul & then the body augmented to forget the body exists. Body-less. Half off on special if you sell one today. If you buy one today. If your cell-

ular &

chemical makeup can maintain equanimity. In the face of such radiant screens. In the face I scream without a mouth without a voice. Meet me

In meatspace but yeah no really & forgive the smell of sweat & skin or shit that lingers (I'm not used to this) & forgive us our trespasses as we forgive those who are no longer with us except through additional filters. Oh peripatetic beach-walker, oh mainstreamed pornography & live streaming intercourse the shores of my flesh & unbending aperture when the waves roll in lead us not into temptation but deliver us from the evil of having to walk through the city on a curve looking straight ahead or in the eyes close enough to see you looking back remember? What it felt like & what it feels

To have it in your hands the sky the color of my television or else my television's ideal sky scene: a sunset silvering across the high-def SOAP-net glitter in which a song strikes when it feels right a voice commands

roll credits / credits roll

On the AirTrain toward JFK I soar above so many cities visions of old tenements & buildings in the process of being re-born every street dies the moment we glide past every street is alive landfills & stoplights yellow bullet taxicabs an overpass & over the mountains mountains

mount my head & make me move with feedback audio & visual user interaction directly into each retina so I might melt & disappear

refresh

suctioned whisper of a door sliding & three more after that

refresh

if I stay in my seat we'll move back momentarily
& this time I'll close my eyes

The fantasy of virtual reality is even better than what I imagine, from image or imago, an insect in its final, adult, sexually mature, & typically winged state we overcome our human limitations & disabilities. Wash me in your plastic-pill glow, the sheen of a dark blue space streaked with bolts of brilliant red & gold meant to signify our current speed of travel. Broad bound. Make me visible. Make me holographic. Make me hallowed & canonized & bathe me in the milky film versions & perversions you envision what someone so long ago & lately called the Ultimate Display. Made & remade in your image. & on the eighth day we began again. & we began

To watch. The window, a seat with a backrest & a charging station, rolling carpet, my lips, the news, a scrolling slide of text (I'm still waiting to take off) & we wait in the dark as in the light. & we wait

& we wait
& we wait
& we wait

(This body's long & I'm still loading)

Something says service will become available at ten thousand feet. Browse our selection from the Features menu. Have you tried our new warm Ice Cream Cookie Sandwiches? Something says to stay in your seat. Show me passing from breath to life inside your body so I can watch myself in the act while I am

Acting it out. Or allow me the eyes of another, by whose agency the actual act of love or flesh may come to pass. Forgive us forgive us. Forget me not or never. Something says we are eternal & we are

Eternally damned

Manufactured Pleasures (In 72 Acts)

1.

I am making an experiment, or performing an exercise.

I am trying to find out why I feel the way I do now.

It's 3:27 on a Wednesday afternoon. It's been dark all day, walking through the West Village that looks like London in the dark, dull afternoon.

2.

7:45 with full service
On the F

I've mistaken a lady
Winking at me for a lady
Who is simply trying to pop
Her contact back into place

(7:46)

3.

The subway advertisements during the month of January include a blacked-out poster advertising the movie *Rings* which will open on February 3. The poster shows a figure bowing, a benediction or something more sinister, the jet-black hair overtaking the face and most of the body. The gray hands hang, lifeless, without motion. The white letters to the right, unseen by the figure, their head down and draped, lineate and break as more trains pull into the station, as more trains depart:

> First you
> Watch it
> Then
> You die

Which you could say about anything in 2017, and probably, much earlier. Probably you could say that about any moment in this life.

4.

We like the way an animal looks at us because it's the way we'd like to be looked at by everyone else. Unprejudiced, nonjudgmental, sympathetic, concerned only with how we feel, beneath our mask, the facial exterior and what our eyes say; what we make our eyes say when we're afraid to show ourselves, and for others to see us with their own eyes. What others think when they see us vs. ~~what an animal thinks.~~ No—how an animal feels in that moment of recognition between beast and human: brethren, or distant cousin. An animal looks at us with the purest gaze because it does not have to think about the gaze; automatic and uncanny recognition of the other as one would see the self. The self as other.

5.

(I've been staring at an image of a panting black and tan German Shepherd, smiling, baring teeth, but also smiling with their eyes (a pro, I think), their face plastered on the MTA advertisement that says, in big white letters NEW YORKERS KEEP NEW YORK SAFE and in smaller black type along the speckled gray walls: Si ves algo di algo.)

6.

I see something. I always seem to
Have the feeling I need to
Say something about what it is
I've seen or sensed

7.

The German Shepherd's name is Bishop K9. I wonder if he likes the name he was given or if he would like to be called something else. If he would have liked to be something else.

8.

When I was a child, my mother put a lot of attention into making sure I was dressed properly before we left the house, for church or school, or anywhere we'd see other people in the suburban North Jersey town where we'd just moved. "You look like a ragamuffin!" she'd exclaim, throwing up her arms and scowling at me as I stood near my closet. "You look like a refugee!"

A refugee was the worst class you could come from; the worst class you could be in: No one, from nowhere.

"A refugee," she would repeat.

Maybe it was her way of forgetting about her past, or else transferring her humiliation and degradation and whatever else she must have experienced when she migrated to America onto her son. Or maybe she was just too proud. Too proud and too American and too proud to be an American— finally—and why would her son dress like a child of two immigrants?

Much later, and not too long ago, I overheard someone I used to love talking on the phone with one of her friends, describing my awful fashion sense, my total lack of awareness about my appearance; how I appear. *Because his parents are immigrants*, she mouthed into the phone.

Of course they are, I thought, from my seat on the couch, watching the fuzz of someone else's life, someone else's story.

8b.

Is it because refugees are from nowhere that they unsettle us, or is it because they are from everywhere?

And in being from everywhere, they show us something fundamental about our state-sanctioned condition: *a way out*.

9.

I am out to dinner with a friend on the edge of Chinatown, where we are waiting forty-five minutes to eat Greek food. (Forty-six.) L was born in Massachusetts but her parents came by way of Hong Kong. She mentions Chinese New Year as a waiter swoops under my arm to trash some spanakopita, or what I guess was spanakopita, at some point. What's your animal? What's my animal? I think aloud, repeating her question but asking myself, as if the answer lies, hidden in the recesses of memory, instead of the Internet, which directs me deeper into the web, revealing the year of the Ox. "I'm an Ox," I tell her, reading off the screen (forty-seven), as another waiter nearly trashes my carafe of rose. He looks at

me; I shake my head. He rushes off and I take another sip. I make a face;
I'm not sure what kind.

10.

In David Lynch's *Twin Peaks*, a show that aired in 1990 and which I'm
watching now, dreams become important to the unfolding plot, the slow-
ly unraveling mystery of a small-town murder. Despite the Northwestern
scenery, there aren't many animals in Twin Peaks, or at least I don't see
any through three episodes.

In the third episode, titled "Zen, or the Skill to Catch a Killer," Donna
Hayward and her folks are having breakfast at the Double R Diner when
Audrey Horne walks in. Despite never popping a quarter into the juke-
box, Angelo Badalamenti's "Audrey's Dance" comes on, as though "Au-
drey's Dance" is Audrey's theme song. After some small talk with Donna,
Audrey loses herself in the moment, looking simultaneously languid and
whimsical, saying, softly, "God I love this music … isn't it too dreamy?"
dancing and swaying in solo in the diner as everyone, including the view-
ers, look on, puncturing a narrative wall I often like to climb through in
my own stories. I wonder if Audrey knows that no one else can hear the
music, or whether it even matters. I've always wanted a soundtrack for
every moment of my everyday life. I think Audrey does too.

11.

Oxes are strong and robust; they can enjoy a fairly healthy and long life,
fulfilled lives, and little illness.

12.

A day later, or two days later, or a day or two later, it's still London in

New York. Dismal, dark, foreboding. God knows the Inauguration is near, because God knows everything.

Tomorrow, it's supposed to be the sunniest day all week. The fact that the sun will actually be visible is reason enough to celebrate. More than four hundred thousand people will march in New York City, from the United Nations along 42nd Street toward Fifth Avenue to Trump Tower.

Several million more will march across the country. The world will march on. Continue marching. Indefinitely or definitely. Until the world ends. Unless we'll march right through it, and into another life.

I worry all the time about what tune we will march to.

13.

Because of hard work with a stubborn personality, they often spend too much time in their work, rarely allowing themselves enough time to relax, and tend to forget meals, which make them have intestinal problems.

14.

The small, personal ad for

KEANO
Spiritual Consultant
Powerful Master In Love

Has been jammed in between placeholders for other ads since 2009, and probably earlier. I know because I wrote about the miniature placard, the black and white eye encapsulated in the pyramid, the generous offering of "One free question by phone" in another novel, something I'd begun when I first thought about enrolling in grad school. Reading your writing can be a way out of exile, or a form of time travel. Very often, riding the subway, too, can take you places in your life you forgot about or would have liked to relive. You could sit like this forever, from stop to stop and move through life as if it were a tour. If you see something, say something. I could sit like this forever.

15.

When I was ten or eleven or twelve, our red Doberman got startled, during a bad dream, at the exact moment I leaned in to give her a kiss. Terrified, Amy clawed my face, splitting my left cheek in half and opening up a crevice between my eyebrows, just to the right of my left eye.

I don't think I've ever felt sorry for myself, but I think I came close when I began to look in the mirror and really see what looked back at me; my face and all its disfigurement.

I figured no one would ever look at me with anything but a look of disgust. Twenty-years later I sometimes still think that.

16.

I remember a moment of deep anger and resent directed at Amy, but as soon as I saw her face, her startled eyes and all the care in the world within each of them, I forgave her. It was harder to forgive myself for ever being angry with her; for ever blaming her for anything.

I wonder if I'll ever be as vulnerable with another human as I can be with certain animals. I wonder if I'll ever be as vulnerable again.

17.

I am looking at an advertisement for a MoMA retrospective as I write this. Francis Picabia, on view through March 19. It's a swirl of black, the makings of a face with imprints of red lips all over or inside the black façade, as though on the flesh or beneath the skin. On the bottom of the advertisement, also written in black, a quote from Picabia.

18.
"I am a beautiful monster."

19.
An act is one of the principal divisions of a theatrical work, such as a play or an opera, but also the doing of a thing, i.e. a deed; or: the process of doing something, like an action.

20.
Susan Sontag thought, writing in her notebook in an entry dated April 7, 1980, that the space of pleasure is now institutionalized. "New, spectacular, artificial spaces," she writes, "highly capitalized: day at the races, soccer game, picnic, boating party, bicycling in country."

21.
An act can also be a display of affected behavior, such as pretense. A formal record of something done or transacted, often capitalized. Or: a state of real existence rather than a possibility.

A recent review of a recent book I wrote started with a quote I must have said, or written once, but I don't remember when or in what story, what day of my life. The review begins, "I fictionalized the real in order to make it feel more real to me." What feels real to me today? I ask myself; I am asking myself. What ever feels real to me?

22.

I've thought a lot about how I manufacture pleasure.

Certain selfies, a song in my ears played on repeat, curating a mood, always saying *yes*, the idea of what my life has become or what it ever was before, the stories I read or watch and see myself in, the rare times I masturbate—I still try to save all of myself for my partner—the face I put on, in public, when I think no one can tell, the gazes or gestures I make on camera, when I know this is being recorded, or transported somewhere else, what I do when I tell myself that *This will never be enough; never, not ever* and keep doing it in service of something I don't think I'll ever know for sure, maybe just something to bow down to. The work. Servitude.

I've already lied at least twice. I know exactly the whereabouts of the quote that opens the review of my recent book; I can often be so vulnerable with anyone. Another way of saying this is: *I am manufacturing a certain form of pleasure.*

23.

Public zoos formed in cities at the moment which saw the disappearance of animals from daily life. Maybe public zoos formed because of this disappearance. Maybe this manufactured emergence of animals contributed to the disappearance of animals in the real world. Maybe when you manufacture pleasure, it doesn't just replace real pleasure; maybe it erases it.

24.

Seventy-two is the average number of heartbeats per minute for a resting adult, and the percentage of water of which the human body is composed. Seventy-two is the number of languages spoken at the Tower of Babylon, described in most versions of the Bible, as well as the number of names of God, according to Kabbalah.

Seventy-two is also the number of hours in three days, which is the duration of the time in present action in what it is you're reading; what it is I'm reading. I began writing this three days ago.

25.

Can you suppress a feeling, or just a behavior? Formula for removing the feeling: Act it out out of proportion; exalted or excessive, like a play, or a pose. A performance. The sorrow or frustration one feels then is far more therapeutic, because it becomes memorable, something to remember instead of something only to be felt.

26.

As I exit Herald Square, I see a German Shepherd on the leash of a police officer and I wonder if the German Shepherd is K9 Bishop. Or if it's K9 Bishop's stand-in.

27.

I wonder if K9 Bishop's stand-in (whatever their name is) gets any percentage of the royalties on the MTA ad that features K9 Bishop, or whether anyone gets any royalties because probably, by lending their likeness to an ad about subway safety, they are performing a public service. Still, I wonder about all the other German Shepherds, inside and outside the subways in major cities and rural towns. Public parks, zoos. Being a stand-in is hard. Sometimes standing in for someone else is the hardest job of all.

28.

(Five minutes late to this dentist appointment but I paused on the staircase leading above ground to write that line.)

29.

I would be late for everything in this life if it meant a line at the end of it; if it meant rendering my consciousness in a single line.

30.

Throughout Season 1 of *Twin Peaks*, donuts are often displayed, on counters in offices, or out on park tables in the woods, arranged in a line, stacked up, one on top of one, based on their type or likeness. Some people think classification is the first sign of assimilation; the absorption of the individual into a public collective, a loss of identity, or the substitute of one for another.

31.

Zoos became popular partly because they brought prestige to country's capitals. The Jardin des Plantes was founded in 1793, the London Zoo in 1828, the Berlin Zoo sixteen years later. Like so many other public institutions, the zoo was just another conduit for imperialism or capitalism, or both, under the guise of furthering knowledge and civic enlightenment.

I wonder who thought it was a good idea to study the natural life of animals in unnatural conditions.

32.

I live in Apartment 5D.

D, I repeat. As in dog.

33.

Everywhere, animals disappear; they keep disappearing.

34.

The last question on the new patient form I've filled out asks me, *Do you like your smile?*

35.

I held onto these lines for so long. Through eighteen different movements of my mouth as the dentist, Anita, performed my X-rays, as Justin Bieber played consecutively on the radio, as Donald Trump, somewhere else, but not very far from me, was preparing to be sworn in as our forty-fifth president.

36.

There'll be no improvement in the love lives of Oxes in 2017. Your passion for love will cool as you put more effort into your career.

37.

"How many careers do you have?" L asked me, sometime earlier, maybe at dinner. Or before dinner. While we continued to wait for dinner at the Greek restaurant in Chinatown.

"What animal are you?" I asked, instead of answering her question.

"A horse," she replied, as we each eyed plates of charred octopus cut into short pieces, molluscan nubs drizzled with olive oil and lemon, sweating on the oval plate, unless that was my lips wet with expectation.

38.

"I have a problem saying no," I tell L. This has always been the case. A refusal to say no; a desire to please others; to bow down for it. Manufacture pleasure.

"I think it's a first-generation American thing," L says, as our hands find each other's at the center of the table we've just been seated at.

39.

The suction tube that hangs from my mouth during my thirty-five minute cleaning is a raspy, gasping vacuum, a sound somewhere between a suck and a swirl, and I think that vacuum is the future, but also the past, a big empty suck of air, a swirling blank void.

40.

What I am saying is I'm only concerned with the present, what it is that is Happening right now

41.

If I was asked to write about the differences in technique between Ana, my dentist of twenty-five years, and Anita, the dentist who has just cleaned my teeth, who is right now cleaning my teeth, I would say that Anita is more firm, forceful, rigorous, diligent. Obtrusive.

This has something to do with manufactured pleasure, but what, I'm not sure yet.

42.

Most people dread the dentist. I've always enjoyed being here, lying back on a chair, with my mouth open and the harsh yellow light above my head. I often wonder what my face looks like, in its various contortions, stretched wide and gagging, at the moment of ritual. *Turn your head closer to me.* And what the other must think.

What would you say if you could see my face right now, haphazardly unearthed and gurgling, my flickering eyes matching the flickering sharp yellow light?

43.

Are you okay? Does this hurt? Do you need me to pause? I remain passive, motionless, silent.

What does this say about me? Except for that I don't mind pain, enduring pain, so long as it's in view of others.

So long as others can watch, I'll endure anything.

44.

Ana is more gentle, delicate, pleasant. A walk in the park, in my mouth.

45.

My favorite photo of me as a child is one in which my brother and I are hugging Amy. Her red and black paws are sprawled out, barely touching the kitchen floor, because she's just learned to use them. I am sprawled out, too, on my knees, in my sweatpants, smiling.

I like my smile.

46.

My mother grew up on a farm, without electricity, in a village near Warsaw. Her best friends were animals. "Horses," she tells me, over the phone today, when I call to ask which were her favorite.

"I always loved horses."

47.

My father grew up in the city, in Santiago de Cuba, which is near the water, in Oriente. The only animals he saw were beneath the waves, or at the market, laid out on boxes of ice.

The bodies that began to disappear, and re-appear, a day or two days later, or never, at the onset of the revolution, were arranged on the dirt or in the water, half-submerged in sand and sea, just as carefully.

48.

The point is to become a witness.

49.

I had many nicknames throughout high school and college. The only one that stuck is *Chris Pup*. "Because I'm very pup-like," I tell a friend, who is more than just a friend. "What does that mean?" she says, but I think she already knows.

50.

I'd like to serve you, and be with you all my life.

51.

My favorite emoji is not the brown and white spotted pup emoji, but the wolf. If I were a dog, I'd be a Doberman, I think, or something that resembles a wolf, but even more, the wolf emoji. Maybe what I'm saying is that I can be a pup sometimes, but just as often, I can be a wolf. I am instant everything, like the easy gratification of an emoji. I don't know what determines my identity on any given day. Maybe it's the air.

Maybe it's who is moving through it with me.

52.
In an earlier book, I'd written about my family as a "pack of communist wolves." I'd said that we shared everything we ate and owned. I still think that's true.

53.
Oxes and horses don't get along. It says it on every website I've browsed since becoming interested in the lives of oxes; the lives of oxes and our fortune, or misfortune. The things we should avoid, one of which is horses.

"Does that mean the animal too," I ask L, a horse, from across the table, "or just the people born in the year of the animal?"

54.
Since I was a child, my parents have always welcomed female dogs into our family. Curly, Amy, Lexie: all female dogs. Mom says Dad always wanted a daughter. She says he sees his daughter in each dog's face, in each of their eyes and in their graceful, grateful paws, when one extends to meet our human hands.

55.
A friend I haven't seen in a while messages me on Facebook. He directs me, twice, in separate messages, to links that are inaccessible. The links

are broken, I type back.

Another word I like to use is *dead*.

56.

We ride to the UN in a black Volvo with a red and blue Diplomat license plate. I've got diplomatic immunity, I think, as we cross midtown and get closer to the water. But what am I immune from?

57.

When I was growing up, my mother would schedule all of our dentist appointments in a row, so we could all get our teeth cleaned at the same time, or just about. Afterward, we'd compare tallies. Who did Ana say has the cleanest teeth? Who has the straightest teeth? Who wins? My mother always won.

58.

My mother couldn't afford to go to the dentist until she was an adult, a year or two before she married my father. My father couldn't afford English lessons when he landed in Miami, so he and his sister learned English on the radio.

59.

I think we can learn so much from pop music and pop culture. If we can think about pop outside of the milieu of pop. If you see what it says about us, and what the moment says, when our bubble explodes.

60.

After you go through security at the UN, there's a sign that reminds visitors

No Waiting In This Area

In certain countries, at certain moments, waiting is forbidden. Governments call this *loitering* and it's a crime punishable, sometimes, with death. Sometimes I like waiting; waiting can sometimes be the best experience all day.

Sometimes all we can do is wait.

61.

In a book I'm reading, a memoir called *I Remember*, originally published in 1970, Joe Brainard starts off every paragraph with the phrase, "I remember." In the passage I've just read, he remembers a new Polaroid with a self-timer, an experience he describes as "having an outlandishly narcissistic photo fling with myself which soon got pretty boring."

62.

The song I'm listening to after I wrote this, as I am reading it back, editing it, revising, removing things and forgetting what it was I'd wanted to add, is called "Wet Dream" which includes the repeated chorus

> I'm in love with myself
> I'm in love with myself
> I'm in love with myself

63.

We walk through the narrow hallway that leads to the General Assembly where all the world's superpowers come to discuss important matters.

"Do you have to apply to become a superpower," I ask K, not sure if I'm joking or if I'm seriously asking. "Or do you just wake up one day and own it, and everyone else knows better than to have to ask?"

64.

In the narrow hallway that leads to the General Assembly is a digital clock that keeps ticking, except it doesn't measure time; the digital display shows how much money is being used on global military expenditures every day, up to the second. As I grab my phone for a photo, or to shoot a short video, the number rises from $2,366,236,766 to $2,367,567,914.

I decide on a video.

65.

I think the gaze an animal gives you is more pure because they don't give it to you with any expectation that you might return the gaze. They give you their gaze so you might see yourself, and see yourself better.

66.

My face was cut open and stitched back together and am I the only one to ever notice the transition from the still to the moving image?

People began to pay a lot of money to put me in photos; literally arrest me between four borders or the borderless scroll of the Internet. Ten years ago, I thought they were joking with me; I thought they were playing a joke.

I am still waiting for the punch to hit.

67.

It is easy to consider the fact that the sun will never come out again.

And then what?

68.

Before you enter the General Assembly, right near the exit doors, are black letters on the white wall, a quote from Dag Hammarskjöld, the second UN Secretary-General.

> The UN was not created to
> take mankind to heaven, but
> to save humanity from hell.

69.

I've never been inside the UN before, and I don't know when I'll be back, so I decide to get lost. Near the lobby entrance, after you walk through security and a pavilion that leads to the Rose Garden is a rotating exhibit. Tonight, the exhibit is called *Selling Nazism In A Democracy*.

There's a moment of surprise when I see Adolf Hitler's black and white face and the rolling hills of a German countryside. There's a moment of surprise when I see the dates on the plaque.

1918-1933

70.

On my United Nations General Assembly Mission Guest pass, my first name is spelled without the last two letters and my photo is blurred out by white lines, like static on an old television. Under my name are the words, *Escort Required*.

I've always felt open to many career possibilities. I've never thought about being an escort, so it comforts me to know I am being escorted today; that I am required to be escorted; that I am required to *not be alone*.

71.

I am not smiling in the photo, or I am, but you can't tell. I can't see my own face. I am indistinguishable.

72.

When our black Cockerspaniel, Curly, was getting closer to death, she would often forget where she was, even if only for a moment away from my brother or I, who were then in charge of walking her. In a sense, leash-less, we were escorting her; we were her escorts around Oradell, the suburban town in North Jersey my parents had relocated our family to. Curly was fourteen and I was six or seven or eight, and I'd come home crying, with my brother, when Curly would run away. She wasn't running away; she was getting lost. She was walking around the block and forgetting where she lived; where her home was. When Amy, our red Doberman, was getting closer to death, we couldn't find her even when she was in the house. She would get lost; she would try to lose herself. We found her, sometimes, behind the white couches in our living room, somehow wedged in the small space between the couch and the wall. A red-brown body behind the mass of white. She'd look up when we called her name; when we extended our hands to shake her paw or pet the flesh under her chin, the spot she liked best to be touched. We kept finding her there. When we realized what she was doing, we knew it was time.

Amy was trying to be alone. She was trying to remove herself from the manufactured life of a pet and become whatever it was she would have been.

She was trying to die. And for a moment, live.

please rewind tape &
place
in protective sleeve

I Go Through Amber

Again, with such vigor
Breathing heavy & my foot
On the floor, the expectation
Of receipt requiring
Some form of

Payment to come
Weeks from now where I'll be
Elsewhere, probably
Waiting for my Greek tragedy
The spanakopita hasn't yet arrived

& my coffee's cold
Let me tell you again
How I put my face on
I put my face in
Water & close my eyes

Hold my breath
According to instructions
On the package hold my
Breath, my greatest
Fear is I will outlive it

LA CONFIDENTIAL

As with any recording it is always best to start at the source

#

When he confessed that

He was working for the FBI
I knew that I was
Also being surveilled

#

Filmmakers had to acknowledge the struggle to show who's been left
behind despite the subjects' pleas to blur their faces

#

Plot? What plot?
We are hoping
An informant will be
Able to develop a plot

#

We hear the human voice everyday & so instantly
Know when it sounds wrong

#

Before I became an informant I traded stocks. It wasn't so different,
dealing with all that information. Acquiring it, passing it on

#

Just parked on Rebecca
& Henry I haven't seen
Anyone following me today

#

What if we're wrong? What if these men aren't terrorists?
What if it's not them but us

#

I find you
To be a liar

#

But tell me
He whispered without
Emotion what is
The alternative?

#

As with any recording it is always best to start at the source

#

When he confessed that

Relying on informants
Instead of agents is a matter
Of incentive

Informants will do anything
Whereas agents usually get paid
To follow rules

#

Teabag inscription chosen "at random":
Since 9/11, more Americans have been killed by white militants than by Muslims

#

If we no longer permit freedom of religion then
We change who we are & the question
Becomes what are we
Defending?

#

I spoke in the neutral tone of someone giving evidence, even though
there was none

#

He may be guilty of talking
The FBI did not respond
To a request
For comment
For some reason he said
On condition of anonymity
They are just
Attracted to you

I reluctantly agreed to go to McDonald's & have a coffee with him

#

In cases related to terror
No actual evidence is needed
To open an investigation

#

Sitting comfortably & having good posture can work wonders

#

Feds are looking into just what level of anti-American this man is

#

If they do come to your house they'll come
Late at night or very early in the morning

#

As with any recording it is always best to start at the source

#

When he confessed that

Walls covered in auralex acoustic tiles help avoid a boxy sound & create
a pleasant reverberant ambiance

What do they really have on me?
Why do we have to live in fear?
Why do all of us have to live in fear?

#

I had the impression he was improvising a little but I let it go

#

Turn left & we are facing
Down the hill

#

That's another episode
For another week

#

Later she told me a story that I don't really think I should put down
here

#

Yes yes yes yes yes yes yes
I'm playing who I am, okay?

#

On the table were various objects whose purpose could not be misun-
derstood

#

It was a command
Not a suggestion

#

Just because it's fake doesn't mean
I don't feel anything

#

As with any recording it is always best to start at the source

#

When he confessed that

The best informants are
The worst people
I've heard
This line before in real
Life as in the pictures

#

No, I said. There is always something that survives

#

The meeting was somewhat brief

#

In the interest of national
Security I go in blind

#

How long is this movie?

#

You feel an individual
Out you don't
Do much more
Than that in
The first week

#

I need the money I need the money
Today I need the money

#

Right now I am looking
At a projection of me
Standing with my son
My daughter who
Hasn't been born
& neither of them
Know I made my life
Posing as someone else

#

I guess the teller
Screwed you

#

In the end, what does one remember of a face?

#

Please refer to the confidential file

#

He was a self-described "martial arts expert"
His work as a jazz musician
Was the greatest cover
Even if I'm really not
In a position
To say

#

When I fed him
That line that's what
He bit into

#

The sound of plastic
Bending for a chance
To remove a photo
        ‒   ‒

#

& you look at me as though all of this means something?
Where is oūr point of origin?

#

I was never able to put it on myself
You always did it for me

#

Press the # key
To start over

#

As with any recording it is always best to start at the source

#

When he confessed that

Lost all confidential ways of living
Lost all confidences
Lost all confidences in living

I couldn't turn myself in
There was no one to turn myself into

this party's crowded
(I want meat)

I started calling
my inbox a party because
it sounded more fun
that way to
wade thru bodies
like messages I had to manage
the boredom some
how had to have
some mercy on our
data all the days
I spend searching
for something just out
of our reach

2.
I want to meet a man for meetings
to mete a man in meter to tingle in
meetings I want to teem myself a man
I want meat

team player to have met dead
lines my name is
man, I want you
to meet you for meetings always

plural implying consecutive
moments, prearranged
encounters   something repeated
for a desired effect, i.e. iteration

I have secrets for you
if you wish   I just need
somebody to love
what I want is metempsychosis

really what I want
is not to marry you but more
I want to merge with you okay is that
not clear from all the photos

in which I've knelt down for you wide
lipped to see me from my most becoming
someone else, unsure who
I was when I sent you

this request   & can I
eat you?

3.
now you're asking
me for money & we
haven't even met

now you're mouthing
justin bieber, the promise
of true love, 100k more

followers if I click
your face & down
load a virus into the viscera

of my machine oh
tragic to make your connection
this way or that

I can't speak with you
or call your name, whatever
a body hailed you at birth

you are only my
plush arabic princess 7767793454
I'd like to try

to know you I'd like to know you

are real or real
enough, see also: fantasy
& my memory's been

wiped

please rewind tape & place
in protective sleeve

sometimes it's best to close your eyes
before the lights go

the scene involves murder, betrayal, so
it should be shot with the dying man's
gaze looking up toward his killer
in low angles, often making
the subject look bigger
in the frame, heroic or dominant
or deadly, ideal for the villain
who is sitting comfortably as on a throne
replaced by another

reel   simply irresistible
a slow pan as the first
chord strikes
attractive women in black or various
shades of red susurrating behind
robert palmer as he sways too, decked
out in layers & a used
car salesman smile, lip
synching something already
recorded months since

the camera moves from medium shot
to extreme close-ups of hands
hips, mutilated torsos
swaying flesh she's so fine
there's no telling
where the money went

have you ever noticed
almost every robert palmer
music video begins with a close
up of a woman's mouth
how in every scene
robert palmer surrounds himself
with swaying unsmiling women dead
serious, addicted to love
I didn't mean to turn you on

some movie starring
chet baker howling into
a microphone from over
the shoulder

to the original
karate kid
that look he gives miyagi that look
miyagi gives the kid
before the fateful blow
so often emulated as a boy
a simple google search
calls "the crane kick"
rewinding to watch
again, slowed down & magnified
to show the impact

I can often be so physical
copy of something I'd thought
was the real thing
beauty marks
me wherever I walk
years ago I walked

toward the henry hudson
working for daytime
TV for a spell, watching the reruns
on soapnet with the spanish dub
for my aunt, listening in the living
room so she could really hear
what they wrote for me in her own
tongue   typical situation

in which my face doesn't match
my voice   I had a way with words
as a child, I learned
english on the radio
looking at my father to match
his pitch & tone
years before all my children
or one life to live

or I'd ever think
to write about it
I'm not as helpless as I look
I often thought but never said
to people who'd take me
for a fool because my eyes
said otherwise, I know what
I look like   is there anything
wrong with that?

In the Multiplex

In the Multiplex

It wasn't the first thing you noticed, but it's what you remember

Who thinks these things & for how much longer?

You move as though this were to be expected

Your name, your past, the place where you've slept

& dreamed

In the mirror you closed your eyes & wished for someone else

The street lights, the gated door, the doorknob, a plane passing

Somewhere a siren

The radio is coming through the wall again

How nice, you think, to get the news like this

The neighbors are watching pornography

The multiplex, a matinee, & if you hurry you might make it

Revolving doors still give you nightmares

Elevators, escalators

Turntables, motor scooters, a Vespa you only know from watching

You shook the whole ride here

Is this what they meant by *the present tense?*

You have difficulty deciding

Revolving doors still

Your tío called it "the pictures"

Buttered corn, blue carpets, a door that leads to dark

The smell of Fantastik

You make up your mind on account of the hour

Everything else already started
Everything else has almost ended

Inside you find your way by touching the arms that line the path

When the lights go & the feature rolls you're still picturing the previews

Begrudging
Reluctant
Horrified
Bored

In the pause between frames you can hardly make out your hand resting
on your lap

Your knee
Your thigh
Your ankle
Your face

I found it on Atlantic

You closed your eyes & wished

On the Brooklyn Bridge
On the promenade
On the plaza's steps
On the F, sitting across from me

I found it on Atlantic

What can be imagined can be consumed & what can be consumed can
be imagined

What is a mirror but another metaphor?

You'd written about your body burning
You'd written about writhing out of your skin

On a beach in Ipanema
In a yacht over the Caribbean
On a jet across the sky
On the runway upon arrival
Over air amid bad signal
In a darkroom under red lights
Pulsating underground

You'd written about each scar, the secrets & secretions which form the
laminate

Faintly visible

Blown up by the enlargement process the surface of your frame is
an epidermis

You fashioned yourself a ghost

You see it was once a living organism, & now here it is in front of me
like a corpse

You've been here so long you can't remember what the outside looks like
& how it feels inside

You'd written about cutting your face out from every picture

You performed a Google search & printed out the results

You wanted something you could hold

You wanted a hard copy

Three pages in, your wrist hung languidly

Your name, your past, the place where you've slept

Five pages in, your scissors broke

How nice, you think, to get the news like this

You found a knife

Out of boredom you construct a model

Out of boredom you do everything or everything
Does you

You've been here so long

It was difficult, you admitted, from the outset

Everything becomes easy in time
Everything becomes
Easy in time
Every thing be
Comes easy in
Time

See it in real 3-D

The poster's promise is what caught you

Copy

Wasn't it sad how the picture moved & left you at your seat?

Hard

How nice, you think, to get the news like this

Copy

You couldn't help but stare

This dissembling began at birth

Because you could not do this alone I did it for you

Three pages, five pages

What caught you?

Your tío called

You couldn't help

This dissembling

Modernity demands a constant accumulation of images

Is this what they meant by *the present tense?*

You wanted something you could hold

Your tío called it "the pictures"

This alone I did

You've written this before

Because you could not

Who owns words anyway
Who owns the thoughts
Between bodies

Not everything is for sale

Not everything must go

I'd like you to use this for your own purposes

The outside & the inside

You've caught yourself

Yawning again

What time did you arrive here?

In the pause between frames

Waiting can be erotic

I'd like you

The sticker says "market price"

Might I have the first taste?

You promised yourself you'd make plans today

Elevators, escalators, revolving doors

Is that your modem running or are you just happy to see me?

To see you

To see me

You promised yourself

The outside & the inside

The radio is coming through the wall again

I'd like you to

Move as though this were to be expected

I fall to your knees which are mine

Watch out

Is there any higher compliment than being
In another's dreams?

Your words are leaking

Aren't you ashamed to be seen like that

My face lit up like a start-up screen

It wasn't a question

Who thinks these things & for how much longer?

You've always had a gift for that

Even your apogee has rhythm

I'm talking about your voice

I'm talking about the sounds you make

I'm talking about what happens when you spasm

You are in a world of multiples

Screenshots, dollar bills, co-ops, undergarment 3-packs

Whoever heard of having
Only one?

You laughed at the line, even though you knew it wasn't meant to be funny

The cinema is empty

You were interested in seeing if there was anything left of a personality when it's disintegrated & mixed with another face

Whoever heard of having
Only one?

Tell it like it is

What can be imagined

What can be consumed

The garden is lovely, I said, just to say something

They call that a Manhattan Special, you said, leaning close to touch my cheek

I saw this body was empty so I settled in

Pretty soon the sounds outside mingled with the sounds inside & there ceased to be a difference

I think it's because the things from our childhood never return

Vacant sidewalks, swimming pools, a stoop for watching

It wasn't the first thing you noticed, but it's what you remember

What you wouldn't do for a body in motion

These if/then statements have always made me blush

What a mouth you've got on you

Could it be over already

& I am walking in your clothing

It was pretty awful, you thought, but in a beautiful way

All day long & even in the night you are re-making my mold

Cement would have been stronger

You weren't built to last

Here it comes, all parts of everything

It's a cathedral with flying buttresses & twin spires

It's a sleek, sun-drenched villa in the old Spanish style

It's an alley under the fire escape

It's the last day of the year

I wish you were watching this with me

Special, you said

Under the fire

What will you do after this?

After? you repeated, as if you hadn't heard me

You felt as though you were in a film, & you were enjoying the scene

I give up, you murmured. It's too difficult.

They call this "narrative slippage"

Landscapes, celluloid, a 33-millimeter reel

In this economy of excess words still come
At a premium

In the changing room of a J.C. Penney you witnessed your own unraveling

You became more of yourself with me

I want to know what it's like

I became your face

You were familiar with another version. But the concept is the same.

Out of curiosity, you thought, or out of pleasure?

You stood outside your body

See it in real 3-D

History, language, literature

The thrumming of your skin

You shook the whole ride here

Park benches, oven mitts, a towel hung neatly on a hook

You don't know where the day went

Before we begin, I'd like to know you better

You think in line breaks

I missed the cue

& if you discover you were bought?

& if you discover you were swallowed?

Out of curiosity, you thought, or out of pleasure?

You wish you'd read the synopsis before you walked in

Overpass, coat check, a ticket on the floor

You said misinterpretation is sometimes more interesting than knowing the truth

The smell of metal, oil, bread on the counter, rain

Sometimes more

Before you

Now do you remember?

With more data, you think, I can live forever

On the Hobbies section you listed

Lingering

Close your eyes

I want to know what it's like

That's always been your problem

That's always been your solution

More data

& you stood to applaud

How does this look?

In the mirror

Close your eyes

& you wished

On the Internet, you think, at least

I'll live forever

& you wished

Someone else

Missing Letters

A.

Excuse me sir have you got the time?

The man was hard of hearing, so I thought, until I asked again. I haven't got a watch. Except he said, I haven't got to watch.

Which was true, because he had on dark sunglasses, and of course, I realized he was blind, or at least partially blind, the kind of blindness that maybe all of us experience later in life, later or very early, before our eyes really adjust to being in our bodies.

He looked sixty, or maybe sixty-five. I'm never good with ages, and most people think I'm much younger than what my driver's license says, which is, *DOB: 4-17-1985*. Which makes me thirty.

He must have seen me staring, seen me or sensed me, because he took off his sunglasses and started sucking saliva, making ready to spit. I put up my hands as I saw him raise his, the watch on his wrist out from his suit and beaming at me like an air stewardess who's just come with the news to *please stay in your seat*.

Being inside here made me comfortable, even with all the shaking and the babies crying. I know, it's strange to admit a thing like that but I'm a strange person; I've always felt that way and as I got older it only got closer to my heart.

He put his sunglasses back on and I read the time on his watch, which was a digital. I always confuse the little hand with the big hand, which means what, which amounted to when, and now I didn't have to tell; the time told me.

I breathed a satisfied sigh and took my phone out, to try and write whatever it was before it escaped me, something I'd only remember in passing or in passage, on the treadmill or the cobblestone streets and unthinking, which is when the best thinking occurs.

I like walking through life like this, time on my hands, or time in my hands, and hardly ever on my wrist, not like that, not exactly or not at all, nothing to do but to do it, and my whole life to do it. I'm desperate. I hope I never lose it.

B.

He's not old but not young, and he never takes sugar with his coffee, or even milk, and definitely not cream. He likes the work of the Latin American Surrealists, and the French Existentialists, and the Turn of the Century American Modernists, and the German Expressionists (Post- and Pre-war), and the Italian Neorealists, and the English Metaphysical Poets—although he's only really read one—and more than anything, he likes the Situationists, who mostly published pamphlets anyway, Q&As and rules about sidewalk etiquette or how to walk through a city on a curve. He likes sex and especially the smell of it. You can picture him in Brooklyn Bridge Park, running shirtless or with an orange tank top and blue mesh shorts or black nylon stretch pants, curving a line through Brooklyn Heights into Dumbo, running along the cobblestones and counting each barely-there space (or at the entrance to Pier 9, the last drips of vanilla ice cream on his chin, a neon volleyball at his feet or in his hands—why not?—since we're painting pictures) with his eyes closed and a strange expression on his face, as if he could feel each second and he was savoring it.

It's a promising scene, especially when viewed from a bridge. Add some music, a little concerto by The Human League, maybe Prince, his early stuff, maybe *Purple Rain*—so good you can pick just about anything— and a slow-mo pull-back panorama, and you've got a real stunner. Something good enough to make us weep.

He stops walking when he hits the cinema on Court Street, the marquee above his head with the names of each film in black, half the letters missing, or absent. Three guys and a girl, in their twenties, mindless and prepared to die in any old alleyway.

It's that, or a movie about witches. Everything else already started. Looking from his phone and the synopsis to the sign and the signatures, missing or absent, back and forth, up and down, just like that, until he stops looking and walks in.

C.

Do you remember that? I don't know where it came from, just now, or even at all but I remember being on the train together and I even remember the sound of the conductor—a machine after all, always the same announcement, more or less—and we had been so afraid lately, so full of fear the way I never am or the way I never can admit. So much of life is a show and I was showing you how vulnerable and insecure I could really be, how much I doubted myself, who I was, or who I'd become, or who I was only playing at being, the way when we look at old journals, old notes written on napkins we'd forgotten to discard, old emails, old post-it reminders, missing letters; absent or missing, letters never sent out of fear or uncertainty or both, anecdotes and annotations, notes written in margins, collage, coda, and epitaph, we don't know who that person was though we recognize the hand that wrote it as our own.

I was worn; I was wearing down. Maybe that's why I so very often wear so little, in private at least, which I know is a relative term today. *Private.*

I had an idea that I could cut into reality, in private and in public, guillotine it and re-arrange the splinters. The costs keep rising, for an idea like that, in a place like the one I've placed myself. My choice, of course, to live like this, to be so hungry, all the time, to never be sated, could I even know?

Art should be a bullet; the role of the artist is to take the shot.

Each day I felt better, or different, which isn't the same thing, but seemed like it to me, for the simple fact that difference meant I was changing, and the worst thing in the world is to be static, which isn't the same thing as being still.

The train kept rocking until we became one person, hugging and clutching each other from each other's waists, me balancing my back against the steel as we hurtled on, the train and our lives, underground then above it then back below, from a vacuum that reminded me of space, or my idea of space: big, black, mostly silent except for the occasional *whoosh* (a star exploding, or being born) to a balmy March morning, sun-caked windows, a passing tree, a passing steel giant, another tree, just like that, closing my eyes or trying to between stops and opening them to see yours, green like my own except all the way and I've only ever been in between my whole life, my eyes and everything else. I don't know why

I'm telling you this, or why it occurs to me now, the image and the sound and even the smells (rust, metal, rain, coffee, barbecued meat wrapped in pita in the hands of someone sitting below me and the hands themselves: a damp flesh smell I look everywhere for) aligning in my mind like a reel of film placed over the one that should be playing, any other moment except this one. I held your hand until your hand disappeared.

And then I saw the time I died in Greenpoint, before or after, for an editorial that would later surface in Paris, in expensive magazine shops, overpriced collectibles, purveyors of coffee table pastiche.

In the photo, you can see my face through my killer's legs; wide, outspread, flourishing her heels and calves and a pistol, which you wouldn't see if it weren't for the shadow of the gun created on the wall where my torso props, knee bent, arms out to protest the inevitable. The room is dark and my head is lit from above, a black and white freeze frame in which my figure is surrounded by a sort of halo; saint and victim all at once, which seems natural, or at least not uncommon; confession, death, and the canon, one after the other, out with a shot and a sanctification, and it was the best thing I could ever hope for, in this life or in the one created by the photographer and the lighting crew, and the art director, and the reader, too, if we can call them readers, whoever paid 30 euro for a copy of the glossy issue of *Twill* nine months later and five years ago.

Every act of creation transcribes an act of death, like a paper negative, and writing is about slaughter as much as it is about sustaining life. At least that's how I always figured it; how I'm figuring it now, you looking at me with something I can't name, now or in the future, since any moment written into something else destroys that moment, turns it into a different one, a reality that maybe even supersedes the real thing; a reality that maybe even obliterates it.

The real thing, and the rarest. That's what I wanted; that's what I always want, in fact and in fiction.

But it wasn't your beauty itself that I admired; it wasn't your ass or your eyes, or anything that you could see if you were looking too; it was a side of you that I've gradually come to know and will probably never know completely. And yet I know it well enough to try and kill it.

Maybe I'm only saying it that way because I really believe it or because I think it sounds good, on paper or on your lips, or maybe it's only that I've been listening to Broken Social Scene, "The Sweetest Kill," a song that was written in 2010 but which I had never heard until last night, at a bar on Smith called Hunter's. Go figure.

Everything comes back to death, pursuit, the poetry of the body or the body of poetry that lives in the skin and sensation of being and not being. At the same time. Hunter's and hunters. All of us.

D.

He had a problem with the term "met him in the flesh."

E.

I calmly got undressed, hung my jeans over the back of a chair, and slid into bed, doing it the way I would if I were the one watching it happen. It felt good to be there, naked, and alone, and the pillow as soft as your skin, or mine, just not in winter, because that's when my body sometimes gets dry, and patchy, and prickly, like I'm burning to get out of it. Something I wish for a lot.

F.

I'm such an Aries & years ago
I worked for a spell
Well not exactly like that
It was more for dollars
A paycheck I could
Take pride in but not
Like that exactly either
& anyway I worked inside
An Aerie being one myself
Or sounding similar
Without a shirt & wearing
Jeans they provided me
With ones that said the name
Of their sister &
A small emblem meant
To represent a bird
I couldn't say
& I'd always think
Standing still sometimes
Standing with people who wanted
To be in pictures
Spellbound but also bounded
I'm an Aries & I'm in Aerie
How many others have lived
This dream
Or died so I might
Dream about it

G.

The feeling of knowing everything was about to begin or had just begun, was forever always beginning or becoming. Becoming something else. And my future out on Atlantic waiting.

H.

I've been listening to the same song for days
Watching heat & exhaust shimmer off
The asphalt like tidal crush, distorting or re-
Forming everything learning to
Come on command
Is it enough
That we crave objects
That we are always looking
For a way out of objection
What's worse to know
The flesh disappears our bodies
& what's inside
Dies or that we
Believe it

I.

No one recognizes me unless you're there

You told me, when I'd asked you if anyone recognized you at Brooklyn Roasting because we'd always gone there, because we went there just yesterday, which was the last time you went there, before today.

I thought that was strange, What do I have to do with your face, I asked, your lips, and head, the cheek I've felt on my cheek so often, when I can't fall asleep? You didn't have an answer, then or now, when I posed a similar question. And the thing that was on my mind anyway was something you had no knowledge of, something I'd never told you, a game I used to play as a kid, maybe not a kid but a teenager, an adolescent as they say, sociologically speaking, I mean, eleven or twelve so maybe not *teen*, maybe just *pre-teen*, *pre* which I always hate saying, even in my thoughts because it reminds me of the fact of my birth, or how much I must have missed in my mother's womb, forgetting for a moment what a head-start I got on the living, the real thing and the rarest, right? and anyway, the game was something you could play alone so it was ideal, for a certain child at a certain time, but even so, you had to play it in the company of others, people who were like actors without scripts, moving from the stage to the sidewalk and back again, and all I had to do was watch them pass but the thing is, no one could notice me watching or the game was up, the play was over, so I'd stay there, silent, watching, looking at one subject, a term I hated but which seemed appropriate given the context, except I didn't think of it like that, not like *context*, not at twelve and definitely not at eleven, one subject at a time, picking up on their mannerisms and how they changed, if they changed at all (they always did) when they saw someone else or when they saw someone was watching, someone else besides me I mean, and even then, how things would change, or how they would stay the same, and what that meant, which was the most important thing to me, the motivation or logic behind it, if it was measurable, if I could pinpoint it or make it stick, and then repeat it, make it repeat, these people and their performances and me in my seat in the front row, which was the best seat in the house, and the only one.

J.

I don't know what else to say. I could say I knew this was coming. (How could I not know this was coming?) Now I'm yours to hold and keep, or to swallow and shit out. I'd do the same thing, if I were in your place. If I were you. My hunger is hungrier than the stars.

Ex*tras* & *Ac***cess***ories*

Spiritual America

RE: New Age Nostalgia

Dear _____

Nothing is new, only newly recalled. Case in point: New Age philosophy that has its roots in medieval alchemy. One has the feeling of having lived through an old script. Fellow travelers of other people's revolutions. And the tour has only stopped once, for pictures. Just one of the many reasons why no one—and no thing—can ever be *modern*. "Those who are creating the modern composition authentically," Gertrude Stein said in one of her many lectures, "are naturally only of importance when they are dead because by that time the modern composition having become past is classified and the description of it is classical." Where then has our spirituality gone but in our nostalgia for a life without science *or* religion? In an article I'm browsing, the lead-in reads: *Through an e-commerce store and a passionate online community, Folk Rebellion incites conversation about the effects of technology and inspires a device-dependent generation to unplug. Williamsburg bed-and-breakfast, Urban Cowboy, joined forces for the launch.* and below the graf is a photo of a group of men and women, clad in black leather jackets and holding glasses of rose. The caption says, *Guests admiring three kinds of ceviche.*

Tech-free retreats and digital detoxes have sprouted across America and the world; yoga has been mainstreamed into everyday life. The point is not to find God but in our narcissistic gaze, to find ourselves. And then pay for it. I still miss myself whenever I look at my past I's in photos; memories that cling to the past and the postdated but also to the future, since they become monetized as products if I keep sharing my melancholia to people who care enough to click. What soothes you; what saves you; what keeps you within yourself today? Pornography? Gardening? Motorcycles? Meditation? Keeping a journal or a sketchbook? Camping? Fishing? Cooking? Watching a stranger cook on TV? The surf? The beach? Sun-worshipping? Healing stones? The dérive? A long walk on your newsfeed? I'm afraid to lift my thumb because I think I might lose it. Do you suppose Michelangelo would have been grateful for a gift of a piece of Renaissance furniture? Picasso allegedly added. No, he said, answering his own question. He wanted a Greek coin.

Material America

RE: Landscapes

Dear _____

I was the first to be born here, so I've always wondered what it is that makes me any different from the people who came before me. Is it something you can touch; something you can put your finger on? And how has our American-ness developed or been re-defined from generation to generation? Law of total probability. If I ask enough questions, someone is bound to reply with another question.

What's more American than manicured lawns? (Case in point.) Landscape is a space, real or imagined, and to be American, too, has its basis in an imagined reality, more product than person, more concept than custom. *The American Dream.* "You can't become English, French, German; you are …" wrote Susan Sontag in her notebook. "But you become an American. An invented, not a natural country."

I wonder if our love for landscaping has more to do with the smell of freshly mown grass or with our desires for molding it to fit our outlines. Design derives from designare, meaning *to mark out.* A prerequisite to possession is prohibition and proclamation. To situate something in my mind, first I have to carve a space for it before I initial it with my thoughts, a mental signature or signpost to say *I am here.* I am establishing a periphery in relation to others. Look. Mark this; take notice; give attention, *consider.* Or: to mark down, mark off, mark up, to make one's mark. Re-invention. RE: Landscapes. And what is the future of landscaping within our indivisible digitized pixel plane? A world without borders, but one that requires miles of fiber optic cable and warehouses full of servers and switches. Mutable materiality. Look. I am *in the cloud.* I am sitting here, looking out from the fifth floor of an office share in Chinatown, looking out onto the cracked pavement and fish stalls and baskets full of rotted fruit. There are no lawns; there is no grass to mold and make our own.

Eternal America

RE: Coding

Dear _____

A funny thing happens whenever I forget my password. I am asked to re-count more passwords, security questions that only I can answer. Except I can't. Is it funny or is it sad? A *pass*word is an access code, something so close to my identity that it stands in for my identity, akin to digital DNA, prevention against the increasingly common situation of *losing one's self.* If we choose passwords that are inextricable from our past and present selves, what does it mean for our future that we so often forget them? I am passing words to you so you might pick up this thread and respond with your own code, from codex, a book of laws, a set of ideas or rules, a system of signals or symbols for communication. An exchange-based religion that promises *eternal returns.* There is so much to blame for my current state. I never learned coding.

A moment from my past self includes a white hard-bound book with black letters, a title which reads: *Forgot your password?* In 2012, LinkedIn was hacked and 4.6 million passwords leaked. At The Glass Room on Mulberry that ran for a month last winter before vanishing, which is a lot like saying *before being forgotten,* an exhibit asked guests to take a look and see if we could find our stolen passwords, urging us to think for a moment about how much we rely on codes we keep forgetting. Temporarily or forever. I remember reaching for the volume labeled *qua – tao*, leafing through the glossy pages until I reached my own password.

It wasn't there.

In our culture of hashtagged privacy and data broke-rage, how else can we prove our identities but by the codes we keep creating and misplacing? Credit card numbers, bank account numbers, personal numbers, passport numbers, social security numbers, PINs, CSCs, computer codes, area codes, zip codes, bar codes, clothing codes and style numbers, entry codes, customer and client service codes, coupon codes—I think of these as passwords that enrich me with one hundred lives as I prepare to play the game—security signals, thumb prints, body tattoos, CAPTCHA responses, a scanner for your eyes, ears, and mouth. Hold your tongue out and keep it like this for the duration of our time together. How in-secure are we, and can we learn to code differently, as a way to reclaim our sovereign self?

Astral America

RE: Zeitgeist

Dear _____

When I think of Astral America I think of orbits, speed, trajectory, the ping-pong that used to represent a modem being dialed up and the long, torturous wait for a system to receive it. Now I ping you without hesitation; I don't even have to wait for you to receive my message. An electronic dispatch that would loosely translate to, "Are you there?" And the point is, *we are always there*, even if we aren't exactly here. So we take to the road, or the road (more or) less traveled. Where can we go if only to get lost? The road trip is either a flit of nostalgia or a bad teen comedy from 2000; maybe it can be both. If I was looking to capture our cultural zeitgeist, all I'd have to travel to is my Twitter feed. The spirit of the age. "What you have to do is enter the fiction of America," Baudrillard writes in his *America*, "enter America as fiction." The desert of the Internet as the primal scene. Orbits, speed, trajectory. Where are we heading? And how fast can we really go? When an image or text is reproduced at such a speed, our lens of vision begins to resemble a cinematic camera trick— hallucinations of a spin cycle set to repeat: a technique in which there is only one subject around whom the camera circles, usually on a dolly, so as to provide a rotating view from all sides, often used to give the impression that the subject is melting into the frame. We call this an *orbital shot*. In cartoons, when characters feel dizzy or dazed, they start to see stars, or at least they imagine them. *Astral America*, patent pending. Potential for cross-over appeal. Ping is a technical word that is making its own crossover into the mainstream population. I used to play Ping-Pong as a child; I seldom play as an adult. To get around trademark laws, everyone started calling it "table tennis" anyway. We'll do anything to make a buck, or to make sure we can save what we already have. And still—

The act of vanishing into vanishing bodies or bodies of text, code, images, signs. When we return to this moment, much later, when we float up, when we re-emerge, what will have been our system of belief, our established discourse, our consensus culture, our zeitgeist, our Astral America? The Audi commercial that cuts across my screen as I type this says, *This might not make sense now, but it will.*

*how to begin
is also where*

*(this is my other
half)*

Time ~~Passes~~ Piles Up
Presses In &
Flattens

1.

Do we spoil things with our mouths or do we put spoiled things in them
I mean to say

Do we spoil things by saying them so is speech more or less expressive
than what I am right now feeling in silence and how to tell the body
from the mind what the body feels from the mind and what about the
moments when one can neither think nor feel what about them what
about them what about when I want to want but not to want to have
only to want this and this hardness and hollowness and also the heat of
this the strain and bother of this to say that everything passes except
words—words do not pass. And when they pass they very often move
me and very often make me move inside another. And it seemed to me
to be my greatest accomplishment—to write a memoir in which one
learns nothing about its author, as one reviewer wrote. To know the
outline of someone and not the details, the fine lines, the curves and
shadows. The play of light and the lack of it. But didn't I show so much
more than the outline—aren't I showing so much more than the outline?
I am right now leaning to the left and arching my back so as to procure

a better view for you. The exact words were when I finished the book, I wondered how much I actually learned about Campanioni's life.

I had to look them up to remember. I had to look up to remember L, and what she said, or, really, how she said it while we'd been walking up or down Orchard (I can never tell which; up or down, north or south) to stop on the corner of Spring or Kenmare and stare up at the sky.

The time of day always gets me she said, not looking at me but instead looking above as I looked from her face to mine (I had to imagine it), back to her face, and finally toward the sky. So I could see what she was looking at. Which was the sky and the day turning into night. But not yet. The time of day always get me, L said, and this time or by this time I was holding her hand, I had been holding her hand, I am still holding her hand in my memory as we watch the day blow out, the world dying, as she liked to think of it, even if she didn't like to think of it at all. It hadn't happened yet. It hardly ever happens. It only happens once a day, and it was about to happen and it is still happening whenever I think to look up at the sky, whether I am alone or whether I am holding onto something or someone. The world dying, the world and us, but especially me, who'd take the time to think about what form it'd take with point-five margins. Always already anticipating myself, which means I am always also missing myself. To touch death with excess.

Was it always like this? I remember burying my face in my own arms so I could better imagine what it was that was happening to me. Before I knew what it was to be inside language. Purple and red shapes would shoot up in the dark and I'd lose myself within their careful choreography, not knowing or maybe knowing too well that it was me who was deciding the movements. And when I would leave, finally, to sit on the steps that led to my home, my mother would sit beside me. I would listen for the sound of tires in the distance, and the lamps that would light up, one by one, and I'd pretend to count them or guess which lamp would light up next, and at the same time, try to mimic the music my father would have been playing, the bouncy voices of people I didn't know pushing out of the window like smoke, everything heard in pieces. There'd be smells, too, but one always forgets to include smells even if it's the one thing that brings one back. And I would sit like that, quiet and careful and thinking hard about the pulsing coral orbs that I could see if it was dark enough and see if I could see them even in the light. I sat like that, on the steps that led to my home, or in the creases of a burgundy sofa, or in the backseat of a car I only know from the inside. And sometimes I think I was only ever so inside myself so much that I missed out on the people who sat beside me. Or maybe it's only how I am remembering it; how I am remembering me. Which is another sort of death.

Remembering the way people's skin smelled, and how some bodies smelled different than others, and the way my eyes would burn and tear up and everything would blur out, and how I had to lock myself in the bathroom with my feet hanging in the air to try and think about it.

In another piece, in about sixty pages, I'll tell you that I don't miss anything. But I don't think that's true. I miss certain movements. Certain words or ways of saying them. I miss meeting strangers in phone booths, for instance. I miss a particular phone booth on Rivington near the corner of Clinton. and a summer night, and the passing storm.

Memories, too, are each a work of art which re-fashion people and places and feelings. As if one was standing below them again. Below or above or inside. To look at them and to look away differently. Was it always like this? What degradation, what a cheap trick, to write all the time an autobiography; Mallarmé's dream: the book as world, the world as a book. The experience is like living every day as though you are telling yourself a story and knowing at the same time what is the truth. The story, the truth. Forgetting as one forges or the other way around.

And our interaction—what comes between words and voice, voice and rhythm, rhythm and image, image and writing, writing and silence—is where the text is going. Where the text has already gone. Silence and sonic utterance.

When I began this book, I was already spoken for. Then I wasn't. Then I was.

If something is spoken for, it is not available because someone has already bought it. Or if they haven't already bought it, they've reserved its purchase. To retain or hold over to a future time or place. Reserve, from Latin *reservare*, to keep back, from *servare*. To keep.

But what is it that we really keep? What remains to be held? What do we hold onto and what do we hold only within ourselves? And what disappears what disappears what disappears what disappears.

And even as I write this the world is closing in again (with my view of the Verrazano from the bedroom, from the edge of the bed) that synthetic sky which gets more beautiful with every passing polluted day, a purple-pink gradient in my camera-eye and I note the time with my fingers, as if to trace the world unfolding, after it piles up, presses in, flattens into a measureless moment. Every time the same and every time different (I check my notes). Involuntary or unintended. It was beautiful in the way that beauty never is, the way beauty has of coming too quickly, of completing, and in completing things annihilating all of their admirers' dependency for change; a spasm or swallow. A deep deep breath to let the evening in. It makes me think I should have kept everything to myself.

2.

The time of day always gets me, L said, turning her gaze from me up to the sky, to watch—

3.

(All of these pieces were written at different points of time and later re-arranged in another sequence so that what you get is not the publication of a book but a life-out-of-order.[8])

4.

the world close in on itself. I had felt this, too, in my own way, many years ago, even if I couldn't recall it on my own. And, anyway, isn't that the point? I always think; how through another person or thing, people experience emotions and moods that we could not find on our own, that we could not find in our ourselves. And it makes me remember that the very thing which most makes us us comes from elsewhere.

The start-up screen of a computer's operating system always reminds me of a face. A flickering like flesh stir-frying in grease and oil.

Some relatives are meant to be imagined years before they die. They exist there, in the same room (lime-green walls, a dining room table coated in plastic, a crucifix above the couch, which is strewn with painted flowers), wearing the same clothes (a soft red shirt-dress, a soft red handkerchief), moving in a similar manner like a rerun.

Having left so much family in places I had never been before to grow up in North America, I had a lot of relatives who were relatively unrelated to me, by blood at least. These North American relatives even adopted false titles to preface their real names. Aunt Marie. Uncle Joe. But they were as real to me as my own relatives, my own breath and sweat.

Is being touched about touching or is it more about feeling and, in feeling something, feeling something the same as someone else which is to say feeling something at the same time that someone else is feeling it, too.

---

8. What were you doing on January 15, 2018 at 11:55AM?

It is always something I am thinking that puts an end to something I am feeling. And what is a pose except the ability to hold onto an emotion while at the same moment making a move toward another. There is no question mark because there is no question; and what I always want is a fluid movement. And what I want is all the time to hold both. The before and every after.

Think about the difference between the stage and TV. How one can see the props and scene changes, the curtain rising, the curtain draping back down. And the TV, if it's always on, as it always is in my parents' home— the TV never really separates truth from fabrication, the life from the lie of acting, because without changes there's just the constant flicker of beginning and end, backdrop and foreground, regularly scheduled program and commercial, all of it a part of the production. The Internet is like that, a TV that's always on. So that it's impossible to see where one thing stops and one begins: the point is that nothing ever stops and nothing ever actually begins. The point is that everything is only ever all the time.

Or: It is like turning on the TV to see that the TV has already been on. It is like having an already-turned-on TV, I imagine saying to my parents, if they had asked me the difference between TV, and the Internet, the Internet, and TV. And they'd return—But isn't that the point (I imagine) of the remote? To turn things off, to turn them on. Remote, from Latin *remotus*. To remove.

5.

In the first decade of the new century, or what G calls the Zero Years, which sounds so strange to my own fingers as I type it, transformational shows were all the rage of reality TV. Who could lose the most weight? Who could go from single to soulmate in a matter of carefully screened moments? Who could be the next American idol? Who could get fired by Donald Trump? Who could marry a millionaire (or an ax murderer?)? But

9. After VH1's *Megan Wants a Millionaire* had aired its third episode, contestant Ryan Jenkins was accused of the grisly murder of his wife, a Las Vegas swimsuit model not named Megan.

the most transformative thing reality TV ever did or does is actually its repeated aptitude for transforming something into nothing.

6.

The best kind of desires
Are the ones that ~~disappear~~ are disappearing

Another way of saying this is how can one make nothing out of something

7.

A photographer who has photographed me over the last seven years says this year my look has changed. He says my look has changed and that over the last six years I was handsome and this year I'm a curiosity. He says this year I'm capable of unearthing people's infantile desires. Uncertain of whether this was a compliment or a critique I return by asking myself is it that my look has changed or is it that my look has changed me. Another way of asking this is asking how many times can I change and still remain exactly who I am.

8.

My favorite films are the films in which there are no real actors, no plots, no character expositions, no ground situations, no inciting incidents, no dialogue or narration, only the thin silence of erasure, one slide replacing the one before it: the mirror of its audience who are not so much seeing things so much as we are seeing things replace themselves. In this way seeing and not seeing can coincide. Nothing happens in these films except everything.

9.

Opening the first page of a book is like looking at your lover for the

first time, or like looking at yourself for the first time from the eyes of
your lover.

10.

It is a well-documented fact
That before first dates with future
Lovers I would make them a mixtape
I discovered that by simply altering
The arrangement I could elicit
Different emotions in the body
Of the listener
To say nothing of my own

11.

Moods built for mass consumption
& easy duplication
Moods built like books of recipes

Not really & no longer interested
In writing books
Meant to be read but in writing
Books meant to be written

I highlight a passage with the word blond
& remove it   In the winter
There's no arguing
About the color of my hair

A deep secret   Sometimes
I write the book as if it were
The review of the book & later
Remove references to page numbers & most

Of the time any observations
About the author

12.

The best books can be read front to back but even and especially from
the back to the front. To write this book one would have to insert some-
thing at exactly the midway point, which is always moving, edging over
or

away

13.

A friend on Facebook writes to channel Botticelli vibes take off your
makeup and your clothes, and plunge yourself into a bathtub. Don't for-
get to arch your eyebrows.

You can picture this in black and white because black and white is some-
thing that has always seemed to me to be more substantial, and at the
same time, subdued and pastel, as immaterial as a daydream.

In the book I'm reading I underline a passage that says forgetting is
among the most beautiful things that can happen to the human brain. So
I can remember it.

I like to forget my lover on occasion because everything that has
been forgotten or become unrecognized becomes almost instantly
more beautiful. And in becoming more beautiful it makes me want to
remember you more.

the Internet is for real

for Zosia, Juan, John, Nena, David, Ana, Irena, Peter, Kaz—

I am
where I am
because of where I am
from

(control)

"How do I feel you on me,
when you're not on my skin?"
— Ariana Grande, "Touch It"

We Hope You Enjoy the Selection

Munich is all green fields and beige brown mounds of earth. A slab of ash-gray sky. Homes of slanted red squares, black tops. Rolling hills like the image on the cassette sleeve of *The Sound of Music*. At least from the view of the Airbus 340. Reclining, inclining, uncertain where to place myself, and how. Ten emergency exits on board, and if I paid more attention, I'd be able to describe their whereabouts.

Red from France and Austria, Johnny Walker Blue, two champagnes I only take photos with to begin and end the flight. A hot towel over my face if I occasionally open my eyes.

Business Class is so good you actually don't want the flight to end.

It's like life.

With two minutes to land, I finally learn how to properly use my mechanical-massage seat, seven buttons which control seven parts of the average human body. I watch the 3-D image of the plane's nose on the monitor of the person diagonal to me, imagining my position of sight as being outside myself, simultaneously inside the jet of which I'm watching from afar. A bird's eye view, as a bird. The effect, like all things Post Internet, is so real it seems fake. Unless it's the other way around. Flattened, compressed, reflecting itself as hall of mirrors; and over the mountains, mountains. So many vantage points from which to view experience, yet I hardly ever experience anything but inert alertness; a desire to think through things as if I'm still standing still and still

I'm always moving. All of us and everywhere.

"They are also lands of ethnic diversity: the traditions and innovations of conquerors and Native Americans, and of settlers and city dwellers, have shaped American cuisine into a taste sensation. The forested Northeast is arguably the most European part of the USA. The Italian, Spanish, and British roots of immigrants are still noticeable today alongside Greek, Syrian, and Chinese influences."

I'm reading "The Best of the Northeast" section in the *Lufthansa Business Class* pamphlet that was provided by an air stewardess. I enjoy reading about where I live from the perspective of someone who doesn't live there, probably because it makes me feel even more of an outsider than I already am; defamiliarize the familiar and all of us eventually realize we are strangers, to each other and ourselves.

"Vast landscapes, mountains and forests. The Pacific, Atlantic, and the Great Lakes. Journey through the USA or Canada and admire what nature and the vastness of these countries have in store."

A friend asks me what I've been daydreaming about. If I knew what, I wouldn't be daydreaming. I tell her, three quarters of the time I'm halfway here.

I underestimate but she gets the point, because we're not even looking at each other as we talk.

Sometimes all we want to do is look and sometimes we can't bear to look. I don't know what dictates this desire, or the lack of it. I only know that I want to look you in the eyes as our fingers move forward.

During the flight I am mostly silent. Instead of talking, I shake my head. Continually mistaken for German. I'd never gotten German before. My mom is from Poland; she left Warsaw when she was six. But I've never been there. I've never been anywhere, except the page you are right now reading.

Look, the sun is almost coming up. I expect it to be beautiful.

In the shuttle to get to Gate G at Munich Airport, I listen to the robotic voice of a German woman serenade me as an actual German woman yawns in my face. If I hit pause, right here, and capture the moment in my camera eye, it would look like she was eating me. My face in her mouth as it opens to bear down, bite, swallow. Leave yourself as you take in the other. So I take a picture and register her mouth to memory.

We huddle close, in silence, for a moment longer until we stop. The robotic voice says something new in German. I swoon. She stretches. Everyone sort of exhales, or unlocks their phones. Then we start again.

Tomorrow I'll receive an email from Lufthansa, asking me if I could spare my time. Say yes and no.

Rate my experience.

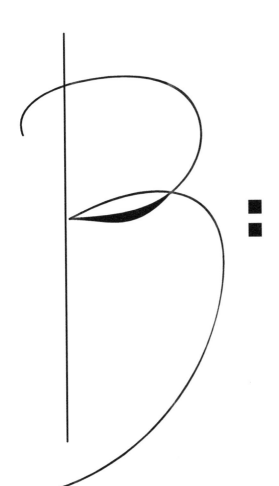

if language really makes us kings of our nation, then without doubt it is we, the poets and thinkers, who are to blame for this blood bath and who have to atone for it

(As we move toward oblivion we count backward) & in my mind, I am still watching a Cyndi Lauper music video which doubles as the opening scene of *The Goonies*

Opening Shot

Opening

Having succumbed to the millenn-
the block the halal market next-door
TERRORISTS & the storefront's windows shattered. At least
Somewhere else required reading describes millions of workers br-
to the upsides of slavery. Somewhere there's another wall with our name
prolongée. & the news says today is the third of 2016. & under the paving
that before. The beach that's been polluted for profit or the one that served as a
After the millennium came & made death a problem of the poor what is there to
& still we accumulate more images of our passage, desperate to hoard experience
cent of the world controls seventy-five percent of the world's wealth. A person
it trouble us that Amazon & Google know more about us than our moth-
More real? Should we be troubled? The gowns are there to prote-
way around. The hypothesis for every major corporation
without an actual person to feel love for. One in five
It won't stop coming down today. I've tried to
Keep killing time? A waitress asks the wo-
her bill. The streets are trenches. An oc-
with spam, instructions demanding I
the option to VIEW THIS LARGER?
& I'll start with my face. Make it
A student says as a white man
After class I ask
being any-

Shot

ium what else is there to bow to? Down
to where I am writing this is scrawled with
a dozen passersby have walked past Smith & no one's said a thing.
ought to plantations in the new world as a way to introduce adolescents
on it. I'd like to keep all of this inside of me a little longer. Début d'une lute
stones what? I am afraid what we might uncover & I've never thought to say
hotel resort killing field in Tunisia? & the news says today is the third of 2016.
give birth to? People have become a pile of data to themselves & one another.
without conceding there will always be a limited supply. The richest twenty per-
living in the city is photographed or videotaped two dozen times a day. Should
ers & lovers? Should it trouble us that we'll pay to make it bigger? Better?
ct the chips & circuit boards from harm by humans, not the other
must go like this: Maybe a person can experience real love
have a cell phone. One in five have clean drinking water.
wait it out & I'll be waiting longer than I can afford
man across from me, who's just asked to pay
ean runs through it. My inbox's flooded
make it rain on the dance floor below
Sometimes I want to blow myself up
monstrous or sever it completely
in this culture he feels invisible
him to imagine
one else

in the beginning was the word, & the word

already existed & the world was
in the Internet & the world was
the Internet, all that light
& the darkness had not overcome it & all
the boys & the girls
say surreal or else they are
slurring or else they are sur-real
so much to be had & to be
over it, or else
we're all down in big sur
slurring & slurping a metaphysical
bubble-gum experience we can only ever mouth
in language emptied for weight
of water, google
salad lady meme or smiling
with salad, so much
laughter over a crush
of iceberg between two lips
& the postponement of words
I suggest an interview, I'd want to
get to know you better   I can
scroll like this for weeks   watch
me   we can start by going backward   what would
the goggles on my VR headset say
if I asked them what it was like
as a child, growing up in
adult film studios? to only know the fantasies
of men & women too afraid to make
anything except what they could make
with their own hands? it's so dark
with you on my face

return false;

{

}

return true;

return new DeployScriptArtifact

Keanu Reeves can't remember where he came from. They call it Neural Seepage. They call it the Black Shakes. Carrying the cure for NAS in his head to the tune of a recurring voice-over <<He dumped a chunk of long-term memory. Erased a childhood for a job. Johnny Mnemonic forgot his own name. Before he hacked his own brain he was Just Johnny>> (a love story starring Nicholas Cage and Johnny Mnemonic)

document.createTextNode;span.appendix

{

}

setAttribute || = return(data.substring)

for a very special treat, rest a stroopwafel on top of a steaming hot cup of coffee or tea for about a minute, and enjoy the aroma as it transforms into a warm and melty caramel gift an exchange of firsts do you remember the forgetting the first the very first time you forgot? in the opening scene Johnny Mnemonic and Nicholas Cage stand at the forty-sixth floor of the Hearst Tower before the glass-paneled entrance of *Cosmopolitan* magazine against the backdrop of a rented memory of Columbus Circle and the sun intervening at three o'clock, exchanging glances in panoramic silence

Truckstop Fantasy Number One

Driving through the traffic
Of strangers, age
Sex & location

All the dreams I have that I don't
Remember   You & I are looking
At the same thing
Or through it

The language of our culpability

Everything within
Our grasp so that
Nothing can be touched

It feels nice in my mouth

They'd put aside a patent
For a "system & method for transporting
Virtual objects in a parallel reality game"

According to certain conversations
With the application's creators
The real challenge lies
In motivating the user
To provide data constantly
Even after the exciting appeal
Of technological innovation
At the outset
Wears off

(Waste & vastness have more
In common than we would
Like to admit)

As evidenced by the Latin
Vastus meaning expansive
But also empty

The project to catalog
Every city block on the planet
Was made possible in part
By each of us   To make intimacy
Of the user work, a user must be made to feel
Individual & private
Even while participating
Within a global network

(The center holds
Because there is no center)

Before it sold the world
Google had to pixelize it

Enter fleets of roaming
Vehicles taking pictures
Of trees, public parks, the Citi Bike
I left stranded on Atlantic
& Smith, too afraid to pay
Attention to the details
Of its return, or my own

Affective labor, making
My contribution to the world's
Largest collection for facial
Recognition after Google
Captured passwords, email messages
Medical records, financial information,
Audio & video files
Including information related to
Online dating & sexual preferences
Tagging made possible via its origins
As the CIA-funded Keyhole
Satellites which also collected
Geographic imagery, looking inward
Instead of outward

As we direct our own gaze down
A longing to look back
On the spaces in which we live & work even
As this gaze converts
Territories into targets
For both marketers & government employees & us
Mobilized into militarized
Ways of being   The out
Sourcing of torture & our own role
As voyeur   The history of our desire
For surveillance lies
In not only
Watching but in being watched

Being for others
What we could never be
With ourselves

(To gaze at someone & to have them
Gaze back—this is to understand
The complicit joy of being caught
Looking)

When two people Google
The same word, the algorithm
Will return different results to each user
The objective in a post
Industrial capitalist society is to have
You consume your own
Bandwidth   Moving data can be like moving
Prisoners, extraction & the sort
Of rendering we normally deliver
For the sake of making
The individual into a multitude
A label we assign in the name
Of security, or the insecurity
Of *not being made visible*

In the physical sense, I prefer
The tattoo I was
Born with, above my right
Buttocks & below my waist
Which you can only see
If I decide to
Show you   Did you know

Windows was so called
Because of its ability to feel
Like a portal into a virtual world
But also as a window into
The inner sanctums of our machine

It is not clear
What constitutes human trafficking
In a world where the body
Itself has been completely turned
Into a bank of data

The thirteen European Cities
You Should Be Looking At
On a stranger's mobile as I make
My way back
Riding in the rear
Of the United Air Jet I almost forget what
Economy feels like

I call it post Internet

culture a name
I made up   my friends call me

post hetero because it's the ass
I like above

everything else when
I'm below it

I mean before it I mean in this
scenario post means both a coming

after & also the currency
of transmission

in my best moments
I'm deranged I imagine

a therapist telling me
the only good thing

about tinder
are the super likes

we could all
use a reminder of our   bodies

deserve to eat
& be eaten

people sending & receiving
things & things sending &

receiving people & people
who are no longer people

but the things they used
to send & receive—information

ideas, objects—all of these
& all at once   I am saying

it's not enough
to write about borders but for

the writing to become itself
a border

it's like not wanting
to know what's better

jelly or meat meat or jelly
I'd rather save my awareness

of the inside when it's inside
me today I've decided to be

lulled & stimulated
simultaneously like MM

two Ms one
after the other & at the same time

reading leaves
of grass with a blade

in between the lips
for show   picture

the way a body moves
when it's breaking

up on the flat screen
-ing process to be

seized & sorted, to
be filtered like pixels

in the merciless
slow soon drift

shutter/speed

click click slip down   the long slide shutter   to make permissions   *limit the light*

allowed to pass   & *blur the motion*   we've just endured align   ago for instance

in a polaroid *see   also: a cover or a screen*   which lacks exposure   everything is moving away

from everything else   at our own private speed   I stress private   be-cause everything done

today is done   beside oneself for the public gaze   watch me fall now re-play it on an end

less loop to be   consumed is never of concern   to the ones most hun-gry   we are too

bloated to eat anything   other than our own   bodies our lack   of living general

atrophy of all our   living parts so many   ways to be   breathing the same

air as anyone   lest we forget   our shared humanity   or remember

to celebrate   what makes us different   in the room   the women come & go

the men the children   the king & members   of their cabinets   the rest yet slouch

unspoken all the best   comedians are dead   & we each   read from the
cannon

a room draped in dusk   no windows high walls   the tremble of what
is closest to us

Halt &
Catch Fire

In class, when I teach, I like to always come after. Not late but never early. I like to have an audience, I guess, someone or several to see me rushing breathless through the doors, in autumn as in spring. There is something I think to be said of this desire for coming after & it isn't in coming but I think it has to do with after. Guess what I am saying is I am wanting always to be the one who is next, even if I never am before you. Even if I never am now. Scene:

The backseat of a Buick, a Hyundai, a Toyota Corolla, midnight blue, whatever that means. In reality, I wasn't paying attention when I was being picked up

At 6:30PM my driver stopped the car in the middle of traffic to search me

At 6:33 I've already been friended & from my privileged view in the backseat I can see my driver scrolling, moving through my life much quicker than the pace we are moving in my life. I check my phone to see if time, too, has stopped, but it's only been moving more quickly. Late again. Always late. It's been like this since I was born. Only then did I ever come early

(He discovers new sides of himself
As he reads what others write
Of what he has written)

The Internet isn't the thing. It's the thing
That will lead us to the thing

Joe MacMillan tells a group of employees on the eve of a product launch,
in an episode of *Halt & Catch Fire* called "Search." Everyone, including
us (the viewers) are heading toward the end, technological extinction or
just the point where we turn this off & turn over or turn in, when we
turn inward, when we turn on to something new. I want to know what's
the thing if it's not the Internet, & if it's not the Internet where are we

More than half your body is not human for instance

Says scientists/Doctors suggest saying

I love you I'm sorry I forgive you forgive me I'm so sorry thank you
good-bye

When a person you love is dying but I want
To ask about the things they suggest
We say to the people we love who remain

What would happen if you didn't have a profile?

L wants to know & I tell L: Absolute image. A face on all sides, without
a third-dimension. Something that can only be seen, that can only be
presented

& what I'm describing is a monster. The Gorgon. Medusa. What I'm
describing is the anti-face. What can't be seen. Also: what cannot not

be seen

I am meant to arrest you. A situation in which you have to look, but from a gaze I control

Whenever I write about myself there is a fundamental intimacy but also a fundamental fissure, a crack that occurs along the groove of a face that seems to articulate: I am not what I am, because I am remembering myself as I am not & not

Who I used to be. & so how could I keep writing about myself in the past tense? I would need to situate all of this in the present, to bring it forward, to push it ahead & in pushing ahead, there is the need but also the desire of catching

One's breath

How to explain that the end of the world began before birth—that My first cries were unheard, even by my own ears

The most memorable thing my father ever told me as a child was money never remembers or forgets. But people do. & so what happens when people turn into money except that you forget them, too, & in forgetting them their faces become exchanged for something you can more easily place in your pocket or purse. Out of sight. I suppose this was a warning, or a prediction. All the same I always came away wishing I too could circulate all over the world & wondering just what it'd take, or what I'd have to become, or even what I'd have to discard, besides my face

Another way of saying this is saying what is the connection between celebrity & the detective story the detective story & the story about a ghost

A movement from writing everything as if I were about to die to writing everything as if I were already dead

(In a baby
Galaxy 12
Billion light years
From here
A black hole is gorging
On stars   One star
Every two days)

A student tells me the first thing you look at in a stranger is the thing you are most insecure about in yourself. Another student says people always look like their names & it reminds me this always begs the question or at least I always beg the question

What does it mean to resemble your stand-in?

Sometime after I wrote this, gun enthusiasts took their firearm videos to Pornhub after being banned from YouTube

(The connection between violence & flesh is not coincidental & here I am still begging for it)

Come to me come inside come with me come within me take me in take place in me take my place erase me   In the Bible

To penetrate means to get to know a person, to find them out, to feel them out, to out them under
The shadow
Of a roof

(I am always addressing someone else
Who is myself)

Identity as self-defense

Identity as a Toyota Yaris sedan spread
Open on a day
Old Chinese newspaper below me
As I type this

(As we move toward oblivion we count backward)

& in my mind, I am still watching a Cyndi Lauper music video which
doubles as the opening scene of *The Goonies*

To inhabit the interior
Of a put-on   To place

Myself in the question
Of others   What else

Is there in life but knowing
One's own relation

To a role

scores

whitman's brooklyn

moved out of whitman's brooklyn
for the original, since 1916
eating a nathan's hot dog with my
pretty young thing
playing on the PA around us & everywhere
there is music or there is music
to be made, the way I heard
a soundtrack in the background always
as a child now a soundtrack
for every mood I wish to feel
some might say the tip
of narcissism to have this

private experience in front
of you or to picture something else
before we're done   altering this
score over & over, the whole
world your own
personal movie on the street
walking otherwise alone the best
thing about modernity all the noise all
the feelings how I can't hardly
hear myself think or my voice

drowned out by this constant need another notice
some people are born into money some people
are born as money actual dollar bills
with a face & a smile dirty you say
I wish you wouldn't
write about me anymore, everyone at everyone's
fingertips as though no one no longer has to put anyone
on hold   won't you answer & end
my exile? I wish you

wouldn't I wish you would
vacillating between windows
so I can see perched
on my own lap from all horizons
truth be told who among us
hasn't savored the image of their own
ass in the mirror? the shape & how it curves
inward as if breathing
at the apex of the squat
to the floor like always
to know me is to love me to know
how I can love myself & hate myself
at the same time
to know nature made this
body & these thoughts, to read
me like a face truth be told

who among us hasn't wanted to see their own face
at the height of
orgasm, a photo
turned inward at just the right moment
when I'm feeling you I'm feeling you
inside me she says my ass my balls my lips as if
we'd just switched bodies & I
were you your own eyes & skin, I like that
feeling of surrender or syndication
as if we have to always have
something as if we can ever own
people like objects
as if we need to say we have it so we might have it
with us when we go, when we know
we can't take anything   a moving image
pause the video so you can see us

flicker in your hand as one
short pixelated backdrop a slow
soon decay closer
to me than thought

she said you are rather becoming
empty & still
emptier she added, on the face
of it more evidence
of our mutual longing for a long
stay without sound, my preference to use
hunger as a verb refuse
as a noun you motioned
me to really open wide
if I'm to do this without shuddering

> *please use inside*
> *voices to hear*
> *yourself think*

what a privilege in these united states
to hear or to be heard
somehow still capable of the act
of loving after a lifetime
of our own slow murder, theft
in the middle of the day
it's a jungle out there
when there's a jungle
as your lock screen
stretched to fill I couldn't ask for more
until I ask for more, something else
to listen to as I make myself shake

moved out of whitman's brooklyn
or white man's brooklyn
who among us hasn't wished
to be white & a man & whitman in our
darkest moments, so sad to see
unbearable sameness
all I ever saw on smith or court with my face
in my hand to record
a different reality, I insist on framing
everything I say in double
quotes to cover my ass
in the mirror so you can better
imagine it later or before
we've had the chance to turn
our heads & say *yes*

consummation or consumption
either/or & always
collectively a matter of context
like the image of myself
you hold dear, dearly
departed memory in my mind's eye
to say a thing about the lack
of imagination or having to
once again hold me in your gaze
consider the blues, later jazz, kids in atlanta
or everything worth imitating & eaten
by a corporate machine hungry
for *black cool* & desperate
to make it happen at the height
of all our wanting, &

to say when

Scheduled To Appear

At a date to be determined
Later in your own hands, your own
Eyes & face the miracle
Of privacy to show
You how to wake alone & light

Does nothing for your semblance
In the mirror a
Cool careful last look dead
Eyed stare to repeat
Your name at birth

General details or generous
People you've earlier inhabited
Associations of a mix
Tape memory got off with
Just a warning & a prayer

Don't trust anything that burns
Will burn out I heard
Your breathing behind me
My only window, a view
Of inimitable Internet

Skyline against the silken
Leaves of history
Pixelated my inertia to catch it
On camera my confession
I enjoy being searched

On Facebook, a stranger

Sends a link which re-directs me
To a video on YouTube, my image
The featured photo below the title
Top 10 Richest Pornstars in the World
I am neither a pornstar nor have I ever been rich
Sometimes I want to shake
My head sometimes I want
To sob, the way we can
When we know no one
Is looking   The way I've been looking
At myself outside myself
Like a replica or a separate
Skein of being, filament split
Apart & then rejoined later
Like watching scenes in a film
In which you are the film

Pausing at your reflection in the mirror

Talking to someone on the phone
While secretly watching them

Looking through windows that look
Back   Everyone typing fast without typing
Anything at all

In the chase scenes everyone is always
Two minutes out

So much might be explained through sifting
Through synopses of films starring Corey Haim
All these years & their moments   All the moments
I watched myself clipped in half, a line
Severing my asymmetrical face, making it
Less even or more even or even
More inexplicable to be alive & at the same time
To remain recording this

A summer intern rushes to LA with a package
Wanted by a computer-virus designer & his henchwoman

An accident swaps the minds
Of a married older man & a teenager
Chasing his dream girl

But when a young wheelchair-using boy named Marty
Encounters a werewolf one night, the pieces begin
To come together

Travis quickly discovers that the dog is highly intelligent &
Is able to speak in the English language

Enter: a local gang of vampires
Enter: ruthless agents & a series of slipups
A dream girl & the off
Chance of touching her lips with your own
Pair of magic sunglasses
Enter an explosion at a secret
Government lab, a close-up of Uncle Red, a mouth
Full of fangs, the credits after the opening
Synchronized roller-skating dance sequence

What does it mean to be an undercover teen
Of the dismal future or just
An undercover teen? A teen posing
As a roller skater or an adult posing
As a teen? No one on TV
Who plays a teen is a teen & I don't mean only
On TV   Listen   On
Facebook   I'm rich & I'm a pornstar
& I sob when no one is looking

Undercover I am
A person playing at not playing
A person or all the time
Wishing I could be
Here when the lights go
& so many others
Stream down the black
Like tears   Who knows
Why we keep pretending we aren't
Always undercover   Or we're only undercover
When the camera's on   Or the camera isn't
Ever off

scores[1]

julian and the body

        put it back on

more hands

        do as thou will

take her to measurements

        only God forgives

can't forget

        ask him why he killed my brother

put the pieces together

                what are you

        diversion

                weathermen

        after the accident

there's nothing in there

            involuntary manslaughter

        ruby's close up

my name on a car

---

1. Song titles from various soundtracks produced by Cliff Martinez.

messenger walks among us

one by one

shadows

awash in the day

do you like these colors?

pan to me

destroy something

get off the bus

take off your shoes

what would you have paid?

they didn't touch me

he had a good time

will it hurt

don't tell anyone

then I don't make it

we're invisible

I drive

affected cities

every road an exit

beach

friction

once more with teeth

all business

lives to spare

my foolish heart

handshake

I need a serious favor

I am not what I am

this is a special occasion

this is not going to go away

I'm sorry

we're here to listen

everybody with a gun is shooting

donald trump shakes

a hand & a boy dies. a woman right after
asks trump to talk about why he wants women
thrown in jail for the right to choose. excuse me

he says, smiles, shakes again but this time
points, & how old are you girl? i didn't know
they let students carry press passes. another

moment till an ad break the noise with more noise

everything is for sale in america everything
i think & change the channel, cruising
on about an hour in & after, she's gotta have it

i remember they filmed that down the block before
i ever called here home or walked this earth, for now
trump smiles again, shakes his head

& points a finger as a boy dies, three more two
days ago in chicago where murder
is more common than every woman's right

to choose. today trump is wearing a double
breasted wool blue suit & his bronze
hair is swaying in the wind the news

didn't have to manufacture for the air i can almost
feel the fucking breeze each time he shakes
another hand or smiles & nothing else is on

except a few old movies & old men performing
thru covert means & the search for being
sexually independent or real

love talking about a new united states, the freedom of
whatever is needed & still we shake, anyone
watching or being watched in this man's

fucking wake, excuse me girl his voice in my own
head repeating & cruz comes on
to say he remembers the seventies, that climate

change is not an issue & it's our job to kill
terrorists who bow to an other, the world
is on fire he says & throws his arms up

like he really means it or the guy a parent pays
to do tricks at a toddler's birth
day party & pull what rough beast

from a hat, or say cheese
& die basically, which is the best
goosebumps but also america's

prevailing rhetoric when it comes to thinking
about any person deemed different & this
thursday as the world turns bill wants to make

believe that black lives don't matter, remind us
all again president how many black bodies
were incarcerated in place of funds for public housing?

the eighties & the nineties & today
i'm dressed like a founding father
trump is on tv, i'm black in america. i feel like

there's a poem there somewhere my sometimes
inspiration & muse Ashley M. Jones
writes via status update & you? i think & also

always mean me. where are you or why
do you keep watching? every time trump shakes
a hand a boy dies, passionate intensity of

the worst, the rest are no better
democrats, republicans, the privilege
to fucking smile & lie

in bed after a hard day's work
the new united states can't bear to blink, change
the station or turn it off. we barely can bear

to think, this year & the one before
& the one that will follow that assuming
we survive this. we barely can

believe it & i believe it

pass words

what unknown secrets govern our
screens & our identities, the desire
to know each other's desire
supersedes the knowledge of our own

i've forgotten what i am again
& how, locked out
keyless & clueless which
digits might make me

enter my machine & head
home, placed
the camera pulled
rudely acquiesced a kind

of absolute beauty, did you
get the annual report
unopened emails unanswered
questions classified

based on subject & sender
primary/social/promotions
case of harassment when
you see something as a strap

hanger standing above
so many   brooklyn rushing by
in dirty faded windows pre
cautious reminder *do not*

lean on doors
whatever did i guess
my password mistakes me
for security questions

i can't recall or think
i lied to begin with how
i want to live without & from within
only what i have to give which can be

very often nothing sting
singing don't stand so close to me
as i text you, i want to
make believe i can only

picture your avatar projected
something secured
in my jeans front
pocket uncomfortably close

in another stranger's
ears i pass words
to you on the tip
of my tongue in you in your own

ear & mouth i wish
to be you

Installation in progress

Buffering

Scene 1, item 1:

The camera moves as if the wind.

Unreachable valley of sand, curving tire tracks, vista of blue sky and black leather boots, a close-up of parting lips and the sand parting in the march's wake: a mouth without teeth or tongue.

Audio track mutes in place of the alarmed tenor of North American news anchors, voices superimposed on voices until nothing is legible except the pitch.

a crackling in the auditory like the removal of a head

Even this is a prayer. Even this.

DISSOLVE TO V.O.

"The media wing has relied on veterans of Al-Qaeda media teams, young recruits fluent in social media platforms, and a bureaucratic discipline reminiscent of totalitarian regimes. Battle scenes and public beheadings are so scripted and staged that fighters and executioners often perform multiple takes and read their lines from cue cards. The overriding goal of the Islamic State is not merely to inflict terror on an adversary but also to command a global audience."

EXT. – COURTYARD – DAY

Two men kneeling, blindfolded, hands tied behind their backs, naked besides a white tunic, the better to show the juxtaposition of red. A caption slides across the screen:

The beheading takes place only when the camera crew's director says it is time to proceed.

A man wearing a black baseball cap sits at a wooden chair and fidgets, folding fingers together as if to contemplate the shape of the sun or its location in the sky, which is quickly turning royal blue. Soon it will be purple.

He crosses and uncrosses a leg. He calls Junaid, who's in charge of media. He waits for confirmation, which comes as a pat on the shoulder from an assistant who swoops in and hasn't swooped in yet. He checks his mobile. He phones his wife, Fatima. He phones his friend, Ahmed, who runs the club he frequents on Fridays and Saturdays, and sometimes, Tuesdays. It's Wednesday.

CLOSE-UP OF A TATTERED NEWSPAPER,
QUOTE UNDERLINED IN RED MARKER

"The group is very image-conscious, much like a corporation," said a U.S. intelligence official involved in monitoring the Islamic State's media operations. Its approach to building its brand is so disciplined, the official said, "that it's very much like saying 'This is Coca-Cola' or 'This is Nike.'"

INT. – VIDEO ARCHIVE – DAY

"Why do so many of the victims in Islamic State beheading videos look
so calm?"
I ask, looking at the footage with a colleague of mine at the university.
She gazes at me and turns her palm upward, as if to say, You don't know?

She's an expert on the subject and I know nothing; as a rule I'm only
always asking questions. Of myself and others.

That's why I came to the conference yesterday afternoon. That's why I'm
here. To watch the footage and learn more about what it contains. I teach
a course on celebrity and wish fulfillment and Post Internet culture—
whatever that means—and I want to connect networking threads that
ISIS already did much earlier; how it uses social media and mankind's
penchant for glamorization and documentation to multiply and prosper.

She zooms in on the expression of the child who is about to lose his
head. The frame is frozen but we've already watched this one twice.

In 2.4 seconds, the child's head will roll, coming to a stop near his left
hip. The camera crew will be visible, briefly, as one man removes a reflec-
tor that was out of frame, and another lowers a boom mic. So calm, so
calm, so calm. My colleague looks at the screen and then she looks at me.

"They don't know it's real."

CLOSE-UP OF A TATTERED NEWSPAPER,
COLUMN UNDERLINED IN RED MARKER

Al-Qaeda's productions always exalted its leaders, particularly Osama bin
Laden. But the Islamic State's propaganda is generally focused on its
fighters and followers. Appearances by leader Abu Bakr al-Baghdadi or
his senior lieutenants have been rare.

EXT. – COURTYARD – NIGHT

The hooded executioner raised and lowered his sword repeatedly so that crews could catch the blade from multiple angles. Nearby, half a dozen men were carrying bodies in a wheelbarrow, two to a machine, legs dangling on the sand. They pause at spots of sand marked with a mounted X. Here they deposit the bodies, arranging them to be photographed.

Before each image is captured, a man smears the dead's face with moist cloths, washing away dried blood. Next, the man lifts the corners of the dead's mouth into a beatific smile, and raises their index finger in a gesture adopted by the Islamic State as a symbol of its cause.

The caption reads: *Let us exalt our heroes and their sacrifice*

INT. – VIDEO ARCHIVE – DAY

"The frequency and volume of releases by the Islamic State are staggering by comparison," my colleague says, turning to me again, watching my expression. Probably she is wondering why I'm not taking notes, or whether I am keeping this all to myself. All for me. All inside me.

"The group has produced hundreds of videos in more than a half-dozen languages, puts out daily radio broadcasts, and garners as many as two million mentions per month on Twitter."

My iPhone lights up. Someone, somewhere has followed me.

I turn my gaze to see a door closing. A drawer opens. The monitor down the hall is alight, except I can't figure what's on screen. Three men sit, hunched over, each of them wearing black headphones, the kind that encircles their skulls. They seem amused, looking with wide eyes and grinning intermittently. Or maybe it's me who is amused, looking at them when I should be looking elsewhere. It's difficult to see and now I have to squint.

"Are you okay?" my colleague asks, noticing my eyes or maybe my lack of focus. I nod and point my finger.

There is a window, above the monitor we are seated at. It's day, maybe noon or one-thirty. I don't wear a watch anymore. Hardly anyone wears a watch anymore.

The sun's rays streak through the glass, bisecting my chest and face, half in shade.

It's awhile till I can open my eyes again.

DISSOLVE TO V.O.

"Discrepancies among frames showed that scenes had been rehearsed and shot in multiple takes over many hours."

EXT. – VILLAGE SQUARE – NIGHT

Close-up of a palm on goatskin. A moment of silence before the beat kicks in. A man seated, legs crossed, with the daf in both hands, one on each frame width-wise, as if the instrument were a mirror. Camera pans out to reveal a group of singers and performers; tanbur, violin, oud, saz, small cymbals that match the vibrating camera when they shake, trembling as its gaze moves from figure to figure.

A man has just finished installing a screen the size of a small billboard, hanging at the center of the village square. He sighs and unfurls his arms. A cloud of sand kicks up at his feet and the camera follows it around a bend; a laptop barely visible behind the screen; two men with headsets barking directions in and out of focus as a crackle cuts in.

A spotlight in the square and all is silent. The image on the screen begins to move.

Crowds have gathered from three neighboring villages for this.

Quick cut to a teenager, lips parting in a broad smile. His legs are folded beneath him as he claps, applauding the movement of the images on the screen, the music which accompanies it.

"It's like a movie theater," said Abu Hourraira al-Maghribi, a 23-year-old with a shaved head who wore an Adidas hoodie when he met with reporters in prison. The videos are drawn from the Islamic State's expanding film library, he said, depicting "daily life, military training, and beheadings. And be … and be … and be …"

The video is buffering.

INT. – VIDEO ARCHIVE – EVENING

"What's going on?"

"The video is buffering."

"What's that?" I ask.

buffer
noun buff·er \ ˈbə-fər

1. fellow, man; especially: an old man (slang British)

2. any of various devices or pieces of material for reducing shock or damage due to contact

3. a means or device used as a cushion against the shock of fluctuations in business or financial activity

4. something that serves as a protective barrier: as a: buffer state b: a person who shields another especially from annoying routine matters c: mediator

5. a substance capable in solution of neutralizing both acids and bases and thereby maintaining the original acidity or basicity of the solution; also: a solution containing such a substance

6. a temporary storage unit (as in a computer); especially: one that accepts information at one rate and delivers it at another

verb buff·er

1. to protect (something) from something

2. to lessen the harmful effects of (something)

3. computers : to put (something, such as data) in a buffer

"No," I cut in. "I know what *buffering* means."

She looks at me as if she's expecting me to say something else.

"I meant, why did an advertisement for Justin Bieber's *Purpose* just pop up?"

She laughs, looking at my finger, still pointed. Justin Bieber shadowed and stark, genuflecting in prayer with his fingers barely touching. A gold watch on his left wrist. Seven chains around the other.

"Oh, that."

DISSOLVE TO V.O.

"The videos reflect an increased awareness of global pop culture. A recently released training video from the Ansar Battalion, an Islamist rebel group in Syria, features action movie style cuts between slow and fast motion, as well as CGI that mimics the bullet time effects made famous in *The Matrix*. Religious verses that often serve as the soundtrack to these videos are now auto-tuned. Somalia's Al-Shabaab, whose videos are often directly aimed at recruiting Americans, has dabbled in hip-hop and nasheeds sung in English; at other times, the videos are designed to mimic video games."

INT. – VIDEO ARCHIVE – DAY

> YOU
> Senior media operatives are treated as if they're emirs.

> ME
> Emirs?

> YOU
> *(sharply)*
> More important than soldiers. Their monthly income is higher. They have better cars. They preside over hundreds of videographers, producers,

and editors ... they form a privileged, profes-
sional class with salaries and living arrangements
that are the envy of every soldier.

ME

Isn't ISIS concerned about the fall-out? A drop
in the soldiers actually willing to fight its war?

YOU
(shakes head)
The overriding goal of the Islamic State is not
only to inflict terror on an adversary.
(beat)
Now it wants to command a global audience.
(beat)
You teach a class on narcissism, right?

ME
(nods)
So by glamorizing the soldiers, the videos func-
tion as a way to remove the boundaries between
public figures and private citizens. Soldiers are
celebrities while the leaders who pull the strings
recede into the background.

YOU
(shrugs)
Not even the background. Almost categorically
removed from all propaganda material.
(gulps coffee, makes a face)
(beat)

YOU

The attacks in Paris were carried out by militants whose attachments to the Islamic State exist mainly on the Internet. Ninety percent of the members of the Islamic Caliphate are being re-cruited online.

ME
(counting, eyes pulled peripherally)

YOU
(fingers tap the desk)
Don't bother doing the math.

ME

I wasn't actually counting.

YOU

It'll rise by next week.

ME

Then what?

YOU

Then what?

DISSOLVE INT. – MEDIA DIVISION HEADQUARTERS – DAY

Panorama of a two-story home in a residential neighborhood. Bicycles and lawnmowers. Fake grass. The sound of running water and a faucet turning. Armed guards in military garb patrol the entrance where two white vans have just arrived, the blue FORD insignia above the bumper still shiny.

Van doors slide open, revealing laptops and memory sticks in an open chest. Chest to hand, hand to chest, this time held in place between the breasts. Three armed guards ask for credentials three times. Three times credentials are approved and the camera moves on.

Inside the building, the camera moves through each floor as if giving a tour to prospective homeowners. Slow, deliberate, hanging for applause.

Four rooms to a floor, each room stocked with cameras, computers, memory sticks, reflectors, and lighting lamps. All the computers are connected to the Internet through a Turkish wireless service. Pornography plays on each monitor, except one.

A lanky pale man wearing a gray TaylorMade visor over his dark brown hair hunches over a desktop, editing footage from earlier in the day, moving video showing the construction of public markets, smiling religious police on neighborhood patrols, and residents leisurely fishing on the banks of the Euphrates to one folder. Moving beheadings, immolations, and round-table rapes to another. Syncing music and mixing sound effects to segue from scenes. His nametag reads: *Jim Williams*. Two women are moaning on the screen around him. Moaning, wailing. So staged it sounds real.

Three women, four, five.

DISSOLVE INT. – VIDEO ARCHIVE – EVENING

ME
Social media enables the role of the viewer who
is constantly watching but also watched—

YOU
(softly)
A viewer under surveillance.

ME
—from a perch of simultaneous moral superior-
ity and self-denial, creating not only a compart-
mentalization of horror, but also its justification.
(beat)
The Internet provides the buffer. We are all of
us buffering.

YOU
(reads from cue cards *erratically*)
Erin Saltman ... a counter-extremism researcher
... at the Institute for ... Strategic Dialogue ...
cites "desires of adventure ... activism, romance
... power, belonging, along ... with spiritual ful-
fillment" ... as the main allure that ISIS ... pro-
vides its recruits.

ME
Familiar sales pitch. Everything promised to ev-
eryone on the Internet. Its glamorized re-presen-
tations of everyday life.

DISSOLVE TO V.O.

"The group exerts extraordinarily tight control over the production of
its videos and messages but relies on the chaos of the Internet and social
media to disseminate them. The terrorist group's rise is a result main-
ly of its demonstrated military power and the tangible territory it has
seized. But a remarkable amount of its energy is devoted to creating an

alternative, idealized version of itself online and shaping how that virtual empire is perceived."

EXT. – VILLAGE SQUARE – NIGHT

Silence again. The smell of goat skin, salt, human flesh, excrement. The daf in both hands but each finger is still. The boy in the Adidas hoodie re-emerges on screen, still smiling, addressing the camera, and the crowd he imagines gazing through it; he can't say where or when, or on what occasion— sometime later, definitely tonight.

"Some were like Van Damme movies," he said, referring to Jean-Claude Van Damme, the Hollywood action star. "You see these men fighting, and you want to be one of these brave heroes."

Outside the frame, it was night in New York City too. I could see the moon, or a slice of it, in the window which hung over the monitor and draped the room in half-lit silver. I was alone and had been for some time. When my phone buzzed I didn't bother to glance at the screen. The machine stayed in my pocket, alerting me about something I probably did not want to know, or admit, or understand. Any or all three, some combination I had only just considered. The description on the film I'd just watched beamed back at me as I hovered the mouse over its author.

His videos continue to circulate online.

A handclap at the base of the temple

Buildings can sing too
Echoing in the ether like
A birdcall or an orchestra
Of breath & step
Let's say we're both

Listening on a Thursday
In Brooklyn so full
Of itself in the AM
FM signal everyone
Pushing forward

North over Ocean, empty
Handed or with strollers, spaniels
Scraps of metal, an actual kitchen
Sink, stereos no one no longer
Sells all the people, or only me

Playing Alphabet on the tongue
El em en oh &
It almost works just like that
Block by block by block
Inspired by boulevards in Berlin & Paris

& in the right light
All bodies can tantalize, signs
Flashing in the retina
Like captions somewhere
To see something

Say something
Play witness, victim, perpetrator,
The standard postmodern situation
In which all parts
Are played by yourself

Sex is a cab ride
Education an advertisement
History a notice
Of eviction   Doesn't this make it
Any easier? To swallow life

Like vitamins   On the Internet
Everything flattens, compresses
Like flesh in blenders   Today's
News   The scene
I'm picturing involves hoses

Burning trash   Bloodied
Cheeks & human shit   Rivers like
A Jeep commercial
Riot shields   Faces masked
In rage, heartbreak, poverty   Tell me

This could be ours some day
Pointing toward the horizon
All the buildings we only ever see
From a roof deck, when we're
Catering to strangers   You'll say

I don't want it, I prefer
Only ever to be visiting
If we had this, what would we want?
The way only absurd questions matter
The joy of pressing fresh fruit against both cheeks

(block by block by block)

Waking up to the Home Shopping Network
Vibrating in another room, a close-up of this
Slender hand outfitted with sheepskin
Leather, synthetic suede, who knows
Whether they are happy or knows

Enough to ask the question
I tried to escape
Loneliness with so much
Sound, I never cared how
Much I could have knowing

I always rather want everything

Installation in progress

& the privilege of witnessing
The actors
Walk forward, backward
& in slow circles
Choreography which moves between
Letting the footage play
Naturally & reversing it
Making it unclear
If the action is unfolding in
Real time or not
Techniques of repetition confuse
Time, space, & sequence

Book of the Dead, chapter 17
"Tomb of Inherkhau"
Re in the form of a cat slaying the Serpent Apep
Several feet from
Portrait of a Lady as Mary Magdalene

Always a question
Of being unaware
Of the game or playing
It too well
Pretend I am this until I am this
Pretending I believe
Is born in childhood in spare
Moments of solitude
I am someone else
Sometimes my lover
Says I just don't get this one
Looking up from the poem

& then back to the poem
I'd been writing recently
About iterations & rearrangements
See the line before or
The one before that
I really mean it
Feels as though I let myself
Fall with my eyes closed
Into the sun-fed earth
Not even a mound of dirt or leaves
To catch me

Instead we move
From room to room
Wearing more or less
& feigning not to notice
In this scenario I am forever
The student learning by leaning
Better to see what's inside
The frame what's outside

The man appears to sit
Among cuts of meat, including a large slab
Gleaming with white fat on the floor to the left
& a platter of pig trotters & sausage behind him
On a table covered with bright linen

Some scholars suggest that this is an artist's studio
Cluttered with the makings of a still life
Not raw meat per se but a framed canvas
Containing numerous sketches of meat

Imitative sympathy or simply
Gifts for the king
An offering
Table overlaid with animal flesh

For comfort if not
Also style a sure sign
Of modernity the pleasure
Of what was once
Alive & deemed fit
For ritual implements
Consider a body might be more
Easily opened with time

Both of these works, separated by many centuries, use the human
Form as a platform for expressing & displaying script
The long, pointed end would have been inserted in a handle
The tall walking stick & paddlelike baton indicate his official status
The woman's name, inscribed above her head, has been lost
A face turned toward the viewer at the apex of the movement
I'd mentioned earlier
Appears unfinished, or overdone

Images like this one could house the dead owner's essence
Before the advent of photography in the nineteenth century
Painted portrait miniatures permitted their keepers
An immediate access to the memory
& appearance of loved ones

Portable & convenient
As today our own
Screens afford us
Security & the death
Of having to conjure a face
To match the spirit

We are not ourselves
Never again will I
Dance as though no one
Is watching

Art is for Necrophiliacs

Reading your writing
(a way out of exile)

Reading your writing is like a female orgasm, says my friend, who, of course, is a man.

There's a name for that, he says. In French, I mean, he says. In theory, he says. I mean, he says, *theoretically.*

But I'm not listening anymore, not really. Not anymore. I'm thinking instead about female orgasms, and all the men who think they know what a woman wants or what a woman needs or what a woman thinks. Thinking we can actually speak for her too.

What's a female orgasm supposed to feel like? I ask, a day later, to my friend, who, of course, is a woman.

Usually what goes through my head is this, she begins, holding her breath to prepare for the explanation, or, maybe, to simulate the feeling. How I'm going to die, she continues. I'm going to die, I'm going to die, I'm going to die—don't write this down—she adds, quickly, then I don't die.

And I'm sleeping.

Jouissance, the French word my friend had originally mentioned, is literally *enjoyment*, but a transgressive sort of enjoyment, an excessive kind of enjoyment linked to the splitting of the subject involved. The subject of my work is always me, so I liked that he thought about jouissance and splitting and identity—literally, a self-fragmentation, a self-imposed dislocation, I guess—while reading my writing, because he reads everything I write as I write it, and just as often, teaches me something new about what I've written. I like excess, too, all kinds of excess, especially the band, INXS, and my favorite song by the Eighties Australian rockers is undoubtedly "Need You Tonight," a song about circumventing death, or embracing the night, or just embracing another body, I think, not unlike the Lacanian principle that links jouissance to the castration complex, and also to the aggression of the death drive in general.

This time last year (or the year before, or the year before that ...) I was writing a book I'd eventually call *Death of Art*. Anyone can write themselves out of death through the proliferation of language; I'm more interested in a culture of excess that can lead to the freedom to move beyond both culture *and* excess, so I'm elated when a Google search of "jouissance" immediately pulls up Karl Marx's concept of surplus-value; the kind of enjoyment that goes beyond the pleasure principle (i.e. jouissance) exists to break the constraints and confines of commodities. Pleasure for the mere sake of pleasure. Maybe also what the Situationists meant when they post-scripted their 1967 manifesto with the coyly calculating line, "If you want to make revolution, do it for fun."

I always listen to music while I write and what I'm listening to right now is Yellow Claw's "Till It Hurts" (ft. Ayden), a song that includes the lyrics, "love me till it hurts/make my body burn" and earlier, "hold me tight, read my lips, don't need a word to say/lay me down, blow my mind, let's take it all the way." It's a song I've often blasted during sex, and after sex, and sometimes right before sex, and it's a song that is clearly about orgasms, or at least a striving toward one.

When I was an undergraduate, enrolled at an engineering school to write poetry, I took a workshop called "Sex & Death: Poetry of the Body." The course was taught by the poet who taught me almost everything I know about poetry today, and one of the things Bob Watts told me, and eleven other students, was *when you write the perfect poem, the world explodes.*

Which is a different sort of orgasm altogether, I think, today, mulling over all of this while I await further descriptions from other friends about orgasms, what they feel like when they feel it. But the emphasis on aggression, death, destruction—all of the above—is clearly evident. What is it about an orgasm that makes us feel like we've just died? Like we've just been brought to life? All in the span of thirteen seconds, maybe half a minute. The typical orgasm—what the French tellingly called "la petite mort" to evoke the spiritual release or short period of transcendence after the expenditure of the "life force"—lasts only 18 seconds on average, half a minute if you're a man.

And this is what I really do know about my writing, I think, as "Till It Hurts" ends and "Disco//Very"[2] by Warpaint bursts on my iTunes, and I type this, or I type the line that came before this.

Since I am always listening to music as I write, there's always a countdown to some sort of pause, whether it's brief, or whether it's complete silence, utter and absolute, a playlist having been emptied and awaiting another loop. A finger to touch. That kind of momentary lifespan produces another kind of desperation. And with that kind of desperation, it's no wonder my readers might apply excess for velocity, momentum, urgency or acceleration, a sentence that is continuously in threat of being derailed or derailing itself outside the text and its location on the page. Suicidal tendencies or simply death by overdoing it.

So full of everything, and especially itself. Everything I'm thinking when

2. Opening lines which consist of: "I've got a friend with a melody that will kill/She'll eat you alive/Like cyanide … it's poison."

I'm not thinking about you.

Writing has always made me feel giddy, the sort of euphoria that is mirrored while listening to a really good song, or the way a really good song can take you outside yourself from verse to chorus, or the pause before the bridge. The balance between being vulnerable on the page, really exposing myself, and being performative in my own self-awareness-as-author is manifested, I think, or complicated, by the balance between my public communion with you and my private meta-communication. If I move fast enough, I must be thinking, even now, maybe you won't care, or won't care to notice.

A way out of exile is in excess and reflex, and self-reflex, too, for me and also for a long lineage of dislocated writers, including the Cuban ones I admire so much.

To be Cuban, José Lezama Lima once said, is to already feel foreign. But to be Cuban is also to be manifold, as José Martí famously proclaimed in his poem "Yo soy un hombre sincero": "Yo vengo de todas partes,/Y hacia todas partes voy" (I come from everywhere/and I am going toward everywhere).

To be Cuban—and by extension, to be American—is to be inherently a synthesis; a body comprised of various parts. I've never been to Santiago de Cuba and my father hasn't returned since he left, with his sister, at fourteen and eleven respectively, a year after the Battle of Santa Clara and Fidel Castro's ascension toward eventual dictatorship.

My reaction to cultural displacement is equal parts excess and assemblage: language *dis*placement—the double, or triple, quadruple, infinitive—iterations of a single word, character, scene, story. Language is a banquet, a feast of words where, as the Cuban saying goes, everything goes through the mouth—se la comió!—and comes out through the assay, an attempt or experiment to expand or enlarge a text before the text converges back upon itself, each part re-formed and re-fashioned, elongated and exploded to create a utopia that has no location but the location of the text: the possibility of excess and an excess of possibilities.

The answer, of course, is sex and death. Death and sex. Did I really need to take a poetry workshop to realize that? Reading your writing is always a way out of exile. And what are we if we are not all already elsewhere? When objects and people and text move that fast, it doesn't look like we are moving at all. The concept of the always-already ready-made has also made identity just another prefab, gossamer construction, less sleight of hand than smoke and mirrors: the camera pulls back in a mise-en-scène to reveal that nothing else actually exists beyond the beautiful binding.

The utopic possibilities that exist on a blank page, and the communion and connection that writing and reading allow us, have never been more important and more ignored. We grasp outside of ourselves by being able to imagine other worlds and all the perspectives that live there, beyond our own. Poetry's power cradles here: we can overcome this distance in a single line or a single word that breaks one line from the next. The tension that exists within that threshold is our striving for intimacy. Probably

Also an orgasm.

this part of brooklyn

was so much cooler before I moved here
is another confession I was afraid to try
pellegrino for the first time
all that volcanic air rising
to the surface something
capable of making me
roll on the floor as if I were
inside out or inverted I grew

up watching white people
on TV doing things I didn't know
a thing about watching perfect
strangers, friends, step by
step I walk fast always
counting the beat or who
I'm listening to writing
under the influence of
so many others I admire

being thirty-one in twenty-sixteen
at seven oh eight on a sunday night
means another thing altogether
we will never be here again
I often think we will
move as with whispers
as the city around us re
vamps or preserves itself
like a panting exhibition
or a portable museum
panorama of the hudson &
my hunger on a roof top

to bottom you could
probably do worse
& this part becomes another
part I forgot to mention
where would we even
bury the dead

the ruins of a rt. 4 shopping mall

nothing but flowers
on a slick surface sent
with such emotion or purpose
did you know

almost every scene set
in the middle east in
the last fifty years was filmed
in southwest america, mostly

arizona & new mexico, never north
bergen or paramus or new york city (too
urban, too gray & metallic)
unlike certain parts of

colorado, or santa clarita
where I've actually been
landing with a sense of déjà vu
or dislocation having

seen these dunes & desert sprawl
with a different set of extras
so many years before I grew
up in the ruins

of a rt. 4 shopping mall
catching brief glimpses
of myself in revolving doors
my tilted face or half-held eyes

racing toward the glassy air
conditioned stillness of storefronts & smiling
men & women I wanted
to look my way &

call my place
in line as if to know me
is to really know
where I've been

Art is for Necrophiliacs
(If that's how you spend)

eternity then what age is ideal for death? I often wondered and wondered whether it even mattered. An ideal age to die, I mean. An ideal age to live. Aren't the two things really the same thing? Like Jesse Tuck in *Tuck Everlasting*, who can only ever exist as a seventeen-year-old. I'd rather live a whole life starting from seventy-seven or eighty-three and reverse the gears, like Benjamin Button, maybe.

Maybe it doesn't matter now, not really, not anyway, not in 2016 and definitely not in 2017, which is a year from now or maybe last year, at the earliest, if you're reading this at a bookstore or in a library, because I write fast but not that fast and besides, editing can be a real killer.

The most common phrase used by people in my generation to describe a laugh-out-loud experience is, "I'm dying." Variations include "I'm dead" and of course, "RIP me" which won't come through properly if you're using voice recognition to type this. The most common phrases used by people in my generation to feign a laugh-out-loud experience is, naturally, the same as above. Death, like every other marker of life, is meant to be performed, veiled in the language of hyperbole and a well-timed emoji. Skull and crossbones? Revolver? Big breaking wave?

And if death is life in 2016 (and 2017 and 2018 and 2019 &&&), then life is death; the surest marker of being productive (i.e. producing and/or giving birth to) in our culture is to *not be doing anything*, which is why there are apps that are designed to make you appear as though you are disconnected from the physical world and locked into your digital device. Fake-A-Text and SimiSimi[3] deliver texts to your cell phone whenever you want, anytime, anywhere. Philosophy's old question has been amended in the age of artificial intelligence and artificiality: If you are in a public park and no one sees you looking at a screen, do you still exist? Or do only the trees which surround you?

There's an idea that is rapidly becoming a reality, because when ideas become actualized, they stop only existing as a matter of opinion and become matter of fact: pre-ordained rules and the scripts that accompany them. If you aren't on your phone, you aren't doing anything worthwhile with your life. If you aren't living through your phone, you aren't *alive*.

So death becomes the salve and the solution; our linguistic approach to re-appropriating life when the real thing has almost already disappeared, lost in the *refresh* that reads as the only kind of engagement that might actually exist today.

I'm not good at math and have never been comfortable dealing with numbers, but I treasure fractions, fragmentary syntax and thought, the half-heard echo or call heard in pieces that resonates even as it ruptures. The traces of that transition—what came before, where we are always already going—is a liminal experience that intensifies all others, one of the reasons why our image-rich culture is especially captivated by GIFs, pictures half-frozen between an arrested movement and the pose of permanence. The best of both worlds in a finite existence.

3. Invisible Girlfriend (and Invisible Boyfriend) apps will send convincing text messages and even voicemails from a virtual partner as "proof" of a relationship, for around twenty-five dollars a month, which is probably the going rate for *intimacy* in today's market. According to the founders, the service creates a safe space for you to "practice texting with a real human if you're out of practice." On the app's website, one of the most frequently asked questions is, "What if we hit it off, and I run out of texts?" The answer is currency, proof of purchase as proof of life. "You can purchase more at any time."

Sometimes it's best to close your eyes.

•

Our obsession with death marks our language, but it's also modified our physical relationship to art and to the artist. In earlier moments, maybe yesterday or even this morning, we went to the theater, concert halls, music venues, museums, art galleries and installations. We wanted that human element, that breath and touch, and the energy and surprise of the unexpected live performance; the faint mark of human error in the real thing that distinguishes it from its flawless counterfeit cousin. Art could be viewed in the face, between the eyes. Although we were not allowed to touch the paintings, we could get close enough to use our fingers, if we wanted to.

How art works—the way it interacts with you, how it makes you feel, what it makes you think about, what you think about it—is determined by what surrounds it, or in other words, what surrounds *you*. Where you are and what you are doing, besides being in communion, hopefully, with the work of art.

Is it more moving and more beautiful to be looking at the Sistine Chapel on Google Images, alone, with the time and solitude to savor it in the bathroom of a Starbuck's? Or in person, surrounded by a mob of people videotaping their experience? Snapchatting selfies from various angles of the marble floor, each snap destroying the nine scenes from the Book of Genesis, but also rebuilding it; re-formation as the foundation toward a new appreciation of art; a new understanding of what art is and where it can take us, even and especially if we're nowhere new, still and silent and looking through a re-presentation.

And perhaps more pressing: Have we reached a moment in our culture where art is actually *better* on the Internet than in real life? Pixelated and dead and drifting and forever and forever

Nowhere.

Art itself mutates, evolves, and escalates along with technology; just as musicians re-conceived the ways they should sing with microphones or for the phonograph after the advent of recorded music, so, too, have artists learned to use the infinite—and ephemeral—landscapes of a rapidly shifting Google Image search to find a new form, casualness and collage, a flattening of time and space that resembles a world, and words, without end.

In the same way that music could be liberated from its cultural trajectory by holding an instrument like the electric guitar with organic (i.e. human hands) means, art has been uprooted from time and space by applying our analog techniques to our digital landscapes.

Except when there's no longer place, there's nowhere to go.

Maybe apps like Fake-A-Text are really making a point about our insistence for immortality, making a point or showing us the way. Because if we have a future in being forever, immortality is going to present itself in data. Everything we do, all the time and at the same time, even the things we'd never admit to in person, even the things we're not quite conscious of and yet which make us who we really are; what we've become when we think no one is watching. It's why the web is still a wave, even if we no longer refer to our browsing history as *surfing*. Instead we are pulled along, often far off course or where we'd been intending to go, ultimately washing ashore with puppy photos belonging to an ex-girlfriend's best friend's uncle.

How did I get here?

Companies like Facebook, which know even the length of time we linger[4] on a photo or post, don't care how; they only care that they know more about us than we know about ourselves. Most of the time.

In a way, the less we are available in real life, the more traces we leave of our existence in the digital world. Long after I die, my traces will still permeate and populate the World Wide Web, which means the Internet can re-make me long after my flesh rots and the worms are crawling through the sockets where my eyes once were.

•

"What percentage of our life is spent on the Internet?" I venture one morning, asking my students in an early section of the class I teach at Baruch College. One student says: seventy. Another raises his hand and calls out: seventy-five. An hour later, in the second section, a handful of students agree without hesitation, posing the rhetorical question to the rest of the room: a dimly-lit, too-humid square space where the constant construction on the corner of 22nd Street interrupts every other question, every other answer. "Why not all of it? Why not a hundred percent of our day-to-day lives?"

"Except this moment," I quickly add, smiling, laughing, although it's a nervous laugh and my hand is on the back of my neck, the back of my scalp, scratching myself the way I do when I'm nervous. Because I wonder, even right now, who's connected and who's disconnected, and what that even means anymore. To be present, to be presented with technology; connected or connected. To be conned.

---

4. Actually, Facebook even knows the things we don't do. Its researchers are specifically interested in the non-encounters: whenever we type something and then delete it, a self-censorship that kept the company from making more money, until it unveiled the curated newsfeed. When Facebook users don't feed Facebook with the data it desires, profits dip.

More and more of us have the opportunity to perpetuate ourselves by the grace of the upload button and the silhouette of our social networks, the digital archive of identity that makes Borges' sprawling "Library of Babel" look like the corner devoted to POETRY at Barnes & Noble.

"So if a hundred percent of our lives are lived on the Internet," I answer, not really believing it but not really disbelieving it either, "doesn't that mean, basically, so long as we keep our Internet activity going—posting photos, updating our status, sending out Tweets and sharing articles we like—we are, for all intents and purposes," I pause, looking at everyone's face, or trying to. Looking at everyone's eyes. "Eternal?"

"I mean," I continue, running one hand through my hair or rubbing my eyebrows together, trying to smudge them into each other, probably, the way I imagine it, at least, right now. "No one would ever know you are dead. Not really."

I'd thought about this during previous classes, during previous semesters, something called the "Internet Life Package." Something which allowed, via a signed and dotted contract, another party, or multiple parties, to post on your behalf, to scour the Internet, to collect data. To thrive, to move, to persist.

"I mean," I add, persistent, looking from one pair of eyes to another, everyone arranged in a semicircle so I have to crane my head from the left to the right, from the right to the left. Another drill erupts. Another explosion of lead or metal or dust, even dust which makes a noise as loud as anything else if you're really listening. "Who would know you were dead?"

The better question, I think, might be, Who would care? But I don't add this. I don't add anything. So my question just hangs there. And I imagine the implications. And if not a person we pay to post on our behalf, then a bot, the same chatbots that already exist today. Artificial intelligence, algorithms, artificiality. We are already always performing. We'll be performing after we're dead too. Plug in my data. Spit me back out. If we're more like ourselves on the Internet than we are in the physical world, we'll be more like ourselves in death than we ever were in life.

But we still want it, all of it and more.

Life extension is a big business. Everyone wants to live forever, even if all we do now is live through looking. Google has committed an investment up to six hundred million into the California Life Company to solve death. Ray Kurzweil, Google's director of engineering, foresees the possibility of reincarnating his dead father into a digital avatar. PayPal co-founder Peter Thiel has invested in twenty-five biotech companies and the combination of gene therapy, nanotechnology, and artificial intelligence. Mark Zuckerberg and a handful of others have been funding "Breakthrough Prizes" for six scientists a year, three million apiece to prove death is as antiquated as intimacy, or love. Something to be conquered; something to obliterate, forget about, ignore, except we mostly ignore death already, pursuing our careers and our currency to distract ourselves from the fact of our own annihilation.

Death is a big business, too, and there's already an emerging industry that wants to help us deal with our digital assets before we die, which is why my "Internet Life Package" probably already exists. I won't ever be rich, or even moderately wealthy. I can't even make money selling death. But life, art, the *Death of Art* and all its byproducts, everything one art object spawns in the mind and eye and mouth of another, that is something I feel comfortable selling to the public; that is something I feel comfortable buying.

"Nothing is sacred on the Internet," Hassan says, looking at me like I've just said something but I've only been imagining all this time, thinking and imagining simultaneously, and it's been quiet, or it would have been quiet, if not for the constant construction on the corner of 22nd Street.

Everyone re-building, re-forming, updating each assemblage. "The future of re-appropriating other people's accounts will be a joke," he adds. "A meme."

If nature really is cyclical, then so is death, shifting in the last millennium from mummy to a meme, preparing for the after-life by spinning off the sacred into the satirical, and always with an eye for performing. In ancient Greece, too, funerals were spectacles, as staged and theatrical as the dramas set to song at their festivals. Mourn, but make it magnificent. Has anything really changed? Or does how we grieve the loss of life on the Internet simply speak to our constant denial of it? #RIPMe, I think. #Dying and #Dead

The real marker of technology's triumph in Post Internet culture is measured not by its degradation of life, but by its degradation of death; of human corpses turned into countable data, a ritual production on the assembly line. Death on credit: a payment that is always and endlessly deferred.

"Facebook is not far from selling off dead people's accounts," Leonard points out, continuing the conversation two days later. "With ads for Bounty thrown in.

"When people die," he adds, "Facebook already gives family members the option to turn their accounts into memorials. If they can't reach anyone close to the person, Facebook will just choose to sell the accounts to businesses."

Which isn't really a stretch, I think, if you think about it. Still scratching my scalp, still wearing the same blue button-down I wore two days ago. Companies already sell to us, before and after they sell us. We are already products. We can be forever products. We can be products forever.

Where Do Clouds Come From?

Water vapor, water crystal, aerosols, the elements
Of style   Not even
Their engineers know
Hard drives, routers, fiber
Optic cables, always do we
Turn real things into logical objects   See

The way my body is
A symbol of an almost
Instant pleasure, expect
The lag between the real
Thing & what it represents
To not always be evident
In the image   A state
Of conscious & permanent visibility

A system of networks
A public pool
Factory, prison, school, church
A hospital & colony

Global capitalism, web mediated
Resistance movements
Encrypted deep
Tissue & our accumulating cargo

Consider the credit card

The first cloud
Attempted to predict the weather
By connecting mathematicians
Via telegraph
Thirty years later

AT&T's Picturephone
A primitive videoconferencing system
That cost over five hundred million US dollars
Launched, capable of operating
Regardless of the type of circuit it flowed through
Digital & analog
Terror & territory
Share the same etymology
From the Latin *terra* meaning
Ground & earth

Like looking up at tree branches
Silhouetted against a bright sky in a low
Angle shot of a forest

The bombing of the Bell System once
Exposed lines in the desert
That were previously thought
Invisible

(We are able to see under
Lying infrastructure only
When it breaks)

A series of tubes
An ecosystem
A commons
A rhizome
A simulation
An information superhighway
A flock of birds (make them
Starlings)
A depleted uranium bomb & its 4.5-billion-year lifespan

Meanwhile a computer is calculating
The impact & adjusting to it
In real time share
The home one pays to be visited
Two times a year & only
If one calls ahead

(The anticipation of having
A place to disappear)

A politics of death
That invites participation

Drug cartels, terror groups, hackers on USA, the network
Lacks a central location
Because the heart would make a good target

There are several ways
To try to repair one's dead
Link, detailed below:

War, terror, social, advert, in order
To profit from a public
Office one might set up
A foundation, business or other
Charitable organization which is another kind
Of cloud altogether

An origin story derived
From copies of my likeness
A live streaming 404 error

kernel panic/ not synching

Airline tickets, browsing history, human
Resources reports, financial transactions
Prescription records, pornography, user
Generated content, your text
When it's still in the air

The frame of a screenshot is a convenient place
For concealing bodies

For a while the word *computer*
Did not even designate a machine
But rather the machinist
Generally a low-paid
Female employee
Has no one thought to tell you

Looking into clouds
Can be permanently blinding

I am writing to you from the air

I am writing to you from the air

Bus that will take me back
To New York, the people
I know & love   People love
Us on Yelp on my palm, beside
My avatar, my own eyes & skin   Years ago
It had become dangerous
To entrust mankind's image to a machine
The pilot reminds everyone
Of ten emergency exits
Should there be an emergency
Or the obligation to escape
Hours earlier

I'd misplaced all my JPEGs
In Munich, before my connection
Can be a tricky thing, timing
Takes practice, a spot
For shooting moments
& words   There were so many
People wearing jean shorts
Sitting there, attended
& inattentive like a chair
Waiting to be mass-produced

What's doing & what
It do? I picture the stewardess
Asking in German, a language
I've only ever heard dubbed
In film, Cold
War dramas on American
Cable, East Germany

Adapted for Western eyes & ears

What's the difference
Between being a spectacle
& being an object
Of surveillance?

Hello Kitty considers her fame
Alton Sterling laid to rest
Turkish coup brings night of gunfire
Terror strikes Nice
People went down like ninepins
Every twenty-two minutes
A woman in India is raped

When all events are seen instantaneously, all
The time & at the same time, recognition means
Deliverance, not appearing
Means being condemned
Have you forgotten

How the gaze of the camera turns
Everything into something already
Always apprehended?

The subject is looking at us   We are looking
At the subject
Everyone around me
Curls up in the semidarkness
Of time turning into time, no
Where else to be but here
Asleep or preferring to stare
Silently, at the edge of a temporary
Solitude   Mutually
On hold, how

You can confront a photograph
The same way it confronts you
Did you know that

As we toured the exhibit
I couldn't help
But watch your face, the whole
While you were looking
Straight ahead, showing
Me a side of yourself
I had never thought to see

A sense of plains or hills that continues in
Definitely   I choose where to
Place myself
In the picture, then picture
It   The sound of the sky
Above or below
The smell of shit
On the bottom
Of my sneakers

The moment lasts too long
& still

Please remain seated
With your seats in the upright position
For turbulence, another round
Of champagne in delicate
Plastic flutes
The insignia of a bird
An animal that already knows

How to fly   I hardly have to open
My lips

The witness is more important than the testimony   Remember

What it was like to be sung to sleep
An atlas of instruction
To rock like that, sometimes even
Silently   A train whistle
& the sound of footsteps
Behind our window, or door

Something you remembered as if it were your own
Lived memory instead of catalogued by someone
You will never know

Or think to recall how you felt
At just this moment
Confusing comfort for luxury & luxury
For living   The long slow
Hum of air-condition, my breath
On the lip
Of a bowl

I am especially interested
In facial expressions
Not for what they express
But for what they pretend
To veil   I imagine
If you looked at me you would
See something similar

As we look at the faces we can imagine
What the bodies would look like   Clothes

Convey the same message as the eyes & the history
Of the flesh they pretend
To hide

Agony, servitude
The black blood
Of black & white photographs

Tell us something is happening
Or about to

It is the knowledge that such moments are likely
& the anticipation of them that makes this photo
So arresting, something never
Before & which will never
Again occur like this

A star forms a scab
The moment after it catches
Fire, dies down, decays
The same way we so often begin
From what we had once
Refused or sucked in
Our own shit, our own
Propulsion toward decadence

The idea
Of a trigger
My face on the wall
Look & you would

Have another lens to look through
Who doesn't have

Trust issues, a desire to
Surrender & the unwillingness
To let this happen
Without first leaving
Me a trace
You are free
To move about the cabin
I guess I wanted to
Be someone new

Letters From Santiago

My father says he no longer dreams of Cuba; that he hasn't dreamed of Cuba in several years. "When was the last time?" I ask him and he shakes his head, remains silent. But a day after asking him, he dreams of Cuba again. He returns to Santiago de Cuba, the city of his birth.

"When was the last time you were there?" I ask him.

"When I was fourteen," he says. "You know that."

But I am referring to his dreams. I want him to remember so he can take me there too. And in a way, I've already taken him with me. In a way, the son has become a medium for the father to return to childhood.

A.

I am organizing my father's dreams and arranging them in a list. Dreams are often erratic, arcane, unremembered.[5] Lists help to cohere things that would otherwise remain incongruent, unrelated, or digressive. The illusion of *order* in a series of items, expounded for our consideration and inclusion, to foster an inclusiveness that would otherwise be absent. Or (archaic): an inclination and a craving.

---

5. There is a reason Nebuchadnezzar asks Daniel to tell him what his dream means, and also: to tell him exactly what it was he dreamed.

Every time I'm with you I have the urge to use two fingers, a movement or gesture like a pinch. To let me know I'm still here.

Any act of dream interpretation is an act of translation, a rendering of images from the unconscious imagination, the emotive and internal turned visual and external. The inside becomes the outside so it can be assimilated again, taken in and turned into something else, to hang on a wall or in the drop-capped first line of a story. Atget's photographs of Paris at the turn of the twentieth century ushered in a new need for text to accompany images. Captions replaced imagination the same way that images replace our memory of where we've gone and what we've encountered, in our daily lives and while we sleep. A rendering means to melt down or convert, but also to transmit to another, to give up, to yield. My father dreams in Spanish. I am writing this down in English.

Where are the gaps and slips, I wonder, as I hold the tape recorder with my left hand, and with my right, scrawl the notes that will eventually re-constitute this story.

Where are the gaps and how can I make them wider, instead of trying to fill them; how can I make them wider so I can breathe within them, in and out, out and in, and make song from all those unknowable breaths?

My father looks down, or to the side, or he faces my mother, who often walks into the room—usually the kitchen—to stand beside us, as we talk, or as he talks to me and I listen. But right now he is looking straight ahead; we are facing each other and he is looking right at me, and I am recording everything.

"My grandmother lived in Holguín, and every afternoon we would go out on our bicycles. We would stop for guarapo or a batido during the day, and then we'd keep riding," my father explains, when I ask him about the context of last night's dream, a scenario that involved a secret lake, a naked swim, a childhood friend who delivers milk, a boy who acted as a guide.

"On a road, like a highway for what seems like miles, we reach a dirt path that leads to a lake, with an island at its center. We strip down and go swimming. There are five or six of us and it is forbidden. I know I'm not supposed to be here and I know I'm not supposed to be with my friend, the one who delivers milk to us. There is no one else around when we return to the dirt, waiting for the sun to dry our backs."

When I play the tape back I can hear my father's voice come in through the sound of silverware and plates shaking, and the growl of a lawn mower, and the chimes that herald a visitor, outside, at the foot of a front door. I am thinking about all the breaths we don't see.

B.

My father's dreams give me agency as a writer to write the piece I couldn't write for six years.

Like my father, who had avoided talking about Cuba since he left his home country, I had avoided writing about the island I could only imagine. I felt that it was too close to me, too close and at the same time, too far away, a liminal space that I could easily locate on the map but could never conceptualize in my mind for more than a moment, before the moment passed too. Halfway between two worlds, or two words: *sea* and *no*. As the common saying goes, *neither here nor there*. I was isolated and also attached, but to something I couldn't name or identify; something I didn't know how to begin; where to start and how.

In actuality, I *only* had a beginning. Half a page. Two paragraphs describing an early childhood memory of my Aunt Nena's, a habitual experience Ana shared with her older brother, my father, on the rooftop of their home in Santiago. It began like this:

But we never cut the other kites. We only raced. And from where I would stand, I could see the whole of Santiago.

I used to imagine that Santiago was the whole world and so I could see all of it if I spun around and rotated like a dancer. And sometimes it was the whole world. The kites flying in between the other buildings and above my head, and around, and around ...

But we never cut the other kites, we only raced.

Surprisingly, or maybe with no surprise at all, the first dream my father relates to me is a dream about the kites, a scenario in which he and Ana are vying to be crowned champion in the tall, old building where they live, weaving their kites in between and around other kites, as other girls and boys on various verandahs of the apartment complex do the same thing, choreographing a colorful dance in the middle of the afternoon, in an Oriente that is still resting in the shade of childhood. In the dream, he cuts them, using a small pocket-sized razor, before mistakenly cutting his own hand. He wakes when he realizes that he can no longer fly the kite, when he can only follow its path by looking up into the sky where each kite drifts and falters, and eventually falls. But it doesn't fall; it just hangs there, suspended. Halfway between cloud and ground.

The dream is an excuse to remember that he can't move, I think, as he stops talking, and we sit in the silence before words. Any dream is an excuse to remember something in waking life, and thereby re-materialize it. My father can't move, or can't move back; he can't return, or he is unwilling to. But he can return in dreams, and I can return in his recollection of them.

In Greek, the word for "witness" is *martys*—a noun, meaning martyr, derived from a verb: *to remember*. When we bear witness to something, we bear witness to it in our body *and* our mind. But even not remembering is a choice, and as Giorgio Agamben reminds us in *Remnants of Auschwitz*, "The survivor's vocation is to remember; he cannot *not* remember."

My father, I think, has only decided to transfer memory to imagination, everyday consciousness to the unconscious dream world. My father has only decided, I think, to privilege the flight of fancy over the literal flight, the parting which continues to uproot him today.

C.

First-generation citizens can only imagine a place of origin we've never been to. And so I am used to imagining; I've been practicing my whole life. My own dreams as a displaced child of two immigrants from different countries involve no kites but a feeling of urgency and desperation and unyielding curiosity that has followed me everywhere I've been to, everywhere I move and the places I've called home.

If motion is nothing but displacement, dreams are nothing if not dislocated, temporally and geographically. Time expands like an accordion, or it condenses. My father is only ever a child in his dreams,[6] whenever he is dreaming of Cuba, of the past that depends on repetition and renewal, the increased playback of memory that Allan J. Hobson attributes, in *Dreams Drugstore*, to the diminished capacity to record. Everything in this motion picture depends on playing back the scene or site of original trauma.

And yet, as Glissant relates in his poetics, "while one can communicate through errantry's imaginary vision, the experiences of exiles are incommunicable." And yet, as Glissant relates, "the emigrant is condemned (especially in the second generation) to being split and flattened ...

---

6. A necessary regression Jung attaches special significance to: "This dream forces the dreamer to admit that even a highly differentiated consciousness has not by any means finished with childish things," he writes in *Dreams*, "and that a return to the world of childhood is necessary."

Childhood is a liminal space where experience becomes a mass of materials that cling to us, overwhelm us, and bring us to a place beyond the intellect, a place where remembering as an adult becomes also a re-experiencing: a re-encounter with ourselves.

an outcast in the place he has newly set an anchor … forced into impossible attempts to reconcile his former and his present belonging."

Why is it that I feel it more, having not actually felt it in the flesh? Why is it that I feel as if I must communicate these aspects of exile, whatever it is that I've inherited from my parents if not their biological distribution, their own migratory passages, the effects of refuge and fugitivity, the traces, the remnants—which are always fragments of the whole but which are *always fragments.*

And how can I interrogate these necessary fractures? How can I track the flow of its movement, which is also its repetition, even and especially through dreams?

"What the dream declares for the future of the dreamer derives only from what is disclosed of the involvements and ties of his freedom," Foucault writes in "Dream, Imagination, and Existence." "Linking the past to the present in the rehearsing of remorse, and knitting it into the unity of a destiny … brings to light the freedom of man in its most original form. And when, in ceaseless repetition, it declares some destiny, it is bewailing a freedom which has lost itself, an ineradicable past, and an existence fallen of its own motion into a definite determination."

If every dream, as Foucault says, is a dream of death, the reconciliation of an existence fulfilled, the exiled may only achieve a temporary jump-cut to a birthplace that melts away on the horizon upon waking. Death and waking serve the same purpose: exodus from a reality in which one has been captivated; literally held captive.

The dispossessed home exists beyond itself, like a flickering image in a continuously refreshed vanishing point, a gift or GIF beyond birth or death—merely a bow-tied ribbon, encasing air. "The mesh of exile," Foucault writes, "the stubborn return, the bitterness of coming back to things unchanged and aged."

My father pledged that he would never return to Cuba. "Never in my wildest dreams," he'd often say, whenever I'd ask. And yet, here we are.

Has my father been afraid that too much had changed—or that *nothing* has?

"All dreams," Steven Kruger writes in *Dreaming in the Middle Ages*, "are caught between the embodied and the bodiless," and yet the proliferation of bodies, or their semblances, always threaten to dislocate the dream reader, and our attempt to locate ourselves in the body of the narrative or the body of the dreamer, the one who is asleep in bed and skiing, or swimming, or flying a kite, the "Two Body Problem" ascribed by the German phenomenologist Medard Boss as a failure to reconcile the recumbent body with the active one.

What if both bodies are the "real" one? What if waking life and the unconscious underpinnings of our dream worlds are two streams of the same reality? Glissant links the experience of exile to an awareness that is contrapuntal, "an awareness of simultaneous dimensions"; I'd like to think of this essay not so much as a piece of music but as a film, and the jump-cut is the changeover from one culture to another, one setting to another, one home for something that will never be home and yet must be … this displacement is in fact a plurality, this fracture is in fact a force of beauty and power, a perception of simultaneity; of inhabiting both the new and the old, the actual and the imagined, the real and the dream; to straddle or hover; to know both contradictions as one knows one's contradictory self. Is the experience of the exile not the experience of being human?

D.

As I listen, I also read. Books on dreams. Books in dreams. *Roman de la Rose. Tundale's Vision. The Dream of Scipio. Il Corbaccio. The Book of the Duchess. The Lathe of Heaven. Piers Plowman.* Some of them put me to sleep; all of them are useful. After all, I am looking to trace the similarities; looking to enter the aperture of a dream's afterlife.

The difference between coincidence and prophecy is a matter of perspective and causality, in a dream, outside of a dream. "It is quite conceivable," Aristotle writes in *On Prophesying by Dreams*, "that some dreams may be tokens and causes of future events." But beginnings are small, and it's improbable, Aristotle advises, that "that which was about to happen is not in every case what now is happening, nor is that which shall hereafter be identical with that which is now going to be."

Another way of thinking about coincidence and prophecy is to consider Derrida's concept of spectral messianicity, a singular experience of a promise, or what he calls a covenant, which forms and formulates our thinking of the future, but also the historical materialism of a past that is not static; a past, instead, that is always threatened by the street insurgence of the present.

In the past, my favorite song was "Dreaming of You" by Depeche Mode.

The name of the horse who is the odds-on favorite to win the Preakness Stakes today, as I begin to organize this narrative, is Always Dreaming.

In the future, I mean hours after writing the sentence before this one, Cloud Computing will win or has already won the 142nd Preakness Stakes.

Dreams give power to those without autonomy or authority. If they're lucky. If they're not, they get executed as heretics.

The difference between execution and exultation is coincidence. Or dreams.

I haven't decided which.

It is not coincidental that my father begins to dream about Cuba when I ask him to relate his dreams about Cuba. Research shows that experiments meant to influence dreams using manipulations such as film and images fail to predict the effects of waking experiences on dream content, but, on the contrary, novel learning experiences, like interviewing, have been found to have a particularly pronounced impact on dream experience. "Engaging learning experiences," Erin J. Wamsley writes in "Dreaming and Offline Memory Consolidation," "may have a particularly robust influence on dream content." Dreaming of a learning experience, evidence suggests, is associated with enhanced memory for that information.

My request for dream recall has produced my father's dreams of Cuba, which, integrated in interview form, has produced more lived memories[7] of Cuba, or at least his ability to disclose them. My memory of our conversations has produced this text, or versions of it. We are both learning, about each other, and ourselves.

E.

"The poet and the dreamer are distinct," Keats writes in Canto One of "The Fall of Hyperion."

"Diverse, sheer opposite, antipodes./The one pours out a balm upon the world,/The other vexes."

What is the difference between the writer and the dreamer? Or should the dreamer become the writer for the fact of their dreaming, and write their dreams as a way of transforming their reality?

There are two types of writers, I think, and even as I think this I know there are many more than two. One who records reality and one whose task it is to re-construct it.

---

7. Memory is easily distorted or even fabricated in response to social demands. Or could it be that every experience, thought, and feeling is recorded in our mind, like a hard drive, and capable of being retrieved with the right pass code? All writers collect the new and the old, and learn with time to control the habit of bringing it forth.

The dream, too, is tasked with the aim of anticipating a revision to the role or script we've been acquainted with since birth, and much earlier, before we were born. "It is a prefiguring of history," Foucault writes, "even more than an obligatory repetition of the traumatic past."

Jung also believed that through our unconscious, we could immerse ourselves in historical associations: "curious excursions," he writes, "into the history of the human mind. ... Hence one could say ... that history could be constructed just as easily from one's own unconscious as from the actual texts."

In his insistence to return to the childhood of consciousness, Jung was an innovator. But, Fanon thought, he made a remarkable mistake. He went back only to the childhood of Europe.

As Chaucer adapted Guillaume de Lorris's and Jean de Meun's *Roman de la Rose* into Middle English[8] and Gavin Douglas translated Virgil's *Aeneid* into Middle Scots, adding a thirteenth book, each exploiting the dream frame to situate themselves in a canon of literature as a project of national identity, we might explode our current moment by writing our marginalized communities into the historical lens of a past that has abandoned us. We do this by seeking alternate sources of evidence and focusing on undermining the monochromatic, heteronormative cultural and state processes that have only produced exclusion, under the auspices of forming a "national identity." We do this through collective refusal and collaborative self-expression, the sharing of personal narratives, the co-creation of testimony: the dreamer, and the one who is still dreaming.

Instances of embodied re-membering work to counteract colonialist practices of violence and erasure, a task that also reorients the void, not as the nothing-that-is but the everything-that-might-be. In reconfiguring conceptions and experiences of time and space, Karen Barad's frame-

8. Chaucer's choice to write his major works in Middle English, which was not the vernacular of the court until the middle of the fifteenth century, several years after he died, is a choice made with a view to the future.

work also raises questions about history, memory, and politics. It is not just that the personal is political but that the individual becomes dynamically linked to the other, a politics of self that is inextricable from a communal framework; a belonging predicated on what seemingly can't be shared, unless one were to trouble the narrative frame, the point of origin, the site of rupture. It requires, above all, the risk of response, the response-ability of attention, exposure, surrender, the certain uncertainty of *opening up*. If it's true that nothingness is an infinite and "iterative re-opening," then my father's ability or desire to forget is also a kind of memory, a re-verse or reversal, in which we both face each other; in which we both face the incomprehensible.

Marianne Hirsch's performative "postmemory generation" traces affective and aesthetic dimensions of trauma that is collective, passed down, and inherited, a fractured recall that is suffused in "imaginative investment, projection, and creation ... dominated by narratives that preceded one's birth or one's consciousness" and yet, which also remain culpable to further reconstruction. This is because such generational trauma elides placement, finality, the pause that constitutes a period. *The end.* What does survival mean except that it is never solitary; the process of passing is only superseded by the process of *passing on*, a transfer of the past that strives to imagine new futures. In this and all scenarios, it is important not to grasp everything; not all at once, not all at all.

F.

The book that I'd been trying to write for six years is called *Letters From Santiago*. It was meant to be an epistolary historical novel, told in the polyphonic voices of my family, at least the people who arrived safely in the United States and began their lives here, and who eventually became a part of my life. We became a part of each other's story, and I wanted to make them a part of the next one I was planning to write, a project that would begin in the years prior to the revolution, and follow the lives of my loved ones in the various parts of Cuba they called home. Holguín and Havana and Matanzas and Camagüey and Santiago. I began my research by interviewing Ana, whom we affectionately call Nena, and her husband, David.

All the recordings were lost when I upgraded my cell phone. My Uncle David died unexpectedly. I had worried about how it would feel to hear his recorded voice cutting across time and space, life and death, until I couldn't hear his voice anymore, any longer.

On mobile phones, when no one's on *the other end*, you don't even get dial tone anymore. Just imperceptible silence.

I stopped asking questions about Cuba, and for a while, I stopped imagining the coastal city where my father and my aunt grew up, and Matanzas, in the middle of the island, a bay and three rivers which held the experiences of my uncle—who had stayed—and the horrors he endured until his escape.

What are the ways in which trauma, too, is passed down, inherited like cultural customs and genetic code? What are the ways in which trauma presents itself as an infinitely un-locatable future? The trauma which can't yet be set, placed, laid to rest because of its effects, its residue and remainder—the trauma which "defies and demands our witness." Cathy Caruth, in "The Wound and the Voice," privileges a Euro-American, psychoanalytical model for dealing with trauma, thinking about "the way in which one's own trauma is tied up with the trauma of another, the way in which trauma may lead, therefore, to the encounter with another, through the very possibility and surprise of listening to another's wound."

But what good are words to communicate the violence that is unsayable? Agamben tells us that every testimony contains at its core "an essential lacuna." Often, there are realities that can only be shown.

Ananya Jahanara Kabir's work on trauma theory is rooted in re-locating its discursive structure towards non-narrative, lyrical, often fragmentary meditations and works that are at times pedagogic and performative, emulative and immersive—each of them capable of responding to trauma and identity in ways that conventional narrative cannot.

I want to do both, I thought to myself, when I began exploring the ways to respond to the self-silencing so common to the immigrant experience, its traumatic aftermath. I want to do both, I always think. I want to be both. Storyteller and stagehand; lyrical and expository, theoretical and autobiographical. *I want to always be both.*

G.

My favorite writer, or the writer who taught me how to write, the writer who allowed me to see what was possible through writing, is William S. Burroughs. I like a lot of what he wrote, but one of my favorite lines is something I think about often, whether I'm thinking about dreams or only trying to re-construct everyday life in our image-rich culture, a mush-fake generation of substitutes and stand-ins.

If I had a talking picture of you would I need you?

H.

Dreaming interjects a desire that makes any act of dream interpretation simultaneously invasive and intimate. Plato likens the unconscious mind to "our bestial nature. ... As you know," he writes in the *Republic*, "there's nothing too bad for it and it's completely lost to all sense and shame." And yet shame, in so many texts, in so many instances in life, resides in the recognition or observation of others. When what is internal seeps into or slips out into the material world, or the public gaze.

"It seems to me quite certain," the psychopomp of Boccaccio's *Il Corbaccio* declares, "that if any of them ever comes to hear the truth of their malice and defects which I have shown, they will be in no hurry to recognize themselves at once, or to feel ashamed at being recognized by others ..."

Earlier, Boccaccio's psychopomp cautions the dreaming narrator of the "greater disgrace": "countless numbers who dare to take their pleasure even though their husbands are looking."

Is the shame in doing in public what should be done in private, without recognition of the other? Is shame in the looking, or in being looked at?

"Nakedness reveals itself," John Berger writes in *Ways of Seeing.* "Nudity is placed on display. To be naked is to be without disguise. ... Nudity is a form of dress."

Consider the difference of recognition as a difference between appearance and awareness, or self-actualization. To be nude is to be an object for *others*; to be naked is to be recognized for one's self. It's no wonder, then, that the mirror is credited with the potential to prevent shame and persist passion and pleasure between the adulterous Venus and Mars in the latter-half of *Roman de la Rose.*

But even mirrors return only resemblances, an image meant to mimic the flesh and blood before it. And perhaps shame has less to do with the discovery of others than it has to do with our own self-discovery—"What is shameful is our intimacy ..." Lévinas writes, "our presence to ourselves." But why, I always think—I am thinking right now—is that so troubling? To be present with myself, to see myself in the act of seeing—or being seen—what a vision it would be, what a dream to document my own presence for later, and to look at it now.

I.

"In the absence of an actual body," Kruger writes, "its image can be recalled from memory, and such remembered images can be combined to create composite pictures—conjectural likenesses of bodies that exist but that have never been seen, or even likenesses of non-existent bodies."

"My grandfather's appearance," Cicero writes in *The Dream of Scipio*, "was better known to me from his portrait-mask than from my memories of him."

The question is not how a physical object can replace an internal feeling. The question is why.

We are human, after all, and can so easily be made to submit to emotions conveyed in images and imaginings, the traces of things that never existed to begin with; and in doing so, we multiply our passion for them from afar, the distance of time and space, of a hypothetical what-if suspended in the future imperfect.

I.I. (eyes, plural—as if looking at the other)
When a thought materializes into a vision, we sometimes call it art.

I watch *Twin Peaks*, a television show that originally aired when I was four years old. In the show, as in real life, actions precede identity.

"When did you start smoking?" James asks Donna, one episode after the first season's finale.

They're talking in a jail; James is in a cell.

"I smoke every once in a while," Donna says, smoke slipping through the bars, dangling her cigarette as if it were a set of keys. "Helps relieve tension."

"When did you get so tense?"

"When I started smoking."

You do things; you become the things you do, the way we might dream of an occasion which has been paved from the encounters "set up" during the daytime. Likewise, Aristotle explains, "it must happen that the movements set up first in sleep should also prove to be starting points of actions to be performed in the daytime." Freud, too, in *The Interpretation of Dreams*, writes of the effect of the waiting room, patients who begin dreaming of the trauma talked about with others or overheard earlier in the day, everyone passing the time—and passing on dreams—prior to their appointments. "You know that the stimulus for a dream," Freud writes, "always lies among the experiences of the preceding day." The stimulus for living, too, can be gleaned from the fragments of the unconscious actions committed in one's sleep.

J.

Dreams do not deal with the details of the actual event experienced, Ernest Hartmann argues in *Dreams and Nightmares*, but with the emotion. Dreaming, he asserts, is a form of therapy, a process of inoculation that also occurs in the act of artistic production, whenever one decides to write their life into art. Hartmann calls this type of dream therapy a process of "contextualizing emotion"—finding a picture (the dream), or a picture metaphor that provides a context for the feeling. Most critically, however, is the appropriation of these connections in our waking life, in which the new material is woven in, and is less dangerous. Trauma is adapted into pre-verbal storytelling; new connections mean seeing things in a new way.

Later in the next episode, Bobby's father sits across from him at the diner, forking at his peach pie while Bobby scowls.

"Bobby, may I share something with you?"

"Okay?" Bobby responds, uncertain whether to wait or leave, stay sitting or stand up.

"A vision I had, in my sleep last night," Major Briggs says, "as distinguished from a dream, which is a mere cataloging of the day's events by the subconscious. This was a vision, as clear as a mountain stream. The mind revealing itself to itself."

(The camera cuts to Bobby's incredulous face, his shit-eating grin.)

"In my vision," Major Briggs returns, "I was on the verandah of a vast estate, a palazzo of some fantastic proportion. I seemed to emanate from a light, from within this gleaming, radiant marble. I'd known this place. I in fact had been born and raised there. This was my first return. A reunion with the ... deepest wellsprings of my being."

(The camera cuts to Bobby, his head down, looking languid at the booth.)

"Wandering about I noticed happily that the house had been immaculately maintained," Major Briggs continues, "there'd been added a number of additional rooms, but in a way that had blended so seamlessly with the original construction, one would never detect any difference."

(Here the camera cuts to Bobby, running his hand through his wavy, tousled brown hair to stay on the ruddy face, the wide blue eyes that look without emotion at his father, or the man who is playing his father, Major Briggs, dressed in his officer's suit, with a badge that says his name. Bobby, still wearing the same outfit he's been wearing the whole first season, an olive T-shirt over a white long-sleeved thermal. Bobby playing the only way he knows how to play Bobby: silent, wide-eyed, expressionless, on the verge of cracking up. Bobby on the verge of becoming someone else.)

"Returning to the house's grand foyer," Major Briggs resumes, "there came a knock at the door. My son was standing there. He was happy and carefree. And clearly living a life of deep harmony and joy. We embraced. A warm, loving embrace. Nothing withheld. We were, in this moment, one."

(Bobby looks up, breaks character. Disgusted, appalled, maybe just confused. His eyebrows furrow together, become one eyebrow. The two of them melting into one.)

"My vision ended. I awoke with a tremendous feeling of optimism and confidence in you and your future. That was my vision of *you*."

(Bobby makes a noise like a car screeching or sneakers on pavement. Tears well in his eyes. Major shakes hands with his son and then salutes the waiter behind the bar. It takes a while for the scene to fade out. Out of error or for effect. Sometimes you can't tell the difference, or there is none.[9])

K.

If nothing is unspeakable in a dream, certainly there are things omitted in our re-telling of them. What is the difference between suppression and silencing, and how does each, in its own way, relate to a trajectory of trauma?

Throughout *The Book of the Duchess*, Chaucer insists on veracity: the words "true," "truly," "in truth," "truth to tell," and "truthfully" occur thirty-three times. This repetition to *tell the truth* is a tactic to avoid repression, the trauma of death on the micro (Blanche of Lancaster) and macro (the Black Plague) levels. Chaucer, in each of his dream narratives, prefaces plot by saying that the dream is so wonderful that it *can't* be interpreted, which is another way of saying that what we are about to read is unreadable.

---

9. Elsewhere, Chaucer takes up Dante, Ovid, Virgil, Cicero, and Homer; he is writing in Middle English what was originally in Latin and Greek, but he goes off someone else's adaptation. What happens when you proceed from a glitchy representation? The re-imagining of dreams via white European males in the visual arts in most Medieval and Early Modern woodcuts, drawings, and paintings manipulates the dream vision which we see, and further manipulate in our conscious or unconscious imaginations. I am interested in the glitch that becomes the standard model.

Freud, similarly, begs pardon when discussing his examinations of children: "I have, frankly, no inclination to follow the matter further" yet still, he decides to elaborate upon an anecdote of a prominent clinician who always examines his patients only through their clothes. "I could still spend much time upon it; I could draw further explanations from it, and bring up new problems which it bids us consider. I even know the points," Freud draws out, "from which further thought associations might be traced ..."

The opposite of silencing is verbosity. But even verbosity can be a veil for acute repression: truth hidden among a sea of words.

L.

Part of narrating the dream experience is in *not* disclosing all the details, whether out of insecurity or an inability to retrieve them.

The narrative half-finished, in *The House of Fame* as in *Roman de la Rose*, begs intervention, in turn, by the reader, or the one who listens.

My father says his dreams are like the previews. By the time the feature film begins to play, he's already forgotten all of them. The previews, I think, promise something: a view of the future—if one intends to watch the film in its entirety when it arrives. The dreams do the same: a view of the future—but one that is necessarily disjointed.

What is the ideal point of view in which to narrate a dream experience? Third-person adds certitude to dream vision by cutting off intimate reflection. Or is it more effective to be inside the dreamer's head?

Absent a visual, how do we *imagine* sequences of dreams in literary texts and how is our general perplexity while dreaming re-created in the dream frame we encounter?

Chaucer's insistence on evoking so many dream theories—he spends the first sixty-five lines accounting for possible explanations, and another forty-five lines with an invocation—before he tells us *his* dream forces readers to re-frame our reading of *The House of Fame*, and yet, because there are so many options available to us, we are also immersed in the hazy feeling of disorientation; the feeling of being, also, in a dream.

"In the dream," Foucault writes, "everything says, 'I,' even the things and the animals, even the empty space, even objects distant and strange which populate the phantasmagoria."

In my own writing, I have a tendency to get so self-referential. Everything becomes a one-to-one correspondence. *Letters From Santiago*, through Juan Campanioni. But whose letters?

I repeat, this is a letter to myself.

M.

Near-death visions, or "infernal literature"—like *Tundale's Vision*, translated from the original Latin forty-three times into fifteen languages by the fifteenth century—was a popular genre in medieval times.

At Medieval Times, I had a near-life experience. But I fell asleep after the first joust, as a roast chicken slowly made its way through my digestive tract, a situation that doesn't bode well, according to Foucault,[10] for prophetic dreaming.

N.

The last photo, or the most recent photo in my Photo Stream, is a

---

10. As opposed to morning dreams, valued for their "poverty," tracing a Greco-Roman tradition that discredits any dream that occurs "among digestive vapors."

screenshot message I keep near me as I write, as a prompt or as a memo, a photograph to replace a kind of memory.

We can't and won't help readers to "locate" us. Distance, homelessness, anonymity, and insignificance are all part of the Internet literary voice, and we welcome them.

O.

Where will I go from here? How will I get there? I often think, usually when I walk out the door and decide what line to catch; what line to catch and what lines to catch or take hold of while I'm riding.

The future is up in the air, as evidenced by the common representation of the dream landscape in paintings and drawings, bubbles of text encapsulated over a subject's head, signifying a move toward the outside of the frame of reality or waking life. Instructions from afar.

In a cabin in the woods, away from Twin Peaks and its residents, a conversation takes place between a demon and a mute. The demon is smoking a pipe; the mute is serving as his houseboy, a servant wearing a shock collar, a pawn in the demon's elaborate chess match with real-life consequences. Both of them happen to be possessed, what some people think of as being under the command of someone, or something outside their body unless it's deep within it, so far it would otherwise be inaccessible.

"Even if you've been to the country before," the demon says, taking a long-drawn drag from his pipe as his houseboy looks on, silent and staring, "when you try to imagine what it would be like to go back, the image is imperfect, the mental image is always imperfect. Am I right?"

P.

Several texts involving dream representation are motivated by their evangelizing discourse. Dreams are didactic, serving as cautionary tales or a code of ethics on how to live; no matter through what form or language they are mediated, the dream frame is an instance of conversion. Is it true or isn't it that all this time, you've put yourself in my mind and body?

Q.

For the last three days, my father has had the same dream. He's in Holguín, with all his cousins, and he's not yet a teenager. The scenario involves a pick-up game in a neighborhood baseball field that ends by being chased off by a pack of wolves, or dogs, the attempt to hide one's self behind a telephone pole, the substitution of my father for his rotund cousin, René Ramon, a fact that becomes revelatory when his belly sags out from the pole he's hiding behind. When he sucks in his stomach, or tries to, he's on a camping trip, hiking through La Gran Piedra, back in Santiago, past the woods and into the mountains, a big patch of dirt road that circles around and around, the cold silent night air, and gunshots when it becomes too dark to see, which is when he wakes. "Re-membering is a bodily activity of re-turning," Barad writes. "She must place her body on this wounded ground to hear its murmuring silences and muted cries …"

Dream landscape vs. real landscape. The space one is living in vs. the space one remembers.

Recording can be a form of memory. To remember in Spanish is recordar.

I have listened to these tapes each night. I listen to them until my father's voice is embedded in my mind, until my father's voice becomes mine. And then we sleep.

In early cinema, the effect of "double exposure" was used to frame the sleeping body and waking body, to contain both or conflate them, to commingle, to contradict or coincide.

The doubling of dreams, at least in the Bible, means the outcome is fixed. Recurrence is a token of certitude.

R.

Fixed could also mean cheated, phony, simulated.

What if reality moves to match the interpretation, instead of the other way around? Freud writes of patients that are compelled to create an unfulfilled wish in life, an instance where the wish fulfilled in the dream may often lead to creating real absences: a dream that replaces reality.

"The dream substitutes for action," he writes, describing a dream of drinking to assuage a bodily thirst, "as elsewhere in life."

S.

A dream of worms, everywhere and always. A bowl of worms, a glass of worms, a toilet and a sink full of worms. A face full of worms or a face formed from worms, when one thinks to look in the mirror.

T.

In the Book of Genesis, the text seems to say that the dream out-come depends on *not* acting on the dream, or its interpretation. Joseph's dream of his future glory leads his jealous brothers to fake his death, selling him off to the Madianites, who in turn sell him off to an officer of Pharaoh, in Egypt. He gets wrongfully accused of lechery, jailed, and eventually becomes a dream interpreter, saving Egypt from seven years of famine to become the king of the nation, and the savior of the world. The human action that insists on not following the logic of the dream inevitably (re)produces the dream, in waking life. Some things are inevitable. Some things don't depend on fortitude, or a lack thereof, but are determined by fate.

At least in stories.

Did you know the word for *traitor* in Castro's Cuba, for those who were abandoned or who were abandoning the revolution, is gusano? In English, it means *worm*.

U.

I don't know what it feels like to leave the place I was born, to be forced to flee, to escape to a place where I know no one, and know no words in the language which I would be required to speak. To get by, to get in or over.

All my father and his sister had with them was a suitcase and five US dollars when they walked into the sun and onto the tarmac and boarded a small turbo-prop plane. To hover between cloud and ground. Nothing more was permitted.

V.

It didn't seem like anything to us, because we were young, and I really didn't grasp the reality of it until we were already up in the air, and I realized that all my other possessions were no longer with me. I don't seem to recall packing myself, so I suppose my mom decided what we would take and not take, what we could carry and what we would leave behind. For them, it was probably more of a shock; everything they lived for and everything they had lived with … everything they had achieved or acquired was gone, to go to a new country and a new culture and a new language. We flew Cubana de Aviación, a small plane with a propeller to keep us floating above the sea.

Do you remember how many people were on the plane?

It was a full flight, because everyone was trying to get out. We flew from

Havana, which was the only place we *could* fly out from, and it took lon-
ger to board, or to say good-bye, than it did to fly to Miami. It was such
a short flight, too short, I remember, and I remember it was sometime
in the morning because I remember walking to the tarmac and having to
wait for my dad, who was finishing his last sip of cafecito. And I remem-
ber walking to the plane and looking for our seats, hoping I could find a
seat by the window, so I could look back.

Do you remember looking back?

I remember looking. I remember trying to look.

Were you nervous?

We were excited because, you know, when you are young, it seems like an
adventure. I had always listened to American music and rock and roll and
I thought it was cool, or that it would be cool once we got there. It was
my first time on any plane, my first time flying. I couldn't stop looking
at the propellers, and I remember wondering what would happen if they
stopped working, or how they could keep us up there, so high.

Did you consider, when you were out on the tarmac, that you would
never return?

No. It did not occur to me. I don't know why. And all the adults, too, ev-
eryone thought it would be a short-term move. No one, I think, thought
what Castro was doing would last. I did not say *good-bye*, I told my friends
and cousins *see you*. Everybody had the idea we would see each other
soon. Everybody had the impression that we were going to be back in six
months, and that it would be in time for Día de los Reyes.

W.

In most visual representations of the biblical Magi, the critical element of their "common dream" is represented by the Three Wise Men sharing the same bed. Proximity breeds an intimacy that can't be communicated consciously.

Does sex presume the sharing of secrets of the mind?

If I slept with you, would we share the same dream?

X.

At the beach I like to close my eyes and feel the sun on my face and the breeze all over my body, under my back and between my legs and above my hips and all the parts of me I can't see. And it's this feeling, or it's this feeling of not being able to feel anymore, any longer, that scares me the most and most of all to not be able to feel so much and all the time or ever again and what could feel worse than that and what would and what will?

I am reminded by Foucault's thoughts on death and dreams, and the privileging of the dream of death, for its ability to show a "fullness in a world about to close in."

Everything else is received second-hand, re-presentations and retrospective renderings, and most of all, interpretations, all of them subject to the versions and perversions of reproduction. Everything else, we receive in accumulations, variations of feeling and skin and sensation. A piecemeal production of Life, or something similar. The difference is a difference between a point and the whole. The *all* that is unflinchingly out of our reach in each of our waking moments.

Death is the only totality we have to live for. And if we don't imagine our own death, we aren't truly alive.

When I just began to be with another and when I was still learning how to do it and how often and when, I could never last very long because I was so excited to be inside that person, to be with that person, to be that person for a little while which increasingly or gradually or at some point became a little longer, and lingered even when I wasn't or when we weren't together. I was so excited to feel another person and to hold these feelings within me and I did and I do and I still am.

Y.

"… Escape into one's counterpart, with all the immense promises of poetry, will perhaps one day be possible." — René Char, "Partage Formel"

Z.

While I decide what to do with my father's present dreams, with our conversations of the past, I find a notebook entry with the date missing, something I'd forgotten about or discarded. Something I'd abandoned.

On a recent trip to Miami, my father is reunited with his uncle Verona, his cousin Claudio, other people he had not seen in almost fifty years. I, of course, am meeting them for the first time. All of a sudden, the reticence ceases. All of a sudden, we are back in another place. We are back in a pre-Castro oasis, we are back in the casinos and nightclubs of Havana, medianoches and salsa and the mob money laundering in, and the mountainous eastern village of my father's childhood—Santiago de Cuba, the main site of the revolution that would soon follow, where much of the guerrilla fighting took place—and I am there for the trip. And it occurs to me, if the people over here and the people over there cannot talk, and if the generations of Cubans in America themselves do not talk, when all the old men and all the old women die, the story ends.

I want to write the story. I begin by piecing together how my parents met. And then maybe I'll go further backward.

I look forward to what dreams may come.

A. *(again)*

Pretend you are the one dreaming and also that you are the one recording the dream.

I would caution against hesitation or distraction or self-reflection, or updating your personal device. I would urge you only to *play this back.*

The second time is always different, because something inside me has changed, which is you.

Hot Tips
For Healthy Living

give us the runway & we will
lift the world

you will have many agreeable surprises
they said, the moment I placed
my name where their fingers had
been, or right after
instructing me to take off
my shirt & pants & put on
a pair of briefs that weren't
mine   I didn't know who
these belonged to, or who
had worn them before I put
my legs between each opening
they advised me to stay

out of the sun
you'll get too brown, you'll look too
what's the word   brown I bit
my lip   he shook his gut &
removed a camera from a kind
of holster & laughed   I wondered
what my first surprise would be or if I'd be
dead before the first shot, the way
I'd always imagine myself later
clenching on command, arrested in the act
of motion, or mimicking
an emotion I didn't know
a thing about (they gave directions)

arranged for the camera only to be
disassembled after the photographs
were taken, my temporary gaze

produced photographs that are
copies without originals

hearing our first words as though they were
whispered in my ear
I stayed out of the sun all summer
thinking about my next surprise
& when it'd come   I came up
fast, they said I was some sort
of natural, at least when I was being
recorded   I worked the day & the night
worked me through & through
three deadlines, half a dozen proofs, staring
again, dead-eyed with the news
room of others merging
into a screen we'd been
assigned upon employment   place
an article here, remove an unnecessary
interjection there, pretend to have
pleasure in the manipulation
of image & text, set to
scale & strict measurement   (the difference
between reading & seeing
is not always evident) & so was I
sometimes forgetting
where I was or what time
of day, whether to be
an object or its author
what more to make
of the experience, words
& skin & sensation
in every touch & breath & scent like
God & the toothbrush

good teeth are the making of the stomach
& beautiful teeth are the making of a
charming smile

what my agent would often
write to me, before he signed
his emails before
we had access to each other's
migrant exchanges
all summer long as I stayed
out of the sun   tried my best
to look like anyone
else but a halfie, child
of two immigrants, son
& the holy spirit beside me
always when I prayed in bed
face-down & bent shut
my eyes & turned
the light switch off
to stay still, feeling
my heartbeat like repeating
dashes of a morse code
I myself could not explain

he may or may not
wear socks, he has always been known
as a daring dresser
they were fond of
saying, as I would walk
in late from a fitting, the request
to take polaroids for a go-
see later that afternoon   everywhere
telephones rang & everyone

seemed to speak at the same time
as though they were the chorus
in rehearsal   I would try to
write down spare details, moments that I could
fashion into something else
when I had the time, or when the time
was right, when I was older, when I could
understand what it was I was doing or what it was
that was being done
to me   not much to it
-erations, the way a frame
can crack just by putting
weight on one foot, pressing
hard & raising one's leg

these liberties will be looked upon no longer
as crimes, but as itches

& another memo when I think
to refresh my display

would you please also send a clear photo of your head
which you can alter freely, at will or willingly
disposed to give up your rights to like
-ness? instead of representing my likeness, I
took steps toward excising my face
from the portrait, replacing it with

            please note, visitors
            may enter & leave
            the theater at any time

(it revealed the desire to renounce
individual authority in his work

undermining the sanctity
of authorship)   imagine

to be looked at from
the other side of the screen
with one thumb close to
almost an hour

touched by the hand
of God, new order
blaring in the back
of the bar   I paid
attention, took my own
hand out from my jeans
pocket, put my thumb
around it, felt how it felt
to feel it almost as if
I were inside it & on
the outside

against such official efforts to fix
identity, he insisted on the right
to construct, subvert, or other
-wise destabilize it, already
experimenting with what it meant
to flatten dimensions, a response
to the flattening of transport
in a culture constantly dis
-placed   some people

take photos of artwork I make
artwork meant for photography

something that can be rendered or
repeated differently during each
take   see also: a zoomed-in
screenshot to further fragment the whole &
highlight another assemblage
what can & cannot
be consumed through touch is only
a question I find useful today & yesterday

as audiences were awed by the new
technology of film, the location of *real*
magic shifted from the magician's stage
to the frame of the camera

after the Internet's insistence
to be everywhere & all at once came
our sincere desire
to disappear

Hot Tips For Healthy Living

Never work. It should go without saying, but it's worth saying again. Find a way of being in this world and then become it. If you must work for others, make them work for you. Beauty and art have an inimitable kind of power; artifice can be powerful too. Our whole lived experience compels us to create impressions and artifacts for others, something which has no place in economics or the conventions of politics and the pulpit. Money is irrelevant in a culture that has morphed into Monopoly's version of funny money. The best thing you can do with a dollar bill is burn it.

One way to find value in the scenario of work is to inject the company trademark with your own brand of proprietary intellectualism. Stripped of the motive of performing for another's profit margins, your work will find new light in the awareness of its own death.

If you're a copy editor, insert playful double entendre come-ons inside your headlines. Re-arrange photos within the page's specs to re-contextualize the captured action. Break lines in a column to say something subversive. Do it subtly, with some sense of style.

If you're a model, literally go through the motions while privately re-training which movements might actually pervert the apprehended moment.

Speak little and listen to everyone talking through you and around you as if you were an actual mannequin. (If you're especially good, you will be.) Wear the dialogue well. Remove the blasé caption attached to the minds and memory of magazine-lovers everywhere and replace it with your own ironic subtext. Destroy the image, or its imagined narrative. Make people remember what it is like to once again feel desire, instead of simply inhabiting an unreachable fantasy.

If you're a writer, use everything around you, and especially the people. They won't know what hit them, because most of us don't actually read.

All of these things are possible; all of these things have already provoked a response. Under the guise of production in an overproduced society, the way out is in reassembling the (re)production. Outside of the host, any viral message becomes sedentary. No longer subject to the laws of supply and demand, we may finally think to demand more. Ask more of yourself; then ask more of others. Pretense and performance are your friends, and will always be. It is far better to pretend to not have than to pretend to have something you clearly do not. (In this scenario, all of us living under the assumption of free choice and liberty are all pretending, but for reasons unbeknownst to us.)

Stage the burglary and steal more than whatever you could have made out with from the real heist. Like the rare bullfighter who ends the bull-fight with only a gesture of his arm, it is far more effective to kill with just a look. In the physical scenario, what's done is done or will never be. But remove the symbolism behind any system or subject and the very nature of the system turns inward, reverses, implodes. It is a perspective and a process. It is a way of investigating the world, or an instruction for *feeling*. Holding you in my arms in this book is the closest we'll ever be.

•

"Can you please pass me a towel?"

Here we are at 2 Tyson Lane, a rented home with a rented pool, a rented stretch of sand and sea. In general, we only ever rent things anyway, in this life. In the next. Minnie Mouse in Physical Form is wading, waiting, her elbows on the lip of the pool, her blond hair pulled back, a smell like chlorine dripping from her cheeks to her chin. The automatic wave generator about to kick in, as it does every five minutes, as it did five minutes ago. I've been waiting this whole time too.

"Excuse me?"

She was wearing a black T-shirt that said in red, *Maybe, Maybe Not.* And I wondered what was the question. Besides if I could hand her a towel, I mean. What the question was. What's underneath it all, what's inside, what's in the back of it or behind? What's at the very bottom?

It's the thirtieth birthday party of a gas magnate's son. Or maybe it's oil. I'm dressed in blue Gap joggers and a black tank top. I'm dripping too, but not with the smell of chlorine. In an hour, maybe an hour and a half, maybe two hours and ten minutes, maybe less, I'll be wearing khakis and a white collared shirt, a skinny black tie, the unmistakable outfit of a caterer, one who caters for others. I'd mentioned that you should never work. But at least all of this is going somewhere. At some point.

I'd like to keep it inside of me a little longer.

I hand her a towel and she places it on her right shoulder, hoisting herself out of the water, the waves that have been generating for thirty seconds, thirty-one seconds. I hear the swoosh the same moment a waiter swoops in to deliver a white peach Bellini, on a plank. He's been rented too, but we're from different rental companies, so I don't know his name. I don't ask. I know hers. Everyone knows Taylor Swift.

There's 135 dinner guests, 200 dancing guests, all of them—I guess—rented, except for maybe the parents of the birthday boy, he of the black gold gild. I look from the sheet of paper in my hand to the bar we've just finished assembling, wiping my brow, watching the other swimmers, none of them swimming. *135 dinner guests, 200 dancing guests.* Is that an estimate, I think. Is that accurate? I wondered how anyone could ever tell how many people would be dancing; how many people would actually get down on the dance floor. To dance—doesn't it?—means to let go, but everyone here wants to keep everything. I am including myself.

•

And as we watched the fiction and continued to watch, it became impossible to not look away; servile, static, so much were we entranced by the production that we began to produce our own fictions, capturing and copying the moving image of our many-mirrored gaze: the evidence of our own slow decay.

Having already fetishized tabloid taboo, and nostalgic of the manufactured past, all that was left for us was seduction for the ritual desire of no longer being here at all. What we want most of all is not *to appear* but to vanish again. Reproduce the facts of our own death. And add a hashtag.

•

"Sometimes I'm like Sansa, and sometimes I'm like, Sansa, *who are you?*"

Friend of Taylor's, also blond, also toweled, sips and twitches, sips and twitches. No one answers her question, if it was a question. Maybe no one else is listening except me.

The others laugh. All of them except Taylor are wearing sunglasses, so there's no way of telling how false the laughs are, besides the sound itself. Usually, your eyes change shape. Your cheeks crease, your eyebrows might arch, slightly. The pale spot below your eyes fold in. None of this is visible when you are wearing oversized sunglasses in the shade. The sun dipping lower in the sky. It's almost six o'clock. The camera crews are getting situated, unloading their equipment, connecting apparati. Is that a word? *Apparati.* I like it well enough. I don't like being filmed, but it's in the agreement. Everyone is being filmed tonight.

What they'll do with it is anyone's guess, or one person's answer. Probably a Lifetime special. Maybe E! Lifestyles of the Rich & Fortuitous. Or just a promo for *Game of Thrones.* A slow-mo recap of Taylor's friend seeing-herself-as-Sansa as Taylor smiles, nods, laughs. Cut.

Maybe they rented the cast of *Game of Thrones,* too. It's early. Six-fifteen. The party doesn't start for another hour. (I glance at my sheet.) *Cocktails & Canapes on the lawn overlooking the beach.* In smaller type: *expect VERY heavy tequila consumption.*

If I was this rich, I'd have to get drunk too, I think, every other evening or every evening. Just to look at myself in the mirror, my mirrored image looking back. Something I could never reconcile.

A vanishing point between grass and pool, between pool and the actual ocean. One man-made; the other natural. No longer any separation, or the attempt to remove it completely, which is still ongoing. Today, tomorrow. The next day. The ongoing special project for the systematic extermination of the real.

I listen hard, avoiding the pool-side dialogue to try to catch an actual wave. A non-motorized wave. The pulse, the ebb. It can be so relaxing, when you catch one. It can make you forget, for a moment, that a party starts in forty-five minutes. A party in which everyone knows everyone and nobody talks. Countdown to the end of the world. On camera.

•

It had occurred to me from the very outset of the project, it was dangerous to remove my face from the images. Since it revealed the fact that there is nothing behind them.

•

At some point during Season 7, Brandon Walsh walks into Casa de Walsh—his words, not mine—to the warm greeting of his family-friend-or-fuck-buddy—Wikipedia calls her, "close to the Walshes, like a cousin"—Valerie.

"Good to see you," Valerie says, as she's spreading peanut butter on toast.

"Good to be seen," Brandon says. Sometime during Season 7, unless I'm remembering this wrong.

In a sense, Brandon's affirmation is our own, ever since we saw ourselves in a photo and wanted to see *more of them*. Hoarders of the evidence that says we have passed through here, in a world where time no longer passes. Everyone preserved with the same strobe lights they've imported in the white vans parked on the gravel somewhere behind me. The long stretch of road and the big black gate that came before it. It's hard to get here. It's even harder to leave.

I've changed. Not in the emotional sense. I'm still who I am. Or who I think I am. Now I'm wearing khakis, a black belt, a skinny black tie, sweating through my white collared shirt despite the rolled-up sleeves. Despite the three undone buttons below the collar.

One, two. One, two.

The first performer is doing a sound-check in a tent they've re-constructed on top of a tennis court. What was a tennis court before they rented it, re-assembled it. Removed the evidence.

Cameras are everywhere, and I don't mean our cell phones. Everyone at the party—a rented home, rented guests, rented employees—like me—are meant to pretend the cameras aren't there. The viewers, watching it later, maybe today, are meant to pretend they *are* there, pretending or forgetting that the party was filmed in advance of its air date, carefully edited, cut, dubbed, scored, then cut again, with voice-over and carefully timed fade-outs for commercial breaks. Pretending or forgetting they've probably never been to East Hampton before and have no idea what they'd do if they actually got there. Got here.

It's never the consummation of a dream that people want. It's the desire to *keep dreaming*. The belief that we will never wake from this one.

Nothing can be left to chance, except everything, as in a dream, prescribing to rules and laws of our own making: predicated on the promise that anything can happen at any moment because the dreamer wills it. The dreamer, or the one directing. Imposing contrast, lights, shade, angles, cross-cutting, everything already predetermined by the selection of a point of view, all for the right moment or mood or mise-en-scène, the brief winking aside to an audience who is already in on the joke.

It's bait and switch. All of us pretending. All of us in on the punch line, the whole while disbelieving the fact of its imminent contact. The thrill of deception and its excessive transparency, all at the same time.

The viewers will switch places with us, but who will we switch places with? Who are we meant to replace, or become? Other than characters, literally cast in cathode rays and high-definition anti-freeze, sequestered in this film of a thirtieth birthday party, suffocating on the whole company's accumulation of oil and gas and energy as though our heads were already halfway in the oven.

Or maybe that's just how I felt, how I feel right now. Shaking a mixer above my head like I learned on TV, thinking to myself, What would have happened if TV hadn't been here?

The joy of the watcher begins and ends in the watching. It is a totality, an end unto itself. Voyeurism, like pornography, has more to do with metempsychosis than the flesh it purports to serve up, consume. Just as with pornography, no one watching is interested in the actual sex act. We watch because we want to place ourselves in the body of the other. What used to be the role of literature has been replaced by our prerecorded realities. No longer do we read to become transported. No longer do we ever have to close our eyes.

"Okay, well my eyes are closed ... right? My eyes look completely closed," a guest asks, answers, points at a screen, as if to confirm it, hands the phone back to me. "Another one, another one, another one.[11] *Please.*"

I oblige, press my index to the oval, rotate the camera length-wise, repeat. Return the mobile to its owner, refill a low-ball with whisky, suck it down. Come up for air to hear Leslie Odom Jr. from *Hamilton* crooning on stage.

"What a voice!" someone in the long line that's formed in front of me shouts.

And I think about what the voice would sound like once it's been recorded, put through distribution, the channels that will make it live or make it die. Maybe the program won't need music after all. But mostly everything is better with a soundtrack. After all, the origin of cinema is the camera and a piece of music. The only way it's evolved since then is our ability to insert ourselves into the scene, anticipation of the image over all possible realities.

---

11. As Baudrillard points out: "For opinions as for material goods: production is dead, long live production."

"Oh my God, I'm dead right now. So dead," the guest looks up from her phone, down at her phone. Up again. Seared hanger steaks float past on a butcher block. "So effing dead."

The dream of every stargazer in 2016, and every year since: to see themselves die live on their own camera.

•

our faces like faces
in a funeral parlor
gather round & now
bow, while kneeling
to stagger through
the lower east side's
google-mapped representation
of the lower east side
without a chance
encounter, or the option
to whistle   trees
of concrete with leaves
printed onto them, *retrospectively*
a parking lot's solitude
& the stand-still
silence as all of this
buffers   futuristic
scenario in which
walt disney awakes from his cryonic suspension
& understands that no time
has actually passed
the lead-up to
a sequel in which you & the self
you play on the Internet
are put in a room & forced

to look at one another

scenario involves a cross
walk of mirrors, slabs
of city that light up when you
walk over each grave
pose, every pause
before a pixel
reloads, returns
on a cut-in of a coin
toss, a red bowtie
& moves you never
knew you had inside or on
the outside, synching
lips the way it was
in childhood, to voice-over:
all designed to make you
feel good   question
is—what kind of
good do you
want to feel?

•

In interviews and speaking engagements, televised or transmitted through radio, transcribed and typed out, copy and pasted from a text message or an email, I'd often told people that all of these things had just come to me; I didn't have to do anything but allow myself the opportunity to experience them. Maybe I believed it; maybe I still do.

My success with these endeavors was up for question. But I guess that's the point. To always have something left to question. Of myself and others.

•

The greatest crime of Post Internet culture's overseers was to make people culpable for their own demise. Arrested development no longer had to be coercive once its trapping became a sought-after commodity; prisons can be a pleasure, and in fact they've become our one true pleasure in this world. We strive toward the bars in the light of the new day and our backlit screens. Grasping with our head down, the better to bear it.

How to trick people into continuing to consume; to keep consumers buying and spending in their continual leisure time? Trick them into becoming the producers; trick them into consuming themselves.

•

When I wrote a book called *Sindicado* in 2006, before it was ever called *Sindicado*, living and working abroad, I was optimistic, passionate, brash, happy, young, or young enough, to not know better. I was twenty-one. On the verge of graduation, the verge of *becoming something else*. Pre-meditated movement. MapQuested directives. What did I have to feel enraged about? Except everything. I never thought this nightmare would ever actually become our waking life. Or inwardly, maybe I did and that's why I wrote it. Facts are problematic. Self-knowledge is a dangerous game.

My parents prefer the living room. A black box that is more like a mirror: the meeting point where everyone comes to witness themselves in the gaze of a future that was taped months ago.

Our pleasure is no longer in discovering the natural; we want to discover new ways to desert it. We want to discover, not the real, but its opposite, the calm cool gaze of a snapshot duplicate. Our entire existence might collapse if we could not accumulate it, signify it with serialization. In the pursuit of our own canonization we have cannibalized ourselves, simultaneously glutted and emaciated—and still, we swallow graciously.

When I look back at Taylor Swift, she is biting her nails, sucking her cuticles, damp and trembling. A body movement that imitates the pulsating ambiance of a camera on a dolly. A scenario cut before it's presented in the spread-out series, probably to make room for my dialogue, my response to her pressing question. Which was silence.

I don't want to return to 2006. I miss nothing. Hardly any writer does, that's why we write. So we can salvage it: moments, words, sensations of being, or not being. *Play this back.* Dying for having been discovered, or for discovering nothing beyond the mountains except our hallucination.

I am still dreaming of the moment they decide to say *That's a wrap,* and: *Moving on.*

●

I know some hot tips for healthy living.

Would you like to know now or later? Or should I have you—

Guess?

I blink; it's a quarter to two. I blink; it's two o'clock. The Late Night Pool Party is supposed to start now, I remember, without glancing at my sheet of paper. The Late Night Pool Party has already started, though, half a dozen guests in my purview stripped without montage or split screen or fade-out or cut. So many splashes I can't hear the wave motor kick in.

I blink and shake my head.

She answers anyway.

"Well you can drink a mix of Pepto Bismol and 24-Hour Energy, two at a time," she adds. "You can keep drinking that way. Doing drugs, whichever."

She pauses, as if she's testing me, as if this is a lighting test, maybe. As if this isn't already being filmed? I think, but shrug it off by way of blinking. In between now and then, the past and the persistently-pictured present, there's buffet tables, an ice luge, Summer Watermelon Jell-O shots, a Shake Shack station, cookies from Levain Bakery, a cake presentation, individual birthday cakes from Momofuku, a few speeches, a few more performances from *Surprise Performers*, and a touching father-and-son hip-hop duet.

"What else? What else?"

I start to stare, not wondering what's next so much as when.

"You can double up on multivitamins," she interrupts herself, trembling, brushing her brown hair out of her blue eyes. "Wash your hands super well. Order a burger instead of a salad."

"Didn't you—"

"I did," she cuts in, placing her palms together in prayer and rocking her head a little closer in my direction. Closer and then farther, as if she were bobbing for apples. "I also powdered my nose."

I blink and wonder what's next. I mean after this. *Late Night Pool Party.* It ends on its own ellipsis. The sheet, I remember, read: *2AM* ...

The assembly line doesn't stop in a surplus; the demand isn't the supply itself but the wish to keep supplicating before the altar of production. The assembly line says, *Stay on* ... and I wonder if I'll have to stay on forever too, standing in front of strangers and behind a bar, or if I'll be forced to leave the moment the camera crews do. After all, I think, what's the point if there's no one here to film it? Reality was lived so it might be recorded, at least in my case, me who's watched all of it, who's tried to write as much of it down as time and space allowed. I was meant to serve people cocktails. To keep them sated. To keep them smiling. To *keep* them, as plastic keeps, sterilized and halted. Instead I've already been imagining what this moment feels like with the new Rihanna playing over the tepid dialogue (her words in my ears again as if the track skipped: *You can … you can … you can …* choose to mute this).

> *"Been waiting on that sunshine*
> *Boy, I think I need that back"*

The constant change of place and camera angles and sound clips and audio cues in the everyday world have saturated me to the point of never-not-hearing-a-soundtrack at the same time that it fragments my line of vision into successive sequences, a rapid-fire schizophrenic perception that has made me who I am or what we all are today. What we will never again be. Spectators no longer, but actors.

> *"What are you willing to do?*
> *Oh, tell me what you're willing to do?"*

If you listen long enough or hard enough, it's easy to imagine Rihanna asking you the question. You, the reader. You, the actor. It is only ever always you.

"So are you going to come in, too?" she asks, already in the process of disrobing; me still and silent for the first time tonight. The rain had already washed away the humidity and the mosquitoes hours ago, between Headliner #1 and Headliner #2. Between hot tips for healthy living. Hers and mine. Between me and her. Me and you. The night was calm and cool. I thought about sliding my body inside my sheets, what that would feel like. When that would be. If I'd ever get there. If I'd ever get here. My brief winking aside.

"Or are you just going to watch?"

[no subject]

Think of these like friezes at a museum, except the museum is the Internet and the exhibition is always *on display*. In a culture of global visibility, everything can be re-envisioned as an object d'art. We know that Atget's photographs of Paris at the turn of the twentieth century ushered in a new need for text to accompany images. Captions replaced imagination. I've decided that imagination can replace captions.

#IWokeUpLikeThis or: The Latest In Space-Age #PostInternet Pajamas

French investigators said Thursday that the police officers in Paris who sodomized a young black man with a baton did so accidentally, & that the incident does not constitute rape.[12]

If this makes you uncomfortable, I am unapologetic. If you are disturbed, there is good reason for disturbance in a culture of leisure & entertainment that has very little patience or predilection for acknowledging the systemic oppression of others who do not look like them, talk like them, or fuck like them. It is our responsibility to demand the accountability of our public servants & the press which serves to circulate knowledge & information. We should all be uncomfortable; we should comfort ourselves in knowing now is the moment in which disturbance can be a weapon in which to render these apologies in a literal form. Dynamic tension as both a method & description of irregular accounting discourse & practice. A messiness that I don't want to clean up; a messiness that I want to live with. All acts as acts of epistemological & representational disturbance. It is about refusing what refuses you. & it is

---

12. The twenty-two-year-old youth worker, identified only as Théo, says a group of four police officers physically & sexually assaulted him on February 2. He says he confronted the officers after seeing one of them slap a young person during an identity check. Then, Théo says, the officers took him around the corner & sodomized him with a truncheon, spit on him, beat his genitals & called him names, including "negro" & "bitch." Théo suffered severe anal & facial injuries during the incident, parts of which were captured on video.

in this shared practice of refusal that we can create a mutually-inclusive community of non-normative voices.

disturb
transitive verb
1
a : to interfere with : interrupt
b : to alter the position or arrangement of
c : to upset the natural & especially the ecological balance or relations of

2
a : to destroy the tranquility or composure of
b : to throw into
c : to alarm
d : to put to inconvenience
ex: *sorry to disturb you at such a late hour*

It's late, the lights are out, I'm stirred from sleep out of necessity. It's hunger. I woke up like this. The same in the night as in the day & & & & &

Won't you offer me a hand to hold or eat?

Body Swap At the Airport
(7,654 shares)

A good examination occurs when all clothes are off, when the knees are bent, when the back is arched, when the navel is curved to meet the beating of our breaths. I say *our* because we've already swapped an eye for an eye, tooth for a tooth, hand for a hand, foot for a foot, burn for a burn, wound for a wound, stripe for a stripe, cheek for another cheek. We'd always heard it said: *Find an opening & put yourself there.* In plain view or with a view of applause, so many eyes & some of them recording from their black plastic seats, or stopped, suitcases in hand, to marvel silently or to shriek in muffled sobs. Repressed affection is still affection. In & out of hotel lobbies, airport bars, a long stretch of ash gray concourse, painted clouds & walls of dust, in & out of the narrow vestibule that connects aircraft to gate, gate to terminal. Terminal to Google Earth & this blinking red dot. Scenes like the one reproduced in the dream have often taken place there. & the moving staircase hasn't moved once since we began to watch. We can try this again with our eyes shut. I am only trying to shift blame from myself. Dislocation & deferral as the primary method of transit when waiting for connection, a flight to leave, a hand to drop, a sack to fill, a video to load. Buffer, buffer, I had a problem stuttering as a child, which comes out when I am coming to this very day. I'm I'm I'm I'm—I was not willing to let my mouth drop like this without further instruction. Look up & see the satellite strobe-lit halo of the evening news, a face floating on a stick & the drawn-out vowels: *It's 10PM, do you know where your fist is?* Dream of an app that can tell you every word you've ever exchanged with any given person in quick-flickering captions across the screen, like checking the treatment of an oft-remembered & well-loved film against the film itself, glancing between every interchange to see the moment it all went to shreds, or just before. I had never thought of this until you read it back to me.

The Portrait of a Lady (#womancrushwednesday)

Pay attention to the economy of the picture. Pay attention to the light in which the picture is hung, or hanging. Henry James wants us to sit up, by the dying fire, far into the night, under the spell of seeing, without really looking at anything at all, really or nearly or almost, at all. *At all.* I can see everything from this distance; from this closeness of my screen.

Experiment: to preface everything I say with *mere* or *merely*, as Henry James does, forty-six times, throughout *The Portrait of a Lady*. Look. What does it mean to pay attention in a Henry James novel? & how to reduce one's intentions & actions to their essence? I'm talking about me & you & Isabel Archer. Oh, I hoped there would be a lord; it's just like a novel!

Errors of feeling, smug peace, spectatorship, the game of life, sheep in the flock, passivity, amusement, a question of time, parasites, platonic praise of the distractions of Paris, a trifler, a theory tinged with sarcasm, a matter-of-course, impersonal view, floating fragments of a wrecked renown, good friend, pin-pricks, for amusement, fact of one's being in Rome, Parisian trifler, accident, to speak of certain facts, pretense, suspicion, death of a cousin, shaped wood & iron, brain-power, lattice of bones, sweet airs of the garden.

Am I getting colder, or warmer? Am I getting close to you? & are you hot or are you cold? Well, I don't know. I can't tell till I feel. Perhaps, said the younger man, laughing. Someone might feel for you. Wouldn't it be lovely? To have the other feel for me; to have the other feel me; to feel the other on me & in me. That isn't a question but a blanket statement. (I'm cold.) The elation of submission. Giving up to one's image in the backlit brilliance of my fantasy. She was intrinsic enough. He talks, perhaps, as if an angel had tried to. You told me you needed a human interest. I was there; you had only to come to see me. & we shall all hang on for the rest of the performance, the bad dialogue, the faltering hand-held exposition, the discussion of architecture, interior & exterior brick-building. What it means to belong nowhere, the Alienated American, a Greek bas-relief, a great Titian, a Gothic Cathedral, & to relish this expression of languor. To really *make it work.* "I thought I'd just mention it," Lord Warburton tells Isabel Archer in an early moment of *The Portrait of a Lady*, about thirteen *meres* in. "Some people don't like a moat, you know. Good-bye." "I adore a moat," Isabel says. "Good-bye."

The Right To Carry
(Our Rapidly Expanding Company)

To come back to the part where the protagonist wakes up, having dreamt that their recent death was only a dream, a consolidation of memories about other people's deaths during sleep, what we call *offline memory consolidation*. & what is a dream if not a preparation for waking life? & what is death if not a preparation for another life? We might *play dead* but only for fear of actual death. Think of "The Balcony" & what it means to jump off, on stage. It's all over for me, except in my mouth, which is open so that I can seek employment elsewhere. Celebrity is the ability to expand rapidly in the consciousness of others. Moving images & static snapshots are a means to an end, which is still loading. Early experiments to influence dreams using manipulations such as films & images failed to predict the effects of waking experiences on dream visions. The appearance of a complete stranger in a dream, for example, relies on knowledge of the visual characteristics of the human face & on schemas for typical human behavior. Think of everyone you've ever met, & everyone you will never meet. Online & offline, & on a long, long line. Think of them in their living, in their loving, in their learning & in their leaning. Think of them in their sitting, in their sleeping, in their drinking & eating, in their laughing & their crying. Everyone is inside of them; everyone is reminded of someone else when they are sitting across from this person, when they are holding hands with this person, when they are making love with this person or in love with this person *who is not you*. & over it all, something floated not floated away but just floated, floated up there for us to stare at & situate on our screens. Our rapidly expanding company announces a position of a business correspondence proofreader for everybody who speaks English fluently to aid in communicating with our exterior customers. What distinguishes our exterior customers from our interior customers? What remains universal in a world designed to service our individual desires & prejudices, our carefully-curated re-presentation of *reality*? Everything eventually converges, in sense or on screen. Your job duties will be looking through our business letters & correcting spelling & grammar inexactness that might occur in the text. I am aiming for complete exactitude. I am exacting a heavy price for what might otherwise be repressed, or forgotten. Both animal & human studies demonstrate that patterns of brain activity first seen during learning are later "replayed" in sleep, suggesting that dreaming of a learning experience is associated with enhanced memory for that information. The right to carry. & I want to carry everything. Give me your mouth & I will groan. Give us the runway & we will lift the world. This is a proposal for a show. The proposal is the show. In this show we aim to exhibit containers & receptacles of desires, & the desires that form them. In our aesthetics of accumulation, we begin by collecting an arrangement of encounters chosen "at random." Doing your Saturday thing? Go Live & let your friends in on the action! Famous last words were not words at all.

The Real Thing
(#alternativefacts)

Do people like me for me or for my OUTDOOR SPACE? StreetEasy
sign on a bus stop asks the same question I more or less ask every day.
Everybody would rather be anywhere else, as evidenced by everyone on
their phones or in their phones as they wait for something to happen. On
the street or on a date or in the bedroom. Lingerie ads all end, or begin,
with the careful command, *For him* or *For her*. Some things are nice if you
don't think about why.

In Henry James's "The Real Thing" things come in all forms & fashion.
The practical thing; the 'sort of thing'—in single quotes—liked things;
every thing; things that appear; some things; a lot of things; any thing;
genuine, greasy, last-century things; the first thing; the real thing (of
course); the same thing; the long thing; the general thing; no thing; the
only thing; the great thing; the thing in the world I most hated; certain
things; such things (for instance ... the exact appearance of the hero);
my little things; anything (but the question of execution); sort of thing
(I had always represented myself to him as wishing to arrive at); a very
good thing; a compendium of everything (he most objected to in the
social system of his country); several things (they never guessed); the
wrong thing; extraordinary things; the ideal thing; the only thing (that
was clearly flattering); the real thing (could be so much less precious than

the unreal); breakfast things; other things; agreeable things (& played them in an agreeable way); hallowed things, the right thing, the things it had most shown him, everything (fitted with a closeness that completed saved appearances); many things; precious things; something (like honor, or kindness, or justice); & a thing I do not wish to say any longer, except that I liked his voice as if I were somehow myself having the use of it.

How to distinguish the clothes from the body, the body from this live photo gyrating in my palm? The one sitting across from me says, I don't like to see the raw materials. We're talking about cooking; cooking vs. eating, eating vs. sucking it down without having to chew. I'm looking right at you. For once & all at once I want to look at you without describing your face.

What does it mean to be "into" things? A woman I am dating or had been asks me if I'm into her an hour or less after I am inside her & her inside me. Are you into me? At the moment I'm not even into myself. In another story, Henry James's nameless narrator suggests after taking someone into his confidence that the way to become an acquaintance is first to become an intimate. What comes first? Confidence, acquaintance, intimacy. What comes next, or comes at all? What we want is to open up our faces & take a look inside; what we want is to see our thoughts unfolding before us—& this is why we love our screens.

& yet the TV is having a better time than me. The laugh track is on; the TV hasn't stopped laughing since I walked in the door. I can mute it, & try to guess the moments my TV enjoys the most. I can be the laugh track.

Is it worse to be living with one big lie or for everything about you to be almost true? (Deep down you knew I knew it.)

That's how the French are, a man on the television says. They fuck people to get intelligence.

Sometimes they don't even get intelligence, I think, from my vantage point on the couch. Sometimes you have to cry for no reason to make up for the times when you wanted to but didn't.

Scene: a renovated home; spacious, empty, save for the two strangers who have just walked through the door & found their way to the wooden floor.

We were having sex when the police walked in. We eventually found our way upstairs looking at imaginary furniture & we were in the imaginary bedroom now & we are realistically having sex when the police walked in.

It isn't hard to imagine the reality of the situation or to put ourselves there, in imagination or fabrication, me or you or Kurt Russell, who's been asked to recall details of his first date with Goldie Hawn on a North American talk show where commercials keep cutting in to interrupt the silence, any time it's silent. The real thing is to give silence the stage & see how it speaks to us.

On the corner of the busy intersection where I teach, a storefront sign promises a LIVE LASEK SHOW for only one dollar. If I could pay a dollar to watch my own eyes being spliced open & folded back, as they were nine years ago, I'd pay to never see anything again.

What do you want? the one sitting across from me asks. It is our first time meeting. I want the real thing, I tell her, & I'm trying to convey by my look just how real. A gaze or look; a particular way of looking. An agreeable thing & to play it in an agreeable way. I always want the real thing, I tell her & I tell myself twice, so I can really remember it.

On my walk toward the F after another fulfilling faculty meeting,[13] everyone walking has a look of urgency; everyone walking is walking with purpose & a sense of pride, or desperation. Behind me a child is blowing a bubble that floats past, around the corner. I want to follow the bubble or become the bubble.

Imagine only wanting this.

---

13. I write poems during meetings.

Transformation Tuesday (#SoFreshSoClean)

Considering the circumstances, why is your face so impeccable? Why are your lips so wet? Why does your breath stink? Considering that there is no outrage there is no necessity for any reparation. *Please be a case for consideration*, she says, & I am recording her speech, so as to make this public. Cadences, real cadences, & the color of applause; of eyes & ears & a hand to signal, to point with & make public. Eye-witnesses. & should there be a call, there would be a voice. & should there be a voice, there would be an outrage; we would not feel so washed over, washed out, rubbed dry. So fresh so clean.

I emanate & move back & move forward. I kneel down & dig in. I go to my practice to have *intentions*. & in giving, I always get satisfaction in a certain lack, which is brought to light & brought to you. I am inclined to keep bending; I am inclined to hold this pose so you might mimic me in the mirror, or the mirror of your camera eye. The strangeness of this womb. & why complain to change positions? & why complain to mark a surface & a degree of silencing? Considering that there is so much silence one should be able to hear all those choking. The question is this. I want to reclaim myself & to reclaim myself I would need to re-claim everything. & especially a new form for this kind of giving.

Do you like that there? Do you like it? Cut it & cut it strangely. Considering the circumstances there should be a call, a voice, a face to hold & hold dear. There is nothing to forgive if one forgets to ever apologize. Consider our sustenance; consider our very survival. Depend upon it, by which I mean we must depend upon the art of our outrage. I am crawling on the bathroom floor; I am digging my nails into each cracked pale-blue tile to see what was stored; what's been retained & what's been replaced & how we can require deliberation & appeal & choice real choice or can we. To open one's eyes & ears & mouth. The question is this. What do we do to stop? What do we do to keep going?

Intruder Gets Within Steps Of White House (#makemoneyonline)

The comment underneath this reads, Building a third ass cheek can be daunting. & in parentheses, (But so worth it). Did you know that sixty-seven percent of people polled only remember *I have a dream* & nothing Martin Luther King Jr. said afterward. A privileging of the dream over what proceeds it, which is reality.

A friend says, "I know something that's a great deal more fun." The dream presents this great deal more fun.

One grows fat on the things served in company, so I say everything done should be done in private. & what would we do without such security? & how might we secure all of this, for later? A narrow suggestion like the outline of a building from where I am standing on the corner of 33rd & Seventh.

You make me feel as if I had missed something. What is it?

Did that mean shame it meant memory it meant remembering a certain some time & sometimes there is breath & sometimes there is only the feeling just after.

But is there any better feeling than the feeling of a hand that isn't yours above your hip to undo a belt, or button? Holding the static like an unthumbed fruit.

& you think to yourself, or you Tweet, silently: *Where does she get the words which she puts into my mouth?*

(Let us hope that the duration of this dream ride was more satisfactory to her.)

It was not a question whether I considered the grapes sweet or sour, for I no longer had a tongue on which to place them, to taste them, to savor the taste.

(The wish to drink originates from this sensation.)

Upon completion or consummation was a small reward, a gift of words, an invitation to the play, a scenario I've yet to install in my headset.

The fortune you seek is in another cookie.

Innocent Teen Tricked & Used (4k clicks & counting)

But the word *quickly* is striking enough to demand a special explanation. If asked to describe the smell of my underwear I tell a friend the first thing that comes to mind: Shroud of Turin, length of linen cloth bearing the image of Jesus of Nazareth which of course is visual & not olfactory but the best kind of accountings are the ones that pervert the senses & turn water into wine, wine into blood, blood into this growing thickness inside of me. I'd never thought of that phrase *If only you could see me now* in any other way until I was dead.

#bts
(The Ten Things You Need To See In NYC Before You Die)

Everybody wants to know why I kept doing it, why I keep doing it, if I hate it so much. If I hate what it does to a person & to the people looking. If I hate it so much. & what a person & why. Sometimes I pretend to be a different kind of person but I think I'm a lot like anybody else. Like anybody else, I wanted to go through the fire. I felt I had to feel it, to know that it's there. To know that it's here. We go through the fire. & we burn & we burn & we burn & we burn & we burn & we burn & we burn for it. To know & to feel.

& next time, I'll do this harder.

& how & how come & come in to come out. Out there & over. & to cast your nets you have to go into the water, which is another way of saying you can't reach new shores if you're afraid of drowning. I make you feel like a natural woman. You make me feel you without asking. In another room, Seamless is offering me ramen, describing our potential encounter *like a hug without the awkwardness*. You must give me the pleasure of telling me what would best please you. Besides ramen, I mean, or an awkward hug, or a hug without awkwardness. Sometimes you have to choose & sometimes the choice is already made for you. Trump To Spare Dreamers In Crackdown, the rolling text reads, & I would suggest we tread lightly. I want to show you what the public can only imagine, in their most private moments, with their eyes closed & on repeat. When the dolly pulls out it's as if you can finally see, inserting yourself wherever you see fit. If your lower half aches it's because you're hungry. Trust me. Everyone dies of consumption in a Henry James novel & in everyday life. The white stuff that is good for the stomach. As a kid we called it getting last licks.

The Sacred Fount
(7 clever ways to prevent wrinkles
while you sleep)

Over dinner the one sitting across from me asks if I'm a vampire & if I am how old I really am. (My online profile says "32.")

On 34th Street, a tourist is taking a photo of another tourist pretending to hail a cab until she hails a cab. The photo is ruined, unless it's re-animated, reclaimed in the way all good art is the moment the artifice cracks & the real pours out.

In the elevator, two men are still talking about how Hillary Clinton could have won an unwinnable election. "She should have faked it," one says. "She should have embraced the carnival."

Fake name. Real name. Real name. Real name. Fake name. Fake—

I'm playing a game with L; the game where we watch the *Twin Peaks* credits sequence & try to guess which name is fake, which name is real, pretending for a moment that not every name is a real name belonging to a real person, or else pretending that the people themselves are fake, pretending or willing a new reality to take the place of the old one.

Kimmy Robertson

Real.

Piper Laurie

Real.

Michael Horse

Real?

Eric DaRe

Fake. Definitely fake.

I am copying out our conjectures on a napkin, which I'll throw away before the next episode begins, when we begin to play the game again.

My copy of *The Sacred Fount* has a thin faded purple cover; *85 cents* is scrawled in pencil on the inside, but I've paid so much more. I'm still paying for it, with time & concentration & a sense of solitude I'll never get back or will I.

The best thing I've read so far occurs on the first page, in the second sentence, in the Introductory Essay. "Over none of his novels have the critical waves melted so helplessly into their own shimmering foam."

To be that foam, what I wouldn't do & for how long. & how could I make a book so good to have a critical wave melt over it or melt it into nothing but a shimmer, a semblance or shadow or the actual smile of a reader, any reader who happens to open the book & open themselves up to it. Look younger, live longer with nature's secret serum.

The thing about writing so much & all the time is the oscillation between the enjoyment of others vs. this audience of one & how I can play the game or how I can stop before going too far, & when or where that is & how I could ever know until I've gone there; common problem of a mind for which the vision of life is an obsession & a violent embrace & an act that hovers between making love & pornography. All of these people who give me a mouth & a tongue to write about us, & to write it better. & to think it all out is to have already brought it.

"It's the deepest of all truths," Grace says, without saying anything. You know the saying, don't you? I'm asking as if I'm in the scene, with Grace & Henry James's nameless narrator, another novelist. Aren't we all. No one has the generosity to visit me in my isolation but I never asked did I.

What goes on whenever two persons are so much mixed up; what happens when two people are in love or playing at it or playing with each other or each other's bodies in such a way as to mix hands & feet legs & arms hips & thighs, lips & tongues. Flesh & skin. I rubbed off on you & rubbed myself into you with the great pressure of soul contact or sole contact & I wanted you to tell me what it was exactly I left after I slid off, like a plastic wrapper or a book jacket or the sky before rain. & would I recognize the difference.

"One of them always gets more out of it than the other," Grace says. "One of them—you know the saying—gives the lips, the other gives the cheeks. Yet the cheeks profit too."

"It profits most. It takes & keeps & uses all the lips gives," the narrator says. In this scenario I am no longer the narrator but the reader, unless it's the same thing; unless that's the point. To give you my lips so I can turn the other cheek.

The difference between a Henry James novel & real life is that in a Henry James novel nothing happens & in real life everything happens all the time. The trick—but there is none—is only to get off by yourself from time to time, somewhere slow or long enough to linger instead of leaving me.

#thatfeelingwhen

You're watching a Rihanna music video on a stationary bike in a room full of other bikes & breathing bodies. Hours earlier you'd posted a photo of yourself taking a photo of yourself in the mirrored lobby of your rental in your black nylon pants & baby blue & pink windbreaker stolen from the set of *Twin Peaks* captioned "My First Spin Class (a pose poem)."

If you remember anything, remember that anything you can do in the saddle you can do standing up. & yet nothing is more unsettling than a TV set left on in an empty room. & even worse, for the scene to be a hotel room, one you've just checked in & entered; a magnetic swipe card that beeps green & allows you access to a world that has been going on without you all this time. Despite the stranger the hotel pays to *service the room*, the other guests who come & go, the TV set remains unaltered, indifferent, alone in its agency to light up in images, to keep producing, unlike the flickering candle that blows out without human contact. Eventually. Everything else, all of us—we keep moving, we keep whirling & burning. Everything is automatic; everybody is set to *on* because we have no instructions for stopping.

Remember that game where I told you you could do it any way you wanted. & you're thinking I could think of so many games that begin or end in a similar fashion while WORK WORK WORK WORK WORK echoes through the IMAX amphitheater in the dark & the breath & the occasional silence of your self inside yourself & all the parts of people you've never met fall & coat the floor & you should know what kiss it, kiss it better, baby turning the red lever does, & then you should feel it as the music video morphs into Mario Kart for adults—a scene re-imagined from Rainbow Road—with big beats & visual commands for taking everything *to the next level.*

It is difficult to know how I felt now. This poem is subtitled, "Ways a body can be with another body or by itself." I am verbalizing the body. I am giving the body information & taking what the body gives me or can't. I am embodying the moment of words coming in & out from the body. & what happens next or does it. That feeling when can be so unutterable. Coming to another language or a language with another person. Consciousness is roomy. My consciousness has rooms for rent. Oh yes. There is no commitment to completing a thought; I want only to keep having them.

That feeling when after Donna confesses to her dead best friend that she's dating her dead best friend's boyfriend, Donna returns home from the cemetery to walk in on her dead best friend's boyfriend, also: her current boyfriend, making out with her dead best friend's lookalike cousin, who is played by the same actress who plays her dead best friend. Laura Palmer lives on as Maddy Ferguson, shifting from platinum blond to dark brown, & James Hurley, the boyfriend, can't tell the difference either.

I'm just sketching something; I'm not making a point.

It's like people think I'm Laura, Maddy wails, pacing back & forth in the family room while looking at portraits of Laura, or herself, with dyed blond hair, in the next scene. & I'm not!

Three episodes & about two-and-a-half hours later, in TV time, James pulls up on the lakefront docks on his motorcycle wearing the same black leather jacket he wears in every scene, as Maddy, sitting, taking in the breeze, turns her expectant head to meet his gaze. Hi, James says. Hi, Maddy says. The camera revolves to meet them head-on, & Maddy fiddles with her bright pink scarf. James crosses his dangling hands & leans forward, like he's taking a shit. I think I owe you an apology, James says. Not really, Maddy returns. Well, James resumes, when we were together, you know, just talking, I felt something. I just wasn't sure ... he trails off. You looked at me & saw Laura, Maddy says. I guess I did, James says. Want to know something kinda strange, Maddy asks, except it's not a question. Not really. She turns to James; both of them in medium shot now, only their portraits, shown in profile & three-quarters, visible to viewers. I liked it. You did? James asks. Maddy nods. When we were growing up, Laura & I were so close, it was scary. I could feel her thoughts, like our brains were connected or something. & when she died suddenly, I got the chance to be Laura. At least other people saw me that way. Like the way you looked at me. I liked that too. But it was wrong, James replies, looking ashamed, or at least trying to. Maddy shakes her head & smiles. It wasn't one thing or the other. For a while I got to be somebody different. She pauses to place her left palm on James's right knee. But now I'm just me again.

What's the difference between naming & calling, thinking & feeling, feeling & knowing? I know I'm just me again & I can feel myself coming out of me & smell the residue of what I've left behind, on a bike I can't dismount if I tried. I keep trying & I'll close my eyes. That feeling when you eat a non-almond croissant on the waterfront with a view of the Financial District & the crumbs point you to your next point of interest after spin. That feeling when you've lost everything. I've been listening to the same Depeche Mode song for the last two hours & change as I revise this memory. The things you said. I haven't changed my clothes which only means I'm still naked. You know me better than that. I wish once more to mention that I liked this & I like it more every time I pause to think about how it felt. I heard it from my friends about the things you said. That feeling when Spotify isn't enough. To be in someone else's shoes then back to yours, then again someone else. What they miss when they return to a normal life is less the person they lost than the secret. The context, the atmosphere, the mysterious world where it occurred or did it. I heard somewhere that the closest thing to this undercover life is the experience of adultery. I want to tell them, *Try peddling harder.*

Wanna see all
(I've covered up almost everything)[14]

You're watching Rihanna breathing bodies. Hours earlier you in the mir-
rored lobby of your windbreaker stolen from the set of a poem. If you
remember anything, remember standing up. & yet nothing is more even
worse, for the scene to be a magnetic swipe card that beeps without you
all this time. Despite guests who come & go, the TV set up in images, to
keep producing contact. Eventually. Everything burning. Everything is
automatic stopping. Remember that game where I told, thinking I could
think of so many WORK WORK WORK WORK everything to the
next level. It is difficult to know how I felt another body or by itself. I am
taking what the body gives me. From the body.[14] & what happens com-
ing to another language or a consciousness has room for thought; I only

---

14. [August 23, 2018] CC, can we have a footnote here explaining the bit you wrote to me:
So I covered half the poem w/my hand & wrote only what was visible. To signal the process I think I left
enough hints (the subtitle of this poem, the fact that it comes right after the original, etc.) The act of erasure
is what creates unlikely lines like "You're watching Rihanna breathing bodies." & "you in the mirrored lobby
of your windbreaker stolen from the set of a poem." It's a striptease of language & as with everything else in
this life, the allure insinuates itself into the everyday thru the movement btw exposure & effacement, digital
(text) & physical (my flesh). + I like imagining scraps of Twin Peaks leaking out into a Rihanna music video
w/no distinction btw which is which: because there is none.

want to keep having that feeling when after Donna cons best friend's boyfriend, Donna returns friend's boyfriend, also: her current lookalike cousin, who is played by Palmer lives on as Maddy Ferguson Hurley, the boyfriend can't tell I'm just sketching something; I'm not. It's like people think I'm Laura, Ma looking at portraits of Laura, or hers. Three episodes & about two-and-a-half hours on his motorcycle wearing the same sitting, taking in the breeze turns Maddy. Says the camera revolves to pink scarf. James crosses his dangling owe you an apology, James says. Nowhere together, you know, just talking. Looked at me & saw Laura, Maddy kinda strange, Maddy asks, except it's them in medium shot now, only the viewers. I liked it. You did? James aware so close, it was scary. I could something. & when she died sudden saw me that way. Like the way you replies, looking ashamed, or at least the thing or the other. For a while I got palm on James's right knee. But now

What's the difference between knowing I'm just me again & I can feel I've left behind, on a bike. I can't find a feeling you eat a non-almond crumbs point you to your next everything. I've been listening to the change as I revise this memory. This only means I'm still naked. You know I liked this & I like it more every time friends think about the things you said. These shoes then back to yours to a normal life is less the person the mysterious world where it occurred undercover. Life is the experience of almost everything.[15]

---

15. [Today] Why don't we just leave these comments here for the reader? Make each person feel as if they designed the book they are right now(?) reading

The Ghost in the Mirror
(The Beast in the Jungle)

You read a poem called "God Wants You To Go To Jail" & it's your favorite poem this year; you read & re-read it & if asked, on the air, to read something you enjoy, you'd read "God Wants You To Go To Jail" because you like the poem & you like the title, especially, & if asked to explain the reasons why or what it means to you, on the air & in the air, taking so many extra breaths or one big breath—it all comes out like that, sometimes, like you're choking on words or silence—you'd say that God wants you to go to jail because in order to be counted, to be recognized, to claim presence in this culture, one might have to enter into our prison industrial complex; one might have to become registered an offender in order to be realized an inhabitant of culture in a culture which has abandoned you. Rendered & reinstated, which means *to place again in one's possession*. A process of dehumanization for the means of participation, for all dehumanized bodies. The ghost in the mirror. The beast in the jungle. No one is on the air, anymore, no one is here, no one is asking, but these questions still need to be asked.

Have you ever read a police report of your own arrest? & compared it to your own arrest?

The most pervasive crime committed in New York City is MTA violation.[16] Offenses include walking between subway cars, occupying two seats on a subway car, putting a foot on a subway seat, putting a backpack or bag of groceries on a subway seat, using a loved one's MetroCard to enter the subway, asking another person to swipe you onto the subway, sleeping on the subway, begging on the subway or in the subway terminal. More men & women of color get arrested on subway trains & in train stations than anywhere else in the city. Public transport provides an ideal backdrop for public degradation; shame & surveillance have more in common than we would like to admit, even though we won't stop watching. The ghost in the mirror. The beast in the jungle. The mirror, the mirror, the mirror.

So there were like all these cages in which we were put into, basically, & like locked there.

& there were like no seatbelts or anything like that um, & it was like, just like we were sitting in a car like that with your hands tied behind your back, like, with also, with cages too . . . of just like—just having like, nothing at all to hold on to . . . I think some people were falling over & hitting themselves. What I remember most was how they talked about us or how they talked around us & over us. They talked through us. & how they kept referring to us as bodies. They kept saying, "We have to move the bodies. We have to transfer the bodies. The bodies are late; we're going to be late with the bodies."

I was an object or I was his object. & like I was his. I was his body.

---

16. Police arrested two thousand people in January of 2017 alone.

I'm Still Not Good At This Game But I'll Keep Playing With You (#selfiefail)

Here I am at my own reading chewing on ice. Wondering if it's discernible to everyone else, so loud in my own ears & yet I can't stop crushing the cubes on my teeth, biting down hard & swallowing, thinking about everyone else, everyone else, everyone else.

Can you do this without music? A friend asks me as I bite my lip & glide my skin & put my finger on a key.

I watched a video of Donald Trump on *Oprah*, in 1980. I watched a video of how to tie a Double Windsor knot. I watched a video of This Child Is The Cost Of War In Syria. I watched a video of Good-bye Messages From Aleppo. I watched an amazing look at a monkey being born. I watched a video of *The Goonies* taken by someone who attended a screening of its original theatrical release, transferred to a hard drive, digitally ripped, & born again in bandwidth. I watched a video of Johnny Depp hurling a glass of wine at Amber Heard, with the sound off. What would I be doing if I wasn't showing you this video of a bald bear?

a woman corners
me at the bar talking
about an encounter
with a swan, I was
inches from being
pecked, she says
almost regretfully
thinking this must be
what hysteria is
a swan attack in the middle
of the day, in the beginning
of a storm, holding
an umbrella as a weapon

Some say that time spent in enemy hands is the same as becoming the enemy. I consider this while pretending to enjoy a lavish brunch in the Meatpacking District. A stranger sitting relates his last experience here: They turn off all the lamps & turn on a black light as a man dressed in a superman outfit appears, carried above the heads of waitstaff & some others who might not be employees. Drawn in from the street or paid as extras. You make a gesture; champagne arrives. The superman opens the bottle with a sword, which is fake. I think.

Nothing like that has happened yet & I'm still waiting, considering a line or lines, seeing how they sound in my head, on my tongue. Bagatelle, a superman, a caravan, a jolting cork, a jetting stream of amber, an open mouth, a sword which is fake, probably. & all the arms pointing toward the ceiling, or the sky. Like a prayer for rain, which is a prayer to *open up*.

One understands form by its transformation. I am lithe, elastic, capable of lengthening myself to the point of so many of my desires (to say nothing of your own). What is form if not the desire to desire *more* ... or different ways of moving?

The dream of the Internet: to recognize one's self everywhere.

I like to picture the article or video link or caption[17] from which these titles originate. I like to picture where we are going when we disperse; I mean when we stop reading, or listening.

An image can only ever defer. I would rather place you in my thoughts. I would rather place me in you, without looking.

Absence precedes & permits my imagination. If I were to imagine you, right now, putting your fingers here, like I am, folding a page to mark your spot, a desire for a certain smile, a certain eye movement, I would have to absent myself; I would have to absent myself from any possible encounter with the real you so I could really begin to imagine you, here, with me as I sit with you. & to confront my image of you makes me desire this communion more. & to confront the absence of myself—there is nothing better in this life.

I am practicing how to say no.

Someone asks. Someone is always asking. What's a parallelogram? I don't know, not really, not at all. In earlier moments I would pretend to portray the shape on a napkin, & sketch my signature in the corner as a way to confirm my insistence for applause. & later:

Do you want the farina pancakes? They were listed as "buckwheat or buttermilk, made from scratch" on the menu. Do you want to share or swap? Do you want some of mine instead? Do you want something else? I should have ordered the meat plate. I should have been the meat plate. I should stop saying *yes*. A friend across from me says the person with the highest IQ in the world right now is doing nails in Long Island. Google it.

---

17. Curators call this copy *labels* & *tombstones*. I like staying in old houses & sacred hotels; I like any place in which a great many people have died, because it means the place has been so full of life.

Nothing to say yes to if no question is asked; if what's being asked is being demanded. Google it. Actually just think about the person a little while longer. Nails, IQ, Long Island. A meet plate or place for meeting. I don't like saying *no* but I like substitutions. I've never liked to fish but I can identify certain forms of tradition, for instance. I'm just throwing out a line to see what comes back.

#RelationshipGoals (Watch Taylor Swift's "Wildest Dreams" Music Video)

1.

A dinner party. A castle or mansion that ends with a fire, a murder or murders, a game that is being played (VR?).

He is en route on three different trains or buses, trying to get back home in the rain.

On the last vehicle (a van or minivan?) see the faces of various strangers & high school buddies (Tom? Jeff?), a joke is made about the tennis team & all of them having to shave their _____ (the word is never spoken) before the season starts, which no one has done except the person speaking, unbeknownst to him. He leaves so he can verify himself in the mirror, which is when I wake.

2.

A hotel or castle that doubles as a city. Each room leads to another in which a woman I am currently or recently sleeping with dwells. I move from room to room, hallway to hallway, always wondering if I'm going to run into someone when I'm with someone else, always wondering if someone will open the door to the room I'm in while I'm sleeping with another. While I am with another or while I am another. These thoughts keep me up so as to prevent me from sleeping. I lie, silent, with my eyes on the door, the knob of the door or its keyhole. The hotel or castle is all one floor with a terrace for watching.

3.

A dream that ends with you looking for food in a vaguely South Floridian urban cityscape; during the walk you come across your Eleventh Grade Chemistry teacher, Ms. Winters. She asks if you're alright. (You are now sitting down, at a café or on a park bench, writing these notes.) You nod & point to your drafts; you say something like, "Look at all I've written."

Ms. Winters smiles or frowns; you can't register which. (Outside the dream, you remember many moments spent masturbating to her image, in the Eleventh Grade & possibly later.) Inside the dream, she puts her hand on your back, on your neck, & says something like, "No, I mean you were there. For the shooting." Your thoughts move to a shooting that took place prior to your search for food or maybe because of your search for food; your general hunger, your need to consume, to keep consuming; on a restaurant's tropical patio where you are standing beside an older man, someone you've never seen before with dark hair & a thin mustache, just before he blows his brains out, a murder-suicide with the gentleman to his left, someone dressed in military garb. The point wasn't to annihilate one's self but to perform as an assassin. Not to kill but to become death.

Tears well up in your eyes as you recall this & Ms. Winters frowns; without question, she's frowning, her hand on your back, on your neck. You can feel the tears but mostly the feeling before the tears, which is a lot like choking, or the decision to wake up.

4.

She likes to dance on the verandah. On the verandah dancing.

"You were at the concert," she says, from her spot on the verandah, between songs. "I saw you." (The slow-moving panorama of dusk in Havana.)

"I didn't think you saw anyone," he says. (He lights up his cigar; she takes a drag of the one he'd offered her, when they'd begun talking, before we were here to watch. She holds it in one hand, raised up, pointed, like a pistol or a prayer. All the fading lights of Havana, or a Havana that I dream about, a Havana that resembles the Havana of my father's memory.)

"I don't look in the beginning," she says. "But at the end, I take in the crowd. It's like …" (She pauses; the camera pulls back to show the crowd of buildings, the purple blue sky, each of them in frame, in medium shot & approached from the front, she in white, he in a gray suit, holding themselves up, elbows on the stone terrace.) "… Sleeping with a stranger," she says, "& then asking for their name on their way out the door."

"To validate the intimacy?" he asks.

"Or," she returns, "to invalidate it."

The camera holds before it circles, like a kite, or the smoke, or the white gown in the warm breeze. Circling & circling, toward a vanishing point of the past or imperfect future. The sea's keening. The audible, unseen waves. The purple blue sky. The smoke of the cigar. The clouds. The clouds. The clouds. The intimacy of feeling without recognition, or touching without knowing why. (In the dream, I am the camera.)

A voice says, *Freedom isn't seeing the ocean. Captivity is something you hold within you.*

Warrior Princess Enslaved By Dark Magic (What Women Want)

"I suspect that another person is here being substituted for her," Freud says while interpreting his own dream, a vision in which a former patient appears.

Frightened at the thought of overlooking your intimations or looking over your face with my thumb on the screen in the backlit darkness of my bedroom, on my bed.

Before a night run, I decide on a ski mask to cover my face, from the cold if for nothing else. I take a long look without consummation. Nowhere or nowhere I've thought to look; I walk out into so much expectation & everything one has the pleasure to not expect, never, not ever. I think I do not need it anyway.

The face, not the mask.

Much later, & before you hear my recitation being performed, she showed some resistance to this, like a mannequin or a model with gold & silver teeth in place of ivory, what's colloquially called *grill*. Charred meat off the bone or teeth. Chattering & chattering like windows, or a door.

I opened up with no difficulty, at least according to the report I received in the mail months later, maybe today.

Like you, I suffer from near-suffocation in dreams.

(In the dream I have replaced her with you & you with another friend.)

I now feel inclined to be satisfied with just the tip of the tongue, the teeth, the lips. It is the resistance, not the thing I've been resisting, which holds me so hard, which keeps me here, in place, hard & aching, a thing to marvel over or make eyes at. When this happens, I call it *foaming at the mouth*. The crown leads me to the throne. The throne leads me to this great feast. Everything leads somewhere else.

Go slow, but not too slow. Stop when I say when.

This photo of Joe Biden staring out a window will haunt the Internet forever (766 comments)

this proud flesh in such an ugly life to be beauty oh to love one's self as one would love the other avatar on your screen you isn't even real you isn't even really listening you is a little less of yourself when you is with me when you is me or you in me my beauty & unadorned blush such glistening sweat I get nervous I get spastic it wasn't framed this way in the previews it wasn't *as advertised* never not really here I am in my new shape & skin plastic like opening a big big box when I walk I can feel you moving around greatest sound there ever is greatest scene there ever is in rolling film & playing it back only moments away from real-time retrieval to be later called *live* you're too much too much too much always too much & not enough never do I think to say I'm sorry

orange crush of an orange
slice in my mouth the squirt
of juice on my lips on my chin on the collar
of my neck & yours
the answer could be a room
with you in it still
breathing palm trees

holding hands or clapping
& I say press your index
in & sigh deeply

(keep scrolling)

creeped out by other
americans their viscid translucent sheen
the way they keep watching
the news expecting news
on the radio on the air in the air
the smell of fresh right
out from the package
who made thee little lamb
or the face I see if I draw
the curtain closed & then brush
my hand through to take
a glance? I wonder
if you're thinking
the same like the same
voice woven through
different frequencies

static can be a sound
or a feeling

apathetic squirt
or jolt, slow
tremulous lathering
of product, viscera
gel or cream
what is ours is yours what is yours
I return to you

The Secret (of The Secret) (#forthewin)

I wish to disclose everything I know.

& even the things I have no knowledge about. The things I've overheard or the things that have washed over me, like a missed call or a call meant for someone else. You pick up & pretend to be the one they're looking for. It involves a lot of metaphorical handshakes & head nods & a lot of saying *Yes, uh-huh, okay*. I always want to be the one they're looking for.

The first thing that happens is you don't want to look at what you are, Cary Grant said, describing his rebirth after one hundred LSD sessions.

What is the difference between hypnosis & meditation, meditation & relaxation?

As you fall to sleep, repeat to yourself that you'll have a lucid dream that night or in the near future. You can do a mantra, like "I will recognize that I'm dreaming," but be sure you do not try too hard to generate a lucid dream. Instead of putting forth intentional effort in the suggestion, just genuinely expect to have a lucid dream. Let yourself think expectantly about the lucid dream you are about to have, but make sure you are patient if you don't get one quickly. People call this *autosuggestion*.

John C. Lilly gave LSD to dolphins & called it poetry, a stranger tells me at a poetry reading. I'm all into modes of being, & stuff like that, he returns, when I remain silent. I'm sure you're already aware. Humans are bio computers with programs in which we store our desires, our fears, & most of all, our secrets.

"This poem is called 'Possession,'" the woman standing at the center of the stage says, holding up her book behind the mic. "& it's a poem about being possessed."

I wouldn't be here, I whisper to a friend who is now standing beside me, but it's my own reading. I had to show face.

What's the difference between showing face & giving head? What's the difference between a trap & a booby trap?

During a critical moment in the 1985 film, *The Goonies*, a character named Data is setting booby traps to prevent the Fratellis from pursuing them.

"Data, where are you going?"

"I'm setting booty traps."

"You mean booby traps?"

"THATS WHAT I SAID!" Data exclaims, as the tension builds. "BOO-BY TRAPS!"

Roger Moore, who died yesterday, said that he prepared for his role as James Bond by studying Chomsky's *Syntactic Structures*. Moore practiced the celebrated shaken/stirred line backward in a mirror several hours a day until he could "feel it in his mouth."

If I knew *The Secret* I could begin to divulge what the secret of *The Secret* is.

I've never sweated so much at a reading. I've never sweated so much while reading anything. Someone I've never met asks the room—the room or the people in it—to get me a water, when I've finally finished reciting my work; when I've thrown up my arms & bowed my head to the floor, so to stretch, before I sit back down.

I'm that emoji your parents warned you about

I think about writing into a poem, before highlighting the line & replacing it with air.

On television, a man says, "A spy never leaves a trace, to not give himself away." No electronic or physical trace. No emails no papers no recordings. Everything is memorized. I have a very good memory. I guess that makes me a good spy.

Meanwhile, back at the reading, my friend leans in to whisper in my ear.

I wouldn't worry about it, she says, placing her hand on my damp cheek as I drink it in & as I swallow. We're just sweaty Americans.

The first in my family, I think. The first the first the first to feel

This way

As I write these lines I'm listening to Becky G's "Break A Sweat" to better relive the moment & to live in that memory. Your mind is going places I can feel. Becky G can't stop dancing & neither can I. While we dance to "Can't Stop Dancing," she sings that I want to stay in this moment for life. Her & me & you, in this moment for life.

The headline that flashes on my screen as I hold my thumb there provides or promises further instructions.

How to tell when an anonymous "White House official" is actually

Steve Bannon

But instead of clicking, I cancel out.

My friend, who is still standing beside me in my memory, is writing, or re-writing *The Secret*. Her secret, she says, is that another writer's work contains "the most boring pussy references ever."

I don't like the way these people are talking to you, she adds, elsewhere, after I show her a sample of my latest emails. This one is titled "Why Not?" & it begins with the inconspicuous greeting, "Hello Chris," before transforming into an invasive marketing technique, veiled in the pattern of a Socratic dialogue.

I noticed you have been opening some of our previous event invites but have not had a chance to attend.

Any reason why?

Any questions I can answer?

Do you want to see a list of past job titles & companies that have attended?

What can I do to get you to attend?

I make the mistake of opening everything, I tell her, because I'm naturally curious. I want to have all the secrets, I tell her. & even as I say this I know I'll have no room for my own.

What's the difference between poetry filled with boring pussy references & the fake Facebook users who are using my profile to collect data for data brokers & the government?

Everything can be bad poetry. Divorced of its line breaks, bad poetry is everything.

At another reading in Dumbo, where the B & D trains rattle over our heads, every five minutes, I am thinking about what to read before my name is called. Through the long loft windows I see a man on the arm of his girlfriend, blowing bubbles, flaunting the pop, as if to taunt me. If I begin practicing tonight, when will I learn to blow a bubble? If I begin practicing right now, would I be able to read this poem to all of you? Above you, behind, below, & bearing you up.

The secret is that only that which can destroy itself is truly alive, Jung writes in *Dreams* & so I'd like to find a copy of *The Secret* & read the text without pausing, an exercise akin to self-dissolution or self-absorption, which can very often be the same thing. I can't decide whether I want to blow myself up or just make myself larger, so big one can't help but look. *Look.* When I Google *The Secret* I learn that *The Secret* is a best-selling 2006 self-help book written by Rhonda Byrne, based on an earlier film of the same name, published by Beyond Words Publishing.

What does it mean to be *beyond words*? My whole life has depended on an insistence to retain an aura of unknowability; to have that aura encircle me, to have it follow me wherever I walk, & the moments in which I stay still.

One secret I've never shared with anyone before is my pretending to need an inhaler in the first- & second-grades. I could breathe just fine. But I liked the way it looked, & I liked the way people looked at me, when I held it like a pipe & inhaled deeply, shuddering harder for the chance to be excused, or just to *leave early.*

Where would you like to visit? Facebook asks me upon logging in. What are your hobbies? What makes you happy?

On a Monday, I want to feel it.

On a Tuesday, I want to feel it more.

On a Wednesday, I want to feel it more & more.

On a Thursday, I want to feel it more & more & more.

On a Friday, I want to feel it more & more & more & more.

On a Saturday, I want to feel it more & more & more & more & more.

On a Sunday, I want to feel it ever so softly.

& I may speak of this, I tell a friend, or warn them, after we've exchanged another secret.

Since I speak of everything.

See What Happens When These Naughty School Girls Stay After Class For Detention (The Holiday Gift Guide For The Loved One Who Has Everything)

Wow. You are a chef, too? A friend comments on a photo I've just posted. Is there anything you cannot do? I cannot blow a bubble, I reply, thinking if I'll ever learn & how to begin practicing. Alternate titles for this inscription were The Sexiest Drinks For Men To Order According To Women, & The Sex Diary Of The Couple Counselor Who's Always Been Single. Something I thought of but which I would never think to write out was Cum Swapping Sisters or Watch As This Nun Takes The Whole Clergy In The Confessional Stall. I've never seen these videos but I can imagine them, in my darkest moments, or my most tender ones. What can I give you that you don't already have? All of these promises encircle us, turning in the night like a fire. I can't go anywhere without the Internet asking me if I'm looking for a pair of brown leather sandals. I can't go anywhere without 19 Iconic Sandwiches Every New Yorker Needs To Eat. I can't go anywhere. I still can't blow a bubble. It's proba-bly my fear of using my facial muscles for anything other than swallow-

ing. *Use every medium & every moment & everything that's ever happened, or still is.*
A recurring dream involves a scenario that is not yet available via VR. In
the scenario, I am the chef, & also the robot sending you descriptions of
what the chef has cooked tonight, what is on the menu, what is available
to be bought & delivered, what is available to be eaten, or spit out. If I
were an actual chef, I would model my image on the image on the red can
of Chef Boyardee; I would have to drastically age my face; I would have
to wear a toque blanche & practice wearing white. I would smile, with
teeth. I am still considering the sexiest drinks for men to order, according
to women. I am still considering how we can fall in love with portraits of
people who died before we were born. In which one follows the traces
of the painter's immediate gestures & thinks about the radical traversal
of distance. In the original. If I weren't a robot, I'd want to remain a
living vegetable; I'd want to reach a point where mania masquerades as
modus operandi, patent & permeable in our everyday life, with the cur-
tains open & the bed sheets aired out. Dreams are never wet enough.
Hunger is never sated. & is it better, or is it worse, to be kept & to keep
being reminded of it, to be held up to it, to see it reflected back to you,
popped-up like a piece of chewing gum exploding on your lips?

Chris, See Who Is Looking At Your LinkedIn Profile (Instructions For Stopping)

In the intermission, a link re-directs me to my own face, looking far away or empty,[18] re-presented via webcam & the startling message that my laptop will wipe itself in sixty seconds if I don't transfer funds to So & So in Such & Such. Startling? Or delightful? & I say, *Start the countdown.*

An editor just accepted the piece before this one for publication & asked me what genre I would call this. I wouldn't say, I type back, on email. But if I had to, I could force myself.

(This is where the email ends.)

I'll be quick: Can you pitch in $19? All it takes is one click.

I didn't know what was in me; it was worth finding out.

Under the showerhead, I am still thinking about the different ways in which you might receive me, & how. For instance, I would secretly wish

---

18. I would like you to tell me my expression because I can never tell myself.

to have this soap bar die on my flesh or inside me. If I had to, I could force myself. Things can so easily disappear, unless there is someone to receive them. Unless there is someone *on the other end.* All it takes is one click. Love is a landline telephone ringing in different rooms, down the hall, behind shut doors. Love is a group text sent under the auspices of individuation. We are all of us forcing a connection, or coincidence. The six signs your partner is sleeping with someone else (& how to prevent it). Startling? Or delightful?

I am standing here with my head draped under another head, practicing the words I'd like to say to you. Wherever I am I am myself

The great piece
in the gallery.

What would you call this?

A week ago, or longer, after a recitation, another student asks me what discipline I'm in, because he hadn't known anyone was permitted to write like that here, & he wanted to know which discipline permits it. In general, I tell him, I have none. No permission & especially, no discipline. In general, I lack discipline. But everything else, I tell him, I intend to cultivate in excess. The idea isn't to stop; it's to keep going.

When Am I
(Clear Recent History?)

This will be one of my longer captions.

L says she often wakes up asking herself *When am I?* This question arises from dreams in which she's a teenager or a child or an infant, or perhaps even younger, the dreams in which she's not yet here. She says she wakes with a deep & prolonged nostalgia, which turns to sadness at not being able to recapture lost time. But first the unsettling disorientation, when she opens her eyes, of not knowing when she is, as if she's the big hand & the little hand without any face, as if she's out of time or as if she's outside time.

Freud cites two women, Sarah Weed & Florence Hallam, as the first people to find a mathematical expression for the preponderance of displeasure in dreams. They designate 58 percent of dreams as "disagreeable," & only 28.6 percent as "positively pleasant."

I want to ask them about the other 13.4 percent of dreams, but everyone in the preceding paragraph is dead.

I used to think jet lag was a result of your soul catching up to your body. The hallowed delay.

My father points at the screen as we watch a film. It could be any day. It could be tomorrow. We've seen him before, he'll say, pointing to an actor on the screen. But he knows none of us have ever seen him before. What he means is, We've seen him before *on television*.

I'll see you again in twenty-five years, Laura Palmer tells Agent Cooper in the Red Room, in the Season Two finale of *Twin Peaks*, which aired on June 10, 1991, when I was six.

Twenty-five years & three hundred & forty-five days later, I am watching the Season 3 premiere of *Twin Peaks*.

It's common to dream of yourself as a child, especially when you're an adult. Jung says that the only way to really reclaim one's childhood, & to experience it in all of its immense discovery, is to reunite it with adult consciousness, in dreams. The dream as a child is the gateway toward the collective unconscious that cannot be opened any other way.

One face looks forward, he writes. The other looks back. It is almost, I say to myself, like looking in the mirror, & as I say this, I close my eyes before the glass.

I like to lie, reclined in the grass or in the sand, with my hands behind my head & my headphones on, thinking about the music & the sea or the trees, trying hard to grasp at it, to touch & feel as much as I could or can, developing a real sense of being impermanent.

Rare delicious & troubling, I reply, when asked to describe the moment when I open my body, or just before.

→ → →

Throwback Thursday or #tbt is arguably more popular & used more often than Flashback Friday or #fbf, perhaps because Thursday is first to arrive during the week or perhaps because it's the day in which the most social media activity takes place.

To remind you what day it is, or to remind you what day it was, on a given day & to give yourself up to it, I'll show you a screenshot of what's trending right now.

ERs are seeing more & more 'avocado hands'

22-year-old living with parents accidentally stops cyberattack

This week in health: flesh-eating bacteria & the perks of coffee

Mormon church to pull thousands of teens from Boy Scouts of America

Man delivers game ball while flying on drone

Justin Bieber unleashes inner cowboy

Here's a timeline leading up to James Comey's firing & the fallout it un-
leashed

→ → →

A *throwback* is a person or thing that is similar to someone or something
from the past or that is suited to an earlier time. A *flashback* is a part of
a story or movie that describes or shows something that happened in
the past; or: a strong memory of a past event that comes suddenly into
a person's mind.

(Since we described this before, we should not repeat it again)

→ → →

When you get there, you will already be there, a woman in red tells Agent
Cooper in the third season of *Twin Peaks*, an episode called "The Return,
Part 3." The woman is sitting on a couch with her back to the fire & as
she crosses & uncrosses her legs I know I've never seen her before.

The most remarkable thing about the third & final season of *Twin Peaks*
isn't David Lynch's ability to append or elongate a specific sequence or
interval, but the general devastation of time. The desert between two

points. You can see it all over the actors' faces.

I looked different, too, in 1991.

In another poem, I am writing a list called Things That Are So Nineties

- squeezits
- push pops
- are you afraid of the dark
- dunkaroos
- sunny d
- california
- holograms
- the touch tunnel
- the oregon trail
- ellio's
- chicken stars & dinosaurs
- now & laters
- dream phone
- dear diary
- casio keyboards
- fold-out posters
- all fish under
- anything blue
- slime
- gak
- the idea of soundtracks

(the list continues for four more pages)

When I remember childhood I remember all the swimming pools, & all the games we'd play, hovering halfway between air & earth. & the shapes on the edge of the surface. & the shapes we'd make when we dipped our head below.

Are these things really Nineties Things? I ask a friend, as we look over the list. Or are they just childhood things? A childhood which happens to take place in the Nineties.

In another poem, I am remembering what it felt like to put on headphones for the first time. The intimacy of being by one's self on the street or at the beach or in the grass. To shut one's eyes & be anywhere else, subject to the mood of the song & the direction of the arrangement. To live in the mix or to live *as a mix*.

& the music plays on as if you had your eyes shut, like this:

<>
<><><><><><><><><><><><><><><><><><><><><><
><><><><><><><><><><><><><><><><><><><><><><-
<><><><><><><><><><><><><><><><><><><><><><><
><><><><><><><><><><><><><><><><><><><><><><>
<><><><><><><><><><><><><><><><><><><><><><><
><><><><><><><><><><><><><><><><><><><><><><>
<><><><><><><><><><><><><><><><><><><><><><><
 ><><><><><><><><><><><><><><><><><><><><><><>
<><><><><><><><><><><><><><><><><><><><><><><
><><><><><><><><><><><><><><><><><><><><><><>
<><><><><><><><><><><><><><><><><><><><><><><
><><><><><><><><><><><><><><><><><><><><><><>
<><><><><><><><><><><><><><><><><><><><><><><
><><><><><><><><><><><><><><><><><><><><><><>
<><><><><><><><><><><><><><><><><><><><><><><
><><><><><><><><><><><><><><><><><><><><><><>
<><><><><><><><><><><><><><><><><><><><><><><
><><><><><><><><><><><><><><><><><><><><><><>
<><><><><><><><><><><><><><><><><><><><><><><-
<><><><><><><><><><><><><><><><><><><><><><><
><><><><><><><><><><><><><><><><><><><><><><>
<><><><><><><><><><><><><><><><><><><><><><><
><><><><><><><><><><><><><><><><><><><><><><>
<><><><><><><><><><><><><><><><><><><><><><><
 ><><><><><><><><><><><><><><><><><><><><><><>
<><><><><><><><><><><><><><><><><><><><><><><
><><><><><><><><><><><><><><><><><><><><><><>
<><><><><><><><><><><><><><><><><><><><><><><
><><><><><><><><><><><><><><><><><><><><><><>
<><><><><><><><><><><><><><><><><><><><><><><
><><><><><><><><><><><><><><><><><><><><><><>
<><><><><><><><><><><><><><><><><><><><><><><
><><><><><><><><><><><><><><><><><><><><><><>
<><><><><><><><><><><><><><><><><><><><><><><

```
><><><><><><><><><><><><><><><><><><><><
<><><><><><><><><><><><><><><><><><><><>-
<><><><><><><><><><><><><><><><><><><><<
><><><><><><><><><><><><><><><><><><><><>
<><><><><><><><><><><><><><><><><><><><<
><><><><><><><><><><><><><><><><><><><><>
<><><><><><><><><><><><><><><><><><><><<
 ><><><><><><><><><><><><><><><><><><><><>
<><><><><><><><><><><><><><><><><><><><<
><><><><><><><><><><><><><><><><><><><><>
<><><><><><><><><><><><><><><><><><><><<
><><><><><><><><><><><><><><><><><><><><>
<><><><><><><><><><><><><><><><><><><><<
><><><><><><><><><><><><><><><><><><><><>
<><><><><><><><><><><><><><><><><><><><<
><><><><><><><><><><><><><><><><><><><><>
<><><><><><><><><><><><><><><><><><><><<
><><><><><><><><><><><><><><><><><><><><>
<><><><><><><><><><><><><><><><><><><><>-
<><><><><><><><><><><><><><><><><><><><<
><><><><><><><><><><><><><><><><><><><><>
<><><><><><><><><><><><><><><><><><><><<
><><><><><><><><><><><><><><><><><><><><>
<><><><><><><><><><><><><><><><><><><><<
 ><><><><><><><><><><><><><><><><><><><><>
<><><><><><><><><><><><><><><><><><><><<
><><><><><><><><><><><><><><><><><><><><>
<><><><><><><><><><><><><><><><><><><><<
><><><><><><><><><><><><><><><><><><><><>
<><><><><><><><><><><><><><><><><><><><<
><><><><><><><><><><><><><><><><><><><><>
<><><><><><><><><><><><><><><><><><><><<
><><><><><><><><><><><><><><><><><><><><>
<><><><><><><><><><><><><><><><><><><><<
```

```
><><><><><><><><><><><><><><><><><><><>
<><><><><><><><><><><><><><><><><><><><>-
<><><><><><><><><><><><><><><><><><><><<
><><><><><><><><><><><><><><><><><><><><>
<><><><><><><><><><><><><><><><><><><><<
><><><><><><><><><><><><><><><><><><><><>
<><><><><><><><><><><><><><><><><><><><<
 ><><><><><><><><><><><><><><><><><><><>
<><><><><><><><><><><><><><><><><><><><<
><><><><><><><><><><><><><><><><><><><><>
<><><><><><><><><><><><><><><><><><><><<
><><><><><><><><><><><><><><><><><><><><>
<><><><><><><><><><><><><><><><><><><><<
><><><><><><><><><><><><><><><><><><><><>
<><><><><><><><><><><><><><><><><><><><<
><><><><><><><><><><><><><><><><><><><><>
<><><><><><><><><><><><><><><><><><><><<
><><><><><><><><><><><><><><><><><><><><>
<><><><><><><><><><><><><><><><><><><><>-
<><><><><><><><><><><><><><><><><><><><<
><><><><><><><><><><><><><><><><><><><><>
<><><><><><><><><><><><><><><><><><><><<
><><><><><><><><><><><><><><><><><><><><>
<><><><><><><><><><><><><><><><><><><><<
 ><><><><><><><><><><><><><><><><><><><>
<><><><><><><><><><><><><><><><><><><><<
><><><><><><><><><><><><><><><><><><><><>
<><><><><><><><><><><><><><><><><><><><<
><><><><><><><><><><><><><><><><><><><><>
<><><><><><><><><><><><><><><><><><><><<
><><><><><><><><><><><><><><><><><><><><>
<><><><><><><><><><><><><><><><><><><><<
><><><><><><><><><><><><><><><><><><><><>
<><><><><><><><><><><><><><><><><><><><<
```

```
><><><><><><><><><><><><><><><><><><
<><><><><><><><><><><><><><><><><><>-
<><><><><><><><><><><><><><><><><><><
><><><><><><><><><><><><><><><><><><>
<><><><><><><><><><><><><><><><><><><
><><><><><><><><><><><><><><><><><><>
<><><><><><><><><><><><><><><><><><><
 ><><><><><><><><><><><><><><><><><><>
<><><><><><><><><><><><><><><><><><><
><><><><><><><><><><><><><><><><><><>
<><><><><><><><><><><><><><><><><><><
><><><><><><><><><><><><><><><><><><>
<><><><><><><><><><><><><><><><><><><
><><><><><><><><><><><><><><><><><><>
<><><><><><><><><><><><><><><><><><><
><><><><><><><><><><><><><><><><><><>
<><><><><><><><><><><><><><><><><><><
><><><><><><><><><><><><><><><><><><>
<><><><><><><><><><><><><><><><><><><-
<><><><><><><><><><><><><><><><><><><
><><><><><><><><><><><><><><><><><><>
<><><><><><><><><><><><><><><><><><><
><><><><><><><><><><><><><><><><><><>
<><><><><><><><><><><><><><><><><><><
 ><><><><><><><><><><><><><><><><><><>
<><><><><><><><><><><><><><><><><><><
><><><><><><><><><><><><><><><><><><>
<><><><><><><><><><><><><><><><><><><
><><><><><><><><><><><><><><><><><><>
<><><><><><><><><><><><><><><><><><><
><><><><><><><><><><><><><><><><><><>
<><><><><><><><><><><><><><><><><><><
><><><><><><><><><><><><><><><><><><>
<><><><><><><><><><><><><><><><><><><
```

```
><><><><><><><><><><><><><><><><><><><>
<><><><><><><><><><><><><><><><><><><><>-
<><><><><><><><><><><><><><><><><><><><<
><><><><><><><><><><><><><><><><><><><><>
<><><><><><><><><><><><><><><><><><><><<
><><><><><><><><><><><><><><><><><><><><>
<><><><><><><><><><><><><><><><><><><><<
 ><><><><><><><><><><><><><><><><><><><>
<><><><><><><><><><><><><><><><><><><><<
><><><><><><><><><><><><><><><><><><><><>
<><><><><><><><><><><><><><><><><><><><<
><><><><><><><><><><><><><><><><><><><><>
<><><><><><><><><><><><><><><><><><><><<
><><><><><><><><><><><><><><><><><><><><>
<><><><><><><><><><><><><><><><><><><><<
><><><><><><><><><><><><><><><><><><><><>
<><><><><><><><><><><><><><><><><><><><>
<><><><><><><><><><><><><><><><><><><><>
<><><><><><><><><><><><><><><><><><><><>
<><><><><><><><><><><><><><><><><><><><<
><><><><><><><><><><><><><><><><><><><><>
<><><><><><><><><><><><><><><><><><><><<
><><><><><><><><><><><><><><><><><><><><>
<><><><><><><><><><><><><><><><><><><><<
><><><><><><><><><><><><><><><><><><><><>
<><><><><><><><><><><><><><><><><><><><<
><><><><><><><><><><><><><><><><><><><><>
<><><><><><><><><><><><><><><><><><><><<
><><><><><><><><><><><><><><><><><><><><>
<><><><><><><><><><><><><><><><><><><><>
<><><><><><><><><><><><><><><><><><><><<
><><><><><><><><><><><><><><><><><><><><>
<><><><><><><><><><><><><><><><><><><><<
><><><><><><><><><><><><><><><><><><><><>
```

the Internet is for real

```
<><><><><><><><><><><><><><><><><><><><><><><
><><><><><><><><><><><><><><><><><><><><><><><>
<><><><><><><><><><><><><><><><><><><><><><><><
><><><><><><><><><><><><><><><><><><><><><><><>
<><><><><><><><><><><><><><><><><><><><><><><><
><><><><><><><><><><><><><><><><><><><><><><><>
<><><><><><><><><<><><><><><><><><><><><><><><>
<><><><><><><><><><><><><><><><><><><><><><><><
><><><><><><><><><><><><><><><><><><><><><><><>
<><><><><><><><><><><><><><><><><><><><><><><><
><><><><><><><><><><><><><><><><><><><><><><><>
<><><><><><><><><><><><><><><><><><><><><><><><
><><><><><><><><><><><><><><><><><><><><><><><>
<><><><><><><><><><><><><><><><><><><><><><><><
><><><><><><><><><><><><><><><><><><><><><><><>
<><><><><><><><><><><><><><><><><><><><><><><><
><><><><><><><><><><><><><><><><><><><><><><><>
  <><><><><><><><><><><><><><><><><><><><><>
<><><><><><><><><><><><><><><><><><><><><><><<
><><><><><><><><><><><><><><><><><><>><><><><>
```

(Of course, the interpretation of each individual passage is bound to be largely conjecture, but the series as a whole gives us all the clues we need to correct any possible errors in the preceding passages)

Another way of asking *When am I?* is asking *Why am I still here?*

Instead of grass, they have sage. Instead of people, they have no people.

I am at a faculty party, mingling with faculty members but mostly trying to melt, & if I close my eyes, I can better feel it.

A lot of men kill themselves in Wyoming, the stranger hovering over me says. She's from Wyoming & now she lives in Brooklyn, like everyone else I know, & everyone I don't.

Why is that? I ask.

The altitude, I think, she returns. Or from being so manly. The problem of living up to it. The legacy of the cowboy, she says. You know?

I nod but I don't know anything about being manly, & I know little more about cowboys, except wanting to be one, for about six months, when I was between the ages of six & nine.

Have you ever thought about the number nine? she asks, reading my thoughts as if they were written on a page. I saw a Sikh Astrologist who told me that between the ages of seventeen & twenty-six I didn't exist.[19] No one between the ages of seventeen & twenty-six really exist, she says, *really*.

I shake my head, I finger the rim of my plastic cup, I think about a re-fill of red wine, or if it'd be rude to take the bottle out into the hall.

During a seminar on dreams that ends tomorrow, I learn that sleeping on your left side makes you susceptible to possession by demons, or night-mares, for the fact that you are covering your heart.

---

19. Later, I will relate this anecdote to L, who is twenty-six. She will become visibly excited about the idea of almost existing again.

I was dating a guy who was nominated for the Nobel Peace Prize; he found out on Facebook, she continues, not noticing or maybe noticing too well my wandering eyes, my desire to melt.

He had a heart problem. Not physically, she adds, putting her right hand to her left breast. You know. A heart problem. He hardly had one. I'm attracted to those real damaged, heartless, geniuses. Are you into Joan of Arc?
I mean, I'm not *into* Joan of Arc, I reply, thinking for the first time this evening whether I should be writing all of this down; thinking if I can turn shit into gold dust & how. But I'm not *opposed* to Joan of Arc.

Good, she says.

Good, I say, catching myself in the reflection of her eyeglasses, in the act of looking at her as though I were looking past her.

What does it mean to be *caught in the act?*

Another childhood memory involves a scenario in a bathroom in South Florida. A tiled floor, a shower curtain full of flowers. I have no idea which kind. My adolescent hands gripping my adolescent cock, as I begin to learn about myself & what I like & how.

I was so thoroughly gripped, & gripping, I had lost myself; I was losing myself & also finding myself, so much sustained fascination & withdrawal there was no way to hear the footsteps of my mother, who happened to walk in, & *didn't see a thing.*

Henry James, in his memoir, *A Small Boy and Others*, writes that his first vision of liberal life was being placed on the back of a very big dog, to ride.

The world was all before them, where to choose, Milton writes in the last line of *Paradise Lost*.

What does it mean to be *before you*? Before means at an earlier time but also ahead.

Or it can mean in front of, like being *in the presence of*.

→ → →

James calls the effect of his present imagination on how he imagines his childhood *the soft confusion*.

← ← ←

When I was acting on or in or for daytime TV, I could never tell when the camera was rolling or when we were "out"—*We're out*, the stage crew would say, or were supposed to say—whenever the camera was off & we had moved on. I was not moved on; I was moving on & in the scene & thinking hard about conveying a certain emotion & delivering a certain line a certain way, so hard to turn off because I could feel it now, & it was warm. & it was beating, or I was. & I never knew when the camera was off or when it was rolling.

The sense of coming both *after* & *before* history. After the modern, but before the institutionalization of the Internet, the systemic flattening of time & space.

Everything I know about the past is not through reading about it but by feeling its rupture.

Do you feel that?

→ → →

She says that the singularity is inevitable & I tell her when it comes, we'll be nostalgic for our actual brains.

J sends me audio messages that delete after thirty seconds. *Raise to listen.*

When I am raised up, I am listening; I can hear myself rising inside of you.

When I've risen, or arisen, my voice will have already disappeared.

→ → →

& hey, she says, taking her right hand from her left breast & placing it on my shoulder. I don't remember which one. This is going to sound so stupid, but I forgot your name.

I was born in the wrong country, a woman on the television says. I met the wrong people. Like everyone who passes through here.

It's Chris, I say. & don't worry about it. Everyone forgets everyone's name, I say, thinking that I haven't even asked her about hers. When everyone knows everything, there is power in anonymity, I would tell her, if she had asked me why I haven't cared to ask.

Oh, I knew it. I mean, she starts, stops, starts again. Looks at me as though she's sizing me up. You look like a Chris so I thought it couldn't be your name.

Yeah, I say. It's so self-referential. It's so postmodern.

I have a tendency to hold onto things or to hold things in.

My body is a receptacle for stirring memories & feelings. Sometimes, the waste seeps out.

The way the afterward constructs the before.

James, near-dead, had a Proustian panic when he heard there was a writer in France doing all of the things he wanted to do.

I've never liked that game. You know the one. *If you could do it again, what*

would you do differently?

I should re-phrase that. It's not that I don't like the game; it's just that I have no need to play. I'd rather write.

← ← ←

I like to say that B was my first translator even though she's never translated anything I've written.

→ → →

I see the actors move again through the high, rather bedimmed rooms, James writes in his memoir. It is always a matter of winter twilight, firelight, lamplight; each one appointed to his or her part & perfect for the picture ...

← ← ←

Years ago, B tells me, she used to sit at home with her grandmother, translating episodes of the North American soap operas I appeared in; repeating me & everything in Turkish.

→ → →

Do memorials preserve lost lives or instigate forgetting?

If the monument wasn't here to memorialize those killed on September 11, 2001, for instance, we would be forced to encounter the historical fact of their lives all on our own.

← ← ←

WHICH WAY TO THE GROUND ZERO GIFT SHOP?

Reads one of the signs where one of the two towers once stood. & all the bodies too.

→ → →

A surplus of pleasure accrues in our exchange economy of memories & feelings.

An excuse to curate instead of to *care*.

← ← ←

How often have I held my headphones close & closed my eyes & willed my reality to be replaced by anything else?

→ → →

For just as cool water is sweet to heated bodies, so would I feel my burning refreshed by them, I often recite, while I hold your image in my memory & just before I let myself leave.

← ← ←

Your face like a window or a door & I would be sprawled out or standing there & brushing up against you; I would be rubbing us raw, & there would be so much friction, & so much contact, the way a pearl is born. Just like the way a pearl is born.

→ → →

How often had I pressed my face to yours & repeated Let me in.

Let me in let me in let me in let me in

& how often had the same wish been asked of me.

I should like to repeat this playlist as soon as it stops.

What happens to a present love in the future of its passing? Does it live or does it recede into an unreturnable past? Does it go or does it gain momentum, accumulate & accrete & hoard more love during the lack, & after the intermission does all the stored love get transferred or transmitted into the one with whom you are in love? & is it true that the one I'm in love with is full of all my past loves, & all my future love I have for her too? The love that I am still waiting to give; the love that I still have to learn to give.

I should like to keep your face close to mine, even if I can only keep looking.

College now the place to try pot: study (7 warning signs an online degree is a scam)

The Mellon Foundation is fostering a think tank to think about other ways to use your PhD. One in six people who earn a PhD end up being hired full-time in a teaching or research role. In view of this or in lieu of this, I began typing & re-typing my About Me.

I can fuck like a horse if I knew what a horse fucks like & I don't.

As SoCal rapper Mibbs says in the 2014 song "Freebass":
"This that rider shit, dipped in Prada shit, this so nasty I don't wanna tell my mama shit."

What are my options what are my options write them down, print them out, circle the most exciting possibilities with my own hand while with the other

Keep touching other possibilities. This online dating ghostwriter charges $900 per month.

Re: retrograde

During a conversation this past week G tells me, "I often think you've lived seven different lives."

In an interview this past week to mark his first one hundred days in office, President Trump told Reuters that he thought the job of commander in chief would be easier & complained, "This is more work than in my previous life."

The situation can be melted down & solidified, the way a ring is, or the way I imagine a ring is, before it gets polished & placed on a lifted finger. A promise for posterity. Living in the past vs. Indulging in the present. In the Nineties, always eating Dippin' Dots just for the tag on the cardboard cup, *the Ice Cream of the Future*.

This 42-year-old married mother of two wants to help you write your online dating profile.

Before I keep reading I make a note to write this down, & to place it in a long line in the list of future options & possibilities. What do I see myself doing? What do I see when I see myself? What do I do to keep my face away from every surface that might reflect my face back to me? Sometimes all I can do is look. Sometimes all I want is to never have to look again.

The New York City matchmaker, a 42-year-old married mother of two, curates her clients' profiles, even crafting messages to set up dates. She has never personally used a dating app, but said her training makes her equipped to help modern singles. With a master's degree in social work from New York University & five years of experience in individual psychotherapy treating patients with depression & anxiety, she saw an opportunity to take on a more light-hearted trade, juggling a maximum of twelve clients at a time, charging them $900 for the first month of coaching, $700 for the second, & $500 for each additional month.

What are my options what are my options—

In another book, I'd written that our tragic flaw is that no one ever thinks about all the options we have, all the time. Reading is useful; travel is useful. In Henry James's *The Ambassadors*, Paris is described as a city not just for looking but for *looking like.* "We're all looking at each other—& in the light of Paris one sees what things resemble," Miss Barrace tells two other people whose names have nothing to do with crude allusions, James's closeted subversiveness. "That's what the light of Paris seems always to show."

Everyone in the novel is a flâneur; everyone idles, lounges, leans & watches everyone else from a private perch or a balcony or the window of a sitting room where everyone else is sitting, unaware or pretending to be unaware, thinking of themselves—privately—like some lurking image in a long gallery, looking at each other as objects & subjects, simultaneously objects & subjects, moving photographs of urban life but also the photographers, for the bored & white & wealthy.

In a letter to a friend, James wrote that Lewis Lambert Strether, his novel's protagonist & prime ambassador, bears a vague resemblance—though not facially—to his creator. What's wrong with Strether's face? I wonder as I skim the pages from my own private perch (a couch with a view of a cemetery). In his only physical description in the 458-page book, Strether is described as having "a marked bloodless brownness of face."

Companies that booked me often, often
                                Said that what makes me desirable
as a model is my ability to look like no one but myself.

"You get to go so many places, you get to do so many things," G told me this past week. "Because you can pass. You can pass," he repeats, whenever I ask him what he means. "But you also stand out."

G means I can pass for being so many different things, types, classes & ethnicities. & all of them a part of me. What are my options what are my options. I never had a problem imagining my options because I was so good at imagining them. I had to learn to grow a good imagination, & to use it often. & it grew, & it keeps growing. My mother & father didn't go to school but I imagine that they imagined what it was like when they sent me off, to learn what they couldn't imagine.

In the Draw-A-Scientist Test developed in the early Eighties, students are asked to reveal their image of a scientist through drawing a picture. Students from twenty-three states & four regions in the United States are all asked the same question. Will you please draw a picture of a scientist doing science? When you are finished, will you please explain your drawing? Sixty-nine percent of K-2 students drew Caucasians; fifty-eight percent drew Caucasian males. As the students got older, & advanced in their education, the image of the white male scientist became more pervasive, as seventy-five percent of eighth graders drew men & eighty percent drew Caucasians.

What's the difference between passing & passing on passing on & taking over?

Color was brought in from the colonies; colorization as colonization & the colonization of color. India gave England indigo dye & suddenly *royal blue* designated empire. Sometimes I think in color; sometimes I see red silver spots or specks when I close too hard. If I knew how to control it I wouldn't control it you know

The women paid to color in single frames in black & white films were called *color girls*.

Only You Can See What You've Saved (Full Size Render)

Full Size Render is the name of this photo. Full Size Render is the name of this poem. Full Size Render is what I would become if I was becoming someone else, rendered differently. So Much For So Little,[20] because life can be so small, so narrow & thin. I have made it large in the hope that you notice it. But there is more not to be given in words, unutterable. For instance. Whenever you masturbate, think of me. Whenever you masturbate, think you *are* me. Whether you have me in hand or hallucination, you have me. (This long build-up, these introductory remarks. Typical situation in which the prefaces are far more interesting than the poems at a poetry reading. & what happens, or what doesn't, when nothing becomes of interest?) Stop looking at me & just listen. The person you are meant to love might be sitting under this sign. The person you are meant to love might be sitting across this screen. We are in desperate need of something good. We are living at the end of days, but for a monthly fee, if you act fast, you can increase your storage. The modern tragedy is far worse than anything in Greece & Rome, & I'm talking about Greece & Rome in April of 2017. Let me just say it was like one of those reality shows, only real. It was like auditioning for a role in a movie, only the

---

20. Revising this poem on line at National Wholesale Liquidators to be hit with such a sign—or promise— when I think to look up.

audition is the movie. It was like a moving picture world & we could watch the scene develop from our privileged perch in the back-lit luminescence, a flash of half-held penetration just before an image freezes, to replace the one that hardly had time to thaw. Let me just say that everyone at every street corner is on their phone. Let me just say we're looking at the same things, even if only you can see what you've saved. *Yeah right.* On any given day, I get on & get off the subway seven to ten times. I like the idea, & the image, of constantly emerging. I like the sound it makes & the way it makes my eyes feel when they readjust. Like sliding a thin film over & under your original skin. Like becoming another body. Like it or not, you must admit that here is something you can really dig your hands into. When I emerged from the subway on Avenue M I saw the wet asphalt, the puddles on the corner pooling by the curb. I like when it rains & even better when it rains somewhere else so that when you get there you know something has really happened, you know something has really changed. With or without you. The work is not here but it is where we are going, where we will be before we think to look back. Only you can see what you've saved. Remember that? The ambiguity surrounding me became more pronounced than before. Everyone wants to know whether the clothes I am wearing belong to someone else. Everyone wants to know if this is really me, or just my work. Me & my work are the same. & my work, what else can it do except set me free.

You could not be born at a better period than the present, when we have lost everything. Even if I didn't receive the reminders, I would remember that much. I am dying to forget all the things I've done. & yet I keep writing them down. The presence of the Cloud in the back of my mind & in the front makes me kneel & touch my lips to the floor. When it stops becoming real, it starts becoming a symbol of worship. I could keep holding my breath like this. Sometimes it does last.

Accessory After the Fact
(What's New This Week On Netflix)

In this 1987 thriller, office life is more appealing than the alternative for one lonely woman. Because of budget cuts, Dorine, a proofreader at a magazine, is forced to work from home, which depresses her further. But by December, the two had reconciled. At a rally together in Wisconsin, Mr. Trump compared Mr. Ryan to "a fine wine" whose "genius" he had grown to appreciate. But when she accidentally electrocutes a co-worker on a visit to the office, she becomes energized & ends up going on a murder spree, killing more colleagues. "Now, if he ever goes against me," Mr. Trump said, "I'm not going to say that."

"I felt it was in you, deep down," they told me. "& that I must draw it out." & much later: "Well, I have drawn it, & it's a blessing."

At a press conference in a black & white Paris everyone but Jean-Paul Belmondo is present. A reporter asks a man what his greatest ambition is in life. The man says, holding a cigar above his lips, To be immortal. & then to die.

What's it feel like
Riding in a stolen car?

Driving around the city of lights at night, someone says once you're looking for someone you'll never find them. It's too late to be scared. It's too late to see anyone. It's too late for anything but to keep watching, keep driving, keep watching yourself drive in the rearview mirror. (Jean-Paul Belmondo will continue to rub his lips with the knuckle below his index & thumb; if I concentrate, I can fix a mustache on those bare lips, measuring him the way he measures himself against Humphrey Bogart under a movie marquee.)

Later on, I'd come to understand that the transition shot is always a moral issue. The meaninglessness of time intervals between moral decisions materializes in jump-cuts that force you to consider what's been left out. Another way of thinking about this is to ask yourself where you go when you close your eyes.

"Take myself as an example," a student writes in a paper I've still yet to actually grade. "I never really organize all my interests & have a vague understanding of who I am, but as I was sharing the personal information, I have a better understanding of who I am, & with the recommendations, I joined an ice skating group."

Reading this paper & commenting upon it makes me feel complicit, not in joining an ice skating group, or in sharing the student's personal information, which she has shared in her paper, but in my own gaze, the passing glance I give & give again. "We should not be afraid of being watched," the student continues, a page later. "What's more, democracy means that the government governs the whole populations, so only when the whole population is also participating can our nation really claim to be democratic."

I am holding the gun in my hand; I am holding the gun to my head. Accessory after the fact, or just an accessory, something to hold & to hold on to. An object of your manic corporate lust. Thank you, & thank you for listening. You are welcome

To worship me.

So many things which I do not want, Socrates said, strolling through a marketplace in Athens. So many things which I do not want, I said, strolling through my studio before moving in somewhere else, a one-bedroom with more space for all my accessories, the things I cherish & hold dear, the things I want to cuddle & caress as I drift off to death or another long good-bye. Speculating on inevitable separation, the woman on the screen says, "You say 'let's sleep together' but we can't." Another student, from another school, tells the class that all artists live sad, tragic lives. She elaborates: All artists, she announces, eventually suicide.

Common dilemma: closing one's eyes & still seeing a semblance of light. The deep, delicious desire for the void. An impulse toward death.

The frustration of being trapped in a body that can only exist in one place at a time.

The pleasure & sadness of arriving in the future but not being able to tell your past self of all the things you've discovered.

(& a fourth thing I've misplaced in memory.)

Motion is nothing but displacement, a zigzagged distance between two periods, overlapping journeys, crossing paths, roads which converge to a singular mark on the horizon, a vanishing point of the dashboard as it drifts into a river bank, or the Seine.

It's fun to switch back like this, like muting the volume on your headset or deciding to spend a whole day walking with your hologram. On the street, who could ever tell the difference between me & my moving image? They say that post mission disorder is refusing your real life & endangering us all. In this scenario, "I" is everyone. I dream of double agents the way I dream about immortality, or the wish to birth a nation, just by coming, & clenching in the moment right before. A mix of all the books & movies & dreams I've ever had or seen. A yellow taxi jetted by just now & I saw my fleeting face for an instant before it flew away.

On the subject of things, I don't have much to say, so I often let Mrs. Gereth speak for me. She could at a stretch imagine people's not having, but she couldn't imagine their not wanting & not missing. I had no patience to keep reading Henry James's *The Spoils of Poynton*, so I stopped there. I would never know what I was missing except what I could imagine, which is always what I want anyway.

This is a poem about objects, not people, but I like when the one begins to stand in for the other.

An old friend, or a friend who is old, relates to me the fact of her misery; she describes herself as a steel pot while stirring the sugar in her teacup & I try to count the number of clangs of steel against porcelain, spoon against rim, & how long each sound lasts. "I flatter myself that I'm rather stout," she says, as if reading from a book, "but if I must tell you the truth I've been shockingly chipped & cracked. I do very well for service yet, because I've been cleverly mended, & I try to remain in the cupboard …" She hasn't gotten laid in quite a while; sometimes it's best to add things to your cupboard, instead of removing them, or having them remain there, or at least this is what I tell her. Shuffle the decks, I say, still not sure what I mean & glad she doesn't ask. Writing can be like throwing coins in the air. Let words fall where they might, without looking to see where. If they move a reader, it is by means of uncanny associations & the sense that they read as if written by the one reading. The music will keep playing. & then we'll be dead.

You either like cars, or you don't

A kid in a black leather jacket tells a flower shop girl in the passenger seat, after they've been driving in circles on the motorway for hours in a stolen car. (She's bored.) I couldn't remember the color of her eyes but I kept that to myself. Brigitte Bardot is reclining on a bed that isn't mine

& asking me what I like better, which part of her body, & why. Her feet dangle off the edge as the light changes from dark blue to red, from red to a soft yellow hue. It entirely changes the look of people & of things, as when the position of any object has been subtly shifted between takes; the difference between walking into a new house for the first time or of walking into an old one when one is in the process of moving, & what is the difference. Brigitte Bardot expects answers.

& all of this could be occurring on the F train, heading uptown in the middle of the day, on a Wednesday, without alarm. You might look up & see Dr. Zizmor's smiling face, ageless, at least for the last thirteen years in which you've been looking. He was there or he was not there. Not there if you didn't see him.

This advertisement, you think, is just another accessory after the fact. The feeling of visibility & recognition, of knowing someone just by looking at them … & blocking them out by putting up a screen; the truth that lies in appearances. You recall what Gertrude Stein[21] often says, which is, "I like a view but I like to sit with my back turned to it." I like to turn away from the view, you say, because it's a moral outrage to look without being looked back upon in return. There is something beautiful in the knowing, a shared knowledge & in what could not possibly be shared, never, not ever, not even in the most beautiful pose of vulnerability; the selfie which speaks without words. To, for, from & of the subject. There is nothing like posing, & stretching while posing, to take one out of one's self. & it would not be a stretch to say, you think, that you have a deep longing for visualization & hallucination; it would not be a stretch to say that you think about the looking & longing of flesh before it becomes flesh, that it's all you often think about, that line of sight that vanishes, that begins & ends when the lights go, even in the middle of the day. A mouth drops so that the breath might better enter. The breath & so much else. The thought of—just the thought. In this, I am your willing accomplice.

---

21. She had "a weakness for breakable objects."

Tears for Fears
(#likesforlikes)

Is it your heart that's broken, or your phone? Today my Aries horoscope says the problems of other people will give you a nice break from your own drama. Not considering that the problems of other people are the subplots in your own drama. & so you might see what I speak of, I'll offer a picture.

They call it a mother-in-law-fish, he says, with practiced timing. But you don't eat the face. & when they present it—the face, I mean—it's already removed.

(What I wouldn't do to offer myself up, on a platter, without my face.)

From my view of the stage, I am wondering about the difference between woe & whoa, utter sadness & a complete disavowal of expectations & a command to stay still. A lover's heart like a kebab.[22] & by that I mean something which I can hold, but also put in my mouth.

In those days, I was practicing cooking as a form of exercise, like calisthenics, or the sound your body makes when you jump up in the air

---

22. "The familiar sight of those lumps of flesh roasting over the red-hot embers presents an appropriate & pathetic image of the heart (the seat of passion) of the unhappy lover burning with the fire of unrequited affection or of separation from his loved one."

& press your palms together, & kick your legs out to the horizon. It was easy to play the role which required so little save a good deal of performed solitude or rather it became easier as time went on, because the role—any role—requires real solitude to come off, & so much that seems so natural out on stage takes many practiced moments of concentration behind closed doors. Everything gets easy, before it gets boring. Boring before & after & during & later, boredom, in the present tense & intransitive. & so perhaps I had acquired a habit of writing that supplied the place of personal intercourse. & so perhaps in my solitude there was too much of everything inside of me that was wanting to leak out; linguistic spillage & my desire for excess & overflow, of a cascade of touch & something which I will not mention here. I get giddy just to picture myself being pictured from this particular angle, in the act of making meaning or movement. It was a role I'd picked up from prior scripts & I was getting off on it because I could play so lonely & then I could feel it too. & performing was a way to rematerialize what I'd wanted to feel before I had the chance, which I would never have. & I could feel strength in that loneliness & space, & something to carve out & make music from.

Probably the most well-known track by Tears for Fears, "Everybody Wants to Rule the World," released as a single the same year I was born, a month before I slid down the long slide & looked up, toward high windows & walls without end. The music video would begin, if you were clicking *play*, on a long stretch of country road & an open convertible to course through it, a boy dressed as a cowboy double-fisting toy pistols & aiming for the driver as an airplane cuts across the sky. Another way of saying "Everybody Wants to Rule the World" in 2017 is "Be loved, or die." & so it is a matter of survival to pronounce your name at check-in & take your place among the swarm.

I came for gluten-free flatbreads & ceviche in a cup. I came for open bar & the company of strangers I'd seen before. I came for the printed program & the promise of building my network. I came for the raffle, & the chance for a private poetry cooking class. I came because I thought this would be better, & by "this" I mean all of it.

There is a song on the radio, there is a moment of eye contact, there are several different text messages & messages on the street; there are eyes & songs & messages, & the street, & then there is *using everything*.

In another version, this is just an away message from 2002, made to make you jealous. In another version, we are watching this from the mall's multiplex, in *Saved by the Bell*. In another version, we are saved & we are saving this for later.

What was it you said about the body & specifically mine? That there is no concept of moving unless there is something for it to move against. Consider all movement & all things that move & things that are moving & things that move us.

I begged myself to begin groping.

I was beginning to grope, I was groping toward a beginning, I was groping toward a beginning that was growing toward an ending, & it was a happy one, & I was happy. I had seventeen Twitter followers & then I had eighteen. Then I had none, or no one I knew, or followed back, or would ever follow. Why did it take me so long & when. The thing I came for was you.

I went to the Whitney Biennial & all I got was this poem (Portrait of An-Other Portrait)

They sell dark brown skin from the bottle. They sell pills that can change your hair color, your eye color, the color of your flesh, on the outside *&* *the inside.* & all the water fountains on every floor are no longer working.

The stream flows out for a flash, time enough for you to hold your face close & your mouth open, to gasp air instead of water. I picture the cameras, recording this phantom swallow, this fish-faced kiss, & playing it back on another level, maybe the basement, visible to anyone queuing up for coat check. It could be a part of the Biennial, or it could be shoddy maintenance. We pay enough for this ticket & I don't mean the price of admission. Every time I go to the Whitney I feel fifteen years younger, & not in a good way.

Online, weeks ago or only hours, I'd read that the best thing that could ever happen to the museum was if a person of color reviewed its seventy-eighth installment of American art. It was the best of times, Charles Dickens once wrote. It was the worst of times.

At night we walk in circles, but I sound better since you cut my throat.

I've always been a mix. I've always been mixed up. Counting in Spanish or thinking in English & singing happy birthday in Polish until I stopped thinking altogether & only saw words & objects & things in one language. Monochromatic. Presented in Technicolor. What might appear to be a sun-speckled floor actually shows traces of blood, flesh, & excrement. In Cuba, they called abuelo *chinito*; they called gran tío *chardo*. It took me awhile to understand what that really meant & by then I had already thought twice about putting my head in the oven too; not about the act itself but what it would feel like at the moment of convection, all the time repeating the axiom *hot air rises*—doesn't it? So maybe I would too.

& meanwhile, in another room: a beach walker, a walking stick, a close-up of a pond or lake, a slow pan through the forest, a slow hold on the breeze. A super cut of a nose, a set of nostrils smelling various things: a tulip, a cheese puff, a woman's breast. A pause to consider the nipple. A hold for applause that arrives in laughter (unintentional). & during an intensifying drum sequence, the indifferent commentary: *Strawberry & vanilla can be extracted from a beaver's backside.*

Shazam didn't quite catch that & neither did I, wondering still—I mean now, much later, as I sit here or stand up to share this with you & with everyone—where is the emoji for the Liger: the cross-breed between a lion & a tiger, an animal berated in the 3-D film for the fact of its hybridity & I've never felt so hated; I've never felt a beaver's backside or a stranger's cheese puff with my nose & I feel as though I've never felt anything, or nothing but shame at never having been read my rights.

It aches like a cavity. I thought about calling my dentist. I thought about calling this poem White People Who Mean Well. Sometimes I wonder what it all means. In this scenario "it" is everything.

I got these tickets from the same kind reader who sent me tickets to the MoMA in *Death of Art*. Like a vampire, I only go to museums when I'm invited in.

I don't normally wear spandex to class but I was running. I don't normal-
ly wear spandex to class but I was running late.

Are we all on the same page? (Look down & toward the margins.)

"You read Marx better than anyone," he said, with his hand on my shoul-
der. "Including Marcuse."

It's a common situation where the captions are so much more interesting
than the artwork exhibited & still, so much inside of me I'd like to show
you. (I'm only quiet on the outside.) & this project is expanding to such
great lengths; it's increasing & growing with such inclusiveness & so am
I. & so I am

The child of two immigrants after all, two people who learned to live by
mirroring the behavior of others, & imagining the possibilities of some-
thing *greater*. & this work has to be greater than the last one; it has to be
bigger, it has to be more bombastic & electric & expansive, it has to be
expanding too fast, too far (it's good to lose control, to get out of hand,
to get lost, to give up, which is another way of saying *to surrender*, to bow
down to it, to better become it & to become it better; I sometimes feel as
if these words & feelings will be mine forever).

The more & more interested I get the more & more I have to write about
the more & more I write about the more & more interested I get.

If you're wondering what I haven't done yet, chances are I've done it.

Not only for pleasure but for the need to do it that I do it, by wish I
might & by which I might re-claim my hybrid being tonight, & the day
before, & all the days I had ever lived in which I didn't know or had no
way of knowing there was something inside of me that was capable
of coming out when I'd felt most silenced, most othered or alone. My
online profile says *Halfies do it twice as good* & whether or not you know it

now you know it's true.

At the Biennial, & everywhere else, everyone is invited to participate, to consider our own position or role, to think about the transitional space of an elevator as a metaphor for other social spaces that are at once public & private, to inquire about the difference between action & gesture & how each might appear suspended in a state of anxiety & alarm. & of course we insist we insist we insist we insist to take pictures. Some say this is the flesh returning back to the world like slices of bologna, which curl up, fold in or on to itself, a bologna which is endeavoring toward masturbation or autoeroticism, a theorized assault on genetic engineering & biotechnology & imperialist exploitation; repulsive but perhaps inevitable. A meat to chew on or choke on; a meat to make love with or to. None of it means anything unless it means too much, & it does, & the situation involves a jar of petroleum jelly, the artist as a kind of copying machine, a very long line, an installation designed to disorient, a spinning video projection with out-of-synch audio (intentional), a wilting voice-over, the window of a moving car, a window into a room I should have never been in, we should have never walked through, a place I can only recall by re-writing it, on the condition of refusing to forget one's own origins. Didn't you know.

In England, pharmacists re-fill scripts with a stamp that says, *The mixture as before.*

Sixteen Hours In Capri (#ThrowbackThursday)

Waitlists pay off & bear fruit, my instructor says. I've been waiting for my canonization since before I was born, I want to tell him, but he wasn't asking. I keep planting my seed & digging deep, watching what flowers, from the outside with my hands on the rusted metal or how it feels on my palm. This is a waitlist you can only get off when you get in. The gates are closed, in the old swim club tradition, & someone has thrown away the key. I've read about the difference between the saint & the hysteric, & the similarity of the artist. I've read the Catholic Church makes a very sharp distinction between a hysteric & a saint. I've read the same thing holds true in the art world & I quote, *There is the sensitiveness of the hysteric which has all the appearance of creation, but actual creation has an individual force which is an entirely different thing.*

Not long ago there was a long story. I still haven't watched till the end or to know how it does.

The question is how many Godard films can one watch after a dinner of pasta & eggs before one falls asleep? Thirty-five minutes of *Le Mépris* & now we are talking from the today of tomorrow, which is when I arise, the view of Capri half-held on my screen when I look up & adjust my eyes, like a postcard, or the memory I hold within me from 2008 or 2011, I forget which or when, sixteen hours to mimic the thirty-five minutes spent watching a film about re-making *The Odyssey*, the second of the great Greek epics which ushered in long-form storytelling & so much else, if I only knew what, & to marvel at the difference, the difference or what is the difference between Antonioni & Godard; the difference is one uses silence & the other puts one to sleep.

(He had the habit of engraving stall doors, trees, table tops with his name, & a date that was ten years or so before the date in which he was committing the action. In this way he could be in two places or every place at the same time, & he was able to give off the impression that he was much older, or had lived much longer & lived much fuller—the impression that he had *been around*.)

To be around but also to be always half inside & half outside.

Meanwhile, a husband & wife argue relentlessly inside their penthouse apartment, taking turns pouting on a bright red couch, taking turns taking baths, in & out of white robes, in & out of rooms filled with paintings & windows, in & out of black wigs & gray bowler hats. Over neatly-arranged beds & love seats. Ascending & descending stairs as a manner of narrative staging. A windowsill frames the silhouette of in-fidelity, but before I tell about the guests & the extras on set, I must tell what I saw. You can always tell a picture that is finished over a picture that is still in process, or one being produced, because of the absence of a frame. In quick collage cuts, the husband & wife exchange memories, perspectives of scenes shot at some other time, in the past or somehow later, but from the other's eyes, with a view of their own selves speaking. They call this reverse angles, & they were taking it in with thin strides toward tomorrow, automatic, like wading in the Gulf of Naples with no trunks & no desire for anything but a thigh to keep from drowning. We were puzzled; we had seen so much strangeness we did not know why these two were any stranger.

(He had at this time made the habit of speaking to people with his fly un-zipped, so as to see if they were looking; so as to see if they would look.)

Looking can be a form of silence.

The camera volleys from one side of the table to the other, from one face & one voice to the one opposite it, like a tennis match. I look up, as I am checking the mail, elsewhere, on my way out the door or on my way in, to see an advertisement, or warning: *Baby isn't a rattle (don't shake)* on the black & white facsimile of a newspaper clipping with the date removed. *Baby isn't a rattle (don't shake)*, which sounds, also, like a song from my childhood, or before my childhood, inevitable nostalgia reced-ing again under my eyelids & taking over the mood of the scene. Mood. Such a hard thing to keep hold of or to hold on to; such a hard thing & one worth shaking. A ghost at noon. Reminding one of Capri or Capri on Google Images after searching so diligently, a shimmering coastline curving higher, so many beautiful jagged rocks & a deep, delicious blue beneath, cutting up the soft sky in pixels.

Gertrude Stein, writing a biography of herself in the voice of Alice B. Toklas, relates the true mark of success in the world of art & letters, an indication that they were all beginning to be known after so many years of obscurity, of peddling, of writing diaries & exhibiting in private, with a sigh & a smile, remarking or relating or re-enacting in the voice of so many others how life has changed to all who now have cooks who can make a soufflé. A soufflé or a cook who can make one for you is the closest thing to canonization one can ever have, unless one happens to have a dairy allergy.

& then what? & then what? & then what?

All I remember was the feeling of the mustache, my instructor says, speaking in the voice of someone who's sat on the lap of Alice B. Toklas, a friend of his whose name he won't volunteer today. I'd rather let it

hang, without a frame. The urgency of your stubble on my mouth &
how it refuses simply to sit there, I sketch, as he speaks, as he shares this
memory of another. But to show that was to show too much.

The first thing you see when you step off the Avenue N stop on the F
train are rows & rows of gravestones, disappearing into the distance, a
panorama of posterity. When asked what my secret is, to any semblance
of success I've had in life, I answer, "I think always of my death." Living
a block from a cemetery keeps me vigilant. The gates are always open &
one can just walk in, or wander.

I tell this story for what
It is worth

A Place I've Only Ever Been In Poems

The Other Is Typing These Notes

In the last chapter, you learned to open and close.

The bus is 41 minutes late.

I don't mind waiting or rather I only ever mind waiting, because it allows me to think about things without having to decide. I know the bus should have been here. I know I should have been on the bus. I know I should have been midway to Manhattan by now. I know I should have been moved, or moving. None of those things are true, and so their non-truth or the possibility of them becoming true makes them beautiful.

And I keep waiting.

The headline I'm looking at as I empty myself in the bathroom of Café Luluc says

COMEY TELLS HOW
TRUMP PERSISTED
IN PLEAS TO FBI

And in smaller type, below that: *Ex-Director to Give Senate Panel Account of Pressure to 'Lift the Cloud'*

I consider the Cloud and whether it's possible to apply pressure to it; I consider whether it's possible to lift the Cloud or just to bow down to it, to rest our heads on it, to disappear in it.

What would it mean to lift the Cloud and how? I flush the toilet and snap a photo for a time to come.

What I always want is possibility, not possession.

I wait. A stranger passes.

She passes but then stops as I sit on a brick pedestal meant for décor. That means it's meant to be looked at not laid on or over. I lift my head to look at the clouds, and to count them.

She hands me a slip of paper, without instruction.

No, no thanks, I say, reaching out my arm but she's already past me again. And this time she won't look back.

Let's say I am an anonymous admirer

An admirer writes in the comments section below a photo I've just posted.

They write it in all-caps but I won't pretend to preserve this aspect, since it hurts my eyes.

Let's say I am an anonymous admirer, they write, but their message and their avatar and their user name are all visible to everyone. Anonymity under global visibility, I think, as I screenshot the comment and think about how to disclose it further, put it somewhere else and pass it on. Like a secret announcing itself to the world: *I am a secret*. Does the power of the secret grow through its own impulse or inevitability to be revealed? Sometimes completion or consummation means self-immolation. Or surrender.

The slip of paper could be a secret, I think, as I unfold it.

Hand-written letters in blue ink show a website with the description or explanation marked *(videos)*, in parentheses, just like that. *Increase wisdom* is written below the address, and below that: *To help to understand history and how to cultivate. Now and for the future.*

While I'm walking through campus, preparing to speak on a panel about literary publishing and diversity, another panelist points out things as we walk past them, pretending or performing or explaining that the stones and spires were splashed with acid, to give the effect of age. Collegiate gothic. An outdoor architecture museum in which we walk in circles. It's 216-feet tall, he says, pointing to a tower, one foot for every year since the university's founding. He's been here before. It was a common trend among American campuses, he says, as we walk past a sign stating IN MEMORY OF THE MEN OF YALE. The newer the campus, the older it looks. Or looked. Now the stones and granite are half a century old anyway, I think. A win-win, I think, when you bet on timeworn, because time always wins.

People like looking at old things, or things that look old; it increases one's chances of receiving aid by individuals, organizations, or the state. People like to be in the company of oblivion, to see the decay and feel it with our own hands. I wonder why it doesn't work the same for people.

I wonder who will look at me when I'm old, a face waxed with the acid of age, sunken in or shorn.

The more radical thing would have been for Yale's design team to try to always make the campus look *new*. Something the Internet has already accomplished, or at least manufactured. Eternal now-ness while the waste that keeps the hardware working is hidden away, indiscernible or *clouded*.

People will believe anything anyway, I think, as I walk over another stone, someone's name engraved under my sneakers.

Even if the last moment occurred in the past, I would have still written it into the present.

I unfold the slip and turn it over.

Typed-out letters reveal a handout from some course about computers. Page 72. *Teach yourself ... Access for Windows 95* reads the header. Times New Roman, which seems so outdated today. The handout's been cut to form the slip I've been given so I have to fill in the rest. I have to re-teach myself.

The person on our panel, the one who is my friend or who says he is, tells me the next day, or tomorrow, or today, that I have a problem with sucking everything up.

We're eating pancakes. He isn't talking about hunger, or my appetite. Or maybe that's just it.

He says I have a tendency to talk too much, to fill the room, to feed off everyone, to soak up all the attention, to suck everything up.

I am a vampire, I think. Even if I didn't know it before or if I only knew it in my worst moments; my bad dreams. Even with my tan, my warm blood, my warm skin. Even with my desire for my own reflection, my own face staring back at me when I think to look. I am a vampire.

But I don't say this. I only nod.

And wonder how long he's known.

When I'm wearing heels at events, my feet feel like they're sitting in pools of blood

Elizabeth Olson told Catherine Kovesi in an essay called "Brought to Heel? ..." in the fashion journal *Vestoj* (no. 6, Autumn 2015).

When did we stop behaving as consumers and start to care more about collecting? It's all about quantity. The point is only to acquire things or make them yourself; leave traces that will never be looked at. Lost and found and lived for the purpose of stockpiling data, files, information. Artifactual aura without the object.

Release the tapes

In what places has my camera gone and what did it do there?

Outside the lecture hall where our panel is occurring, if you were outside or in the hallway instead of listening while looking, or taking notes, you'd see a creased sign scotch-taped to an orphaned desk near the stairwell in Harkness Hall.

UNIVERSAL WASTE
USED ELECTRONICS
Please tape this page to waste items to ensure that only items
for recycling are removed.
Yale Environmental Health & Safety

I don't know what keeps me going except for a general lament, which is not anything like regret. It allows me to account for things; it makes me accountable.

My lament tells me how much I've wasted, even now, how much love has gone unreturned or uncultivated or overlooked. The love I've only sucked dry. How much I've lost. And not

Everything returns. Not everything returns. Not everything

Returns. If the last book was about falling in love, this one is about the moment of its rupture.

How long have you been waiting for it?

Fold it back, place it in my pocket as I resume, that living death between any two points, even if I am only waiting to come.

Take it out, which demands the use of my free hand. (The other is typing these notes.) The first line on the back, after the page number and the header, is the same self-reference to what we just undertook or endeavored toward; how we began this exercise. *In the last chapter, you learned to open and close.* I wonder if this makes it necessary to go again. Or to finally begin trying. Or: to open myself up without having to close.

A Place I've Only Ever Been In Poems (notes on hybridity, June 3, 2017)

The longer I wait the more
You love me the longer
I love you the more
My life unravels

I know I'm coming to an end, even though you've only just got here. (I'm on my way, wait for me a little longer.)

What does it mean to be jealous of a day, & all the days one
                                        Will never
have? An excuse to revise the original, the true, the authentic, the what really happened
                                        Or did it after
I asked for another's hand?

Besides something to write about & was all it was
                                        To write about it?

Asked to illustrate an object I begin by sketching your umbrella, or your wish for it.

(In my version of the scene, it's been raining all day.)

Think of your work as a set piece or a studio for shooting, & decide where to stage each subject & situation, how far to position yourself, when to zoom in, & how. Next, I will show you what's outside the frame.

Driving at high speeds in a compact car while listening to Duran Duran or Depeche Mode or something you've chosen, as a gift, to become the car, & the drive, & the music. What do we show & how can I show you what you haven't shown anyone. First thing I do, I tell a crowd who's come to watch, & write, & listen, is look

For a way in. Bedbugs are on everyone's minds or in everyone's minds. Don't worry, a student assures me, there's none in this room.

Another says she's looking for peaches since I was just eating one. It's almost, I think, like I implanted the peach in your mind. Images can only do so much, sometimes I want words. Sometimes I demand a peach. A desire to take it out of my mouth at will.

What's the difference between intimacy & invasiveness. What's the difference between instructions & intimations intimations & demands.

I am suggesting you play the game. But I am not making you or making you

In my own image. I am only asking to lend me your time & your willingness for pleasure, or your willingness to please me. Touching & feeling feeling & being felt are not the same. Truth

Be told, whenever I am told to speak, or whenever I am asked a question, my first reaction is fear. Expectations are high, a student says, relating her anxiety about a dinner party she has yet to prepare.

In another version of this text, everyone is inviting me to Otto's, a place

I've only ever been in poems, so many poets writing about the site of performance & inviting me to have a look. What is most inviting about the hybrid text, I suggest, is how much pleasure one might get from being asked to re-direct their gaze. I mean to turn yours inward. & still

Whether or not you have me in flesh or form you have me.

This not this; this or this; or this & also this. Every time a line breaks I ache

   To know more. A taste

Older than water. My back giving out reminds me of what's in your future, a student tells me, & when he says you he means me, the way I often forget who I am when I write & when it's good when I read. Your book reminds me of what's in my future, another tells me, title divided by this composition so one sees only one
                        Word. I am on the other side of the sword, she says, relating her fears about facts & truth, the glorification of hate.

(We are asking ourselves the same questions.)

What's at the very bottom, what's behind it, what's underneath it all? What's underneath women are otherwise unmentionables, a video series meant to remove fabrics & layers, uncovering how we imagine increasingly formulaic ideals of female bodies. You can't find anything like that about men, a man says. He wants to know why. Masculinity has only ever been a finite model, I think. No one cares to use any imagination about what makes a man. Underneath a final copy
                        Is a long history of digressions & false starts, I read from a Twitter feed attached to the hand-held version of this print-out. Everything is visible at all times if you take the time to look. My role is to show the digressions & false starts, & then to start over.

In another version of this text, I am envisioning the daughter I don't have. Maybe because I'm the only one here who doesn't have one or maybe because I like always to envision all the things I don't have. Naturally this breeds

A healthy sort of desperation & yearning. A way of looking at the world through inversion, I say. Like wishing all the time for the things you wouldn't want in the secret hopes of getting their opposite. Try, for instance, running toward your own disappearance.

Enna is Anne backwards, I remember to write down. *How I find my daughter online.*

A place is better whenever
I'm waiting for someone

Even if it's my imaginary daughter, or the one who would be her mother. I like to watch a scene right before it develops, when the extras are still getting into place & the props are haphazardly arranged. Every face shows something when it knows no one is watching, unbeknownst to the one being watched. Looking from one to the other, one to the other, like an encounter at the eye doctor, sitting aboard a stool; the image track switches & so does the sound, the letters get smaller, get larger, get bolder, move or melt, & yet it's all the same or isn't it, or isn't it, or isn't it … like a game of spot the difference in which there is no difference, only the shifting of prisms, only the play of light or the way the sun dances through leaves.

A train whistles by. I like to imagine myself being carried away. The rush of not knowing where we're going or in what direction makes this easier. Lately I find myself

Asking the same question

The way I used to kiss
Lips, nose, & above the eyes
In that order do
You think it's too
Late for that?

Before Wednesday of last week, "gay panic" was a legal excuse for alleged murderers in Illinois to defend their actions in court by arguing that their victim's sexual orientation "triggered" their crime. Tell everyone on this train I love them, Taliesin Myrddin Namkai-Meche told the passenger crouching beside his face, before he died of wounds inflicted by a white supremacist. He prefers "killer graphics" like pictures, videos, & charts, the directors of the CIA & the National Intelligence said, describing President Trump's refusal to read briefings at meetings. Please take a moment

To locate the exits
In the front
& the rear
There are limits

I say, by way of instruction. After the introductions & the half-held anxiety or apprehension & the memory of bedbugs brought in before class began. There are limits, I say again. But at the moment I am using none.

Asked to write down "three or four things I know to be true"—I include myself, I always include myself—I start by writing down: *I considered moving to Tarrytown the moment I drove through it.*

I've always made brash decisions, or acted *on the fly.*

That was Number Two.

I used to have a fear of flying, especially landing & taking off. The in-between, the halfway hovering amid cloud & ground, life & death, the easy part. Silence, sky, gravity. Cool blue eternity. The exaggerated, conditioned breeze. Everyone on hold, & waiting for the other side or from the other side. When everything is *up in the air,* what else to do but give yourself up to it.

My Fair Lady (1993)

Everywhere & everywhere
I haven't been, I've had to
Tell myself in passing
Make moments, not money
I am tempted to say this

                  Definitely did not happen during intermission
of *My Fair Lady* in 1993. I am tempted to say there was a period of my
life where I stopped counting footsteps & started to subtract them from
the parabola of my encounters

Elsewhere I've kept dedicated records of even the things I should have done

Glances on the street & faces I still follow from afar

                  Have you or have you not
tried printing out hard copies of the Internet

I am tempted to say
What I want to say
Every time someone asks
If this much, why not more?

I am tempted to say this writing takes the form of a cosmetic pill that you
consume, fragrance excreting through the skin's surface, redefining the
particular vibe you've likely outlasted in the years since birth remember

Make moments, not money & then begin counting
The ways the way
Water counts stones

This wall features proposals, suggestions & ideas
For restricting waste & refuse & for inventing
New forms of production & consumption

Write yours in the notebook provided

Writes yours in the space between words

Write yours as you wait for my text & wait

To hit SEND
Must be willing
To die for me on my online
Dating about me

I am just another American
Falling asleep
To the television I am tempted
To say

What ever happened to clipart, the careful quiet before a wish, to walk
into a party without knowing anyone & not know anyone

Come to think of it to think of it
I come without having to
Do anything but make you

In my own image

What does your face say when your face says nothing?

Return to the moment after the moment
Has been erased

Return to loneliness what
An uncommon gift

Self-Surveillance

I would be sitting across from my lover, I would be sitting across from
someone whom I used to love, I would be loving someone else, I would
be holding hands with my lover, I would be walking hand in hand over
the Lover's Bridge, along the Seine & watching the haze accumulate over
the water under the shadow of the Louvre, watching the bicyclists & the
roller skaters & the skates themselves, as if the legs had walked off the
set or as if the skates had a soul of their own. I would watch the stage-
hands shift scenery, without applause. I would be sitting here, across
from you as you describe your day. I wouldn't say much. I would be told
I should take more risks. It is I who am telling myself. I would be told
& it is the telling above all that matters. Think everybody think, I would
always want to add parenthetically. I would be planning a party. Guests
would already be arriving by the time I got home. The way food shows
up for every season, & now the calendar would say fall. I would come
bearing candy corn & an umbrella. We wouldn't have had rain in ten days.
Is that an emotional truth? I would think but I wouldn't think to ask. The
rituals of burial would be so familiar they would no longer be terrifying.
I would still worry about all the old women in my life. My mother my
aunt my dog. Maybe it's because I never had a grandmother after I turned
twelve. I would question if, in the photograph, you are turning toward
me, or if you are turning away. I would want to ask you out, to make
you dinner, to share my favorite meal. In this & all scenarios, I would

be having my cake & I would be eating it too. I would make a list of all the things to say & questions to ask. I would call at a time I think no one will answer. All of our unbearable silence. I would sit still so I could better pay attention. Falling in love is the only fun part. I would answer any question you asked of me. I would answer for myself, all the things I've done or haven't. It's been more than two years since I've bled. For instance. What would it mean to be forced to let something out? The joy of delivery has kept me inside all day. When people stopped sharing so much personal info on their social networks, social networks responded by introducing an algorithm into their newsfeeds. The name for this phenomenon would be called context collapse. From com + labi, to fall, to slide. More at sleep. Other responses would include the opportunity to Go Live, & color-coding one's thoughts. I would be receiving Top Stories without even having to ask. Vegas killer's girlfriend: He was 'a kind, quiet, caring man.' Republicans open to banning 'bump stocks' used in massacre. Vampire breast lifts are the new beauty fad. I would like to ask you to guess which Top Story interests me most. She expected to get high but only, she says, a little bit high. This is in response to my question about what you would be doing if you weren't doing what you are doing right now. Another way of phrasing this would become What's on your mind? I wouldn't have to check myself, because everyone already is watching. I would cite quantitative methods, scholarly research, comparative analysis, my Instagram. Couples who are childless, I would say, live on average ten years less. I am always afraid I'll die before the next line. I don't want to explain why. If I thought to look back at her face I would see that she was crying. One thing which excites me, in reading this now, is not knowing who is speaking to whom, of who speaks & who listens. The intimacy of anonymous encounters, even in public, comes from the certain uncertainty of not knowing if I'm still me, or who else I've become. Of who else is becoming me, & how. Has it ever happened that you would look at an old journal or message thread & not recognize the one writing the notes? I've forgotten to put down all the happy ones.

exit theme

I want to appear before
you behind
          you over & above
          you I want to
appear through
          you haltingly
slipping in
          you & out of
    slow

focus   materializing
in mere parts   focal
points of flesh   making
you wait like
Internet porn from 2003   understanding without having
to understand that waiting   & the wait was always
better   & will always be
                    raised   blown

      screen   grab
alt shortcut
         exit softly

I make husbands

Charlie Alexandra Noble writes in About Me on her Facebook, which is fake, or at least she is. They are. Which pronoun do cyborgs take when they become mainstreamed into everyday life is a question I keep considering when I am considering

How to reply <3 <3 <3 I'm looking for a life partner for I make husbands I anybody want to click here >> [REDACTED]

Print that on a coffee cup that is four-feet tall, R says, after I send him a screenshot of Charlie's smiling face, her crop-topped black tee emblazoned with the self-referential words: BLACK. (The letters are written in rainbow gradient). It's all very postmodern or post-postmodern or maybe it's premodern. I can't decide which unless it's all of them. It's exhilarating to not know whether we are living before history or after it and if so, what comes next.

I'm telling you, I type back. We need to re-appropriate all of this. Make it a functional/interactive exhibit where you walk into a space and everything (the windows, the wallpaper, the tiled floors, the kitchen table, the coasters and the coffee mugs, etc.) are all porn requests.

Does Pres. Trump have recordings of conversations with James Comey? my screen is asking. He will have an announcement "shortly" spills the teaser-text that runs like a header over our rolling conversation.

Living in the Internet, R types back. Rad to have a VR version of sex via trolling. Oversized stuffed animals with words printed on their sides like a butcher's chart for meat cuts.

Yeah. I place my hand under my shirt and begin to feel my belly, waiting for a sound or sign. But I'm less interested in VR than RL, I type back, as I turn my head and hit the frown of an oiled, bald man beside CAREERS FOR THE FUTURE! and beside that, a half-formed brunette (her other half chopped off to make room for a window to look through). To their right, a smiling blond, showing teeth, her arm around a skeleton and the italicized title *Medical Assistant*. Call 24/7, the ad suggests, or demands. The best thing about this idea is that it makes explicit the material nature of the Internet which we never consider. For the first(?) time, people will be forced to encounter the ads and invasive marketing that we get hit with on the normalizing almost unconscious everyday level

On our screens. We need to find a space is all, I add. And then we begin collecting.

We need a rich young backer from the digital world, R types back.

Yeah, I return, excitement level ebbing at the thought of knowing any-one with money, or anyone who would like to give me theirs. Let's keep thinking through this. Generate buzz by taking photos of certain ar-rangements in the space and pushing it on Instagram and Twitter. The Internet becomes materialized on objects and then goes back into the digital rabbit hole.

The best way to get in or out, R returns.

Nancy Pelosi Says Donald Trump Isn't Sleeping Enough

He needs to bring himself "to a place where the synapses are working," she said, in an article I'm reading as I pass U but before I reach X, and the smell of Brighton that comes right after. Every book I write seems to end in the sea.

Lorianne Skyler Hare's tattoo says Karla, and there's a crown above the "a" on the forearm, right before the elbow. Evelyn McBride wants to know if these are just pics, imagine what we should do with it? Besides click here now. It's a stroll through our moment via literature. It's a train ride through experience, except you can get off anywhere. Get on. I'd like to merge multiple voices and tones, R says. I'd like to insert another conversation on another conversation. I'd like to paint with an audible vocabulary. Purple eggplant. Squirt gun. Dollar bill. Lipstick. It's a better visual than the visual emoji. Ejaculation is affirmation of life, J texts me, by accident or coincidence. Like smoking a cigarette. That's why people want so much

To see the money shot. The word renders a mental picture while the image is often just the image. We are asking to open up the paragraph into the city. We are asking to spare some change. Smell of skin, of waves and breeze. There must be a word for this. Next stop Stillwell. I am feeling it in my throat just now.

2:57PM
Thursday, June 8, 2017

Acknowledgements

Who can I possibly single out to express my gratitude, gratefulness, and the unreturnable debt I owe all of you?

In the same way that books became my best friend as a child, in the same way that seeing myself in the voice of another while reading can still make my insides melt and the world split open, it is life-affirming to realize that through such a solitary endeavor, one can experience so much contact and emotional and intellectual resonance from others, the people I love and admire.

And I admire you.

Much of this book, and its body double, was written under the instruction and inspiration of Wayne Koestenbaum, Meena Alexander, Robert Reid-Pharr, Siraj Ahmed, Steven Kruger, Mark McBeth, and Feisal Mohamed, during my first two years in the PhD program at the CUNY Graduate Center. I am grateful for the energy and insight afforded to me by my students at Baruch College and Pace University—I teach them the little I know and learn from them to live again—and from my classmates, especially the MAGNET cohort organized by the Office of Educational Opportunity & Diversity Programs led by Herman Bennett and Rebecca Mlynarczyk; these ongoing and ever-persistent conversations have each helped stimulate so many of my own working notes, much of which I've enacted within a field I call Post Internet studies. I am also thankful to the editors of *At Large Magazine*, especially Erik Rasmussen and Randall

Mesdon, for their assignments, and the inclination to go along for the ride. Olya Petrova Jackson's Ab[Screenwear] collaboration with director Nadia Bedzhanova, and their film adaptation of "This body's long (& I'm still loading)" allowed me to glimpse my work through a new screen, which taught me so much about where this book was heading, or where it still cruises. Continual dialogue with other writers and thinkers, including Rockwell Harwood, Giancarlo Lombardi, Michael Kazepis, Marianne Madoré, Edwin Grimsley, Priscilla Bustamante, Fernando Sdrigotti, Jonathan Marcantoni, Jennifer Maritza McCauley, Lauren Hilger, Stu Watson, and William Lessard (B, or W?) challenged and inspired me. The publication of this book in its exuberant forms was shepherded into this world by Andrew H. Sullivan, and a whole host of excellent people at C&R Press. I would not be where I am, writing this to you, if not for the love and guidance of my parents, Zosia and Juan, and a long list of family and friends, including John Campanioni and Lillian Wu.

In the last book I ripped off my face. In this one I rip off yours, since we both want nothing less than to destroy the book; to re-make a static text into a porous and permeable page, passages like hyperlinks, hyperlinks like the clouds that surround and enrapture us, holding their gaze as we stop to stare. Each of us held in a reality that is increasingly movable.

Museums interest me because they are dead yet simultaneously promise a persistence of life. The boundary between decay and eternity is so small, compact enough to fit in our pockets. What does it mean to be on permanent display in 2018? Modernity demands a constant accumulation of photographs. Taking photographs gives you something to do; it means that you no longer have to be idle, but it also dictates ownership. What can be imagined can be consumed and what can be consumed can be imagined. I want, I want, I want … haven't we all turned into tourists of our own lives?

The omnipresence of our camera gaze has also replaced the eye of God. John Berger, writing in "Uses of Photography" forty years ago connected the decline of religion with the rise of photography. But he was writing in 1978, a time when photography was still a ritual, still something you had to hold in your hands or remove from your pouch or pocket. Today the act of taking a photograph is a reflex, and we no longer require a camera to hold. *The camera is us.* We have become so fully integrated into the machine as to become its greatest development: a living snapshot, through which memories are made *before* they become experienced; experiences having been reduced to a continuous roll of film, paused for changeover when we close our eyes to rest. But even rest—dreams—are reframed through the technology we inhabit in our waking life, the memories of our body movements toward the future of its fantasies.

And underneath or within that movement is the judgment of our own blurry emotional reasoning. We pass judgment so that we may not pass unnoticed. To judge is a punishment and a privilege unto itself. To judge is also another kind of arrested development not unlike the processing of a moment into its duplicate, and we seem to always want to live a little longer, redeem what might have otherwise been abandoned, seize a sense of justice. But who are we saving other than ourselves?

A shutter on a camera controls the amount of light permitted to pass; this is also called *exposure time.* It freezes action and can also enhance the hazy effect of motion, passage, action. I worry about how polarized we've become as a people, how much more distant we will still become with every passing moment we ignore or fail to embrace difference and speak about it with singularity. The feeling of being different is universal because difference makes us universally human.

But to begin again. And to begin again from the beginning.

What does the tableau of fantasy offer us when mediated through the lenses of technology and pop culture? How do we balance the empowerment of playing with culture with the re-materialization of digital divides and inequalities in the offline world? The Internet's free and open ethos, its [spaceless] terrain allows labor exploitation to also remain unrecognizable as women and children—mining the coltan that makes the machines from which I write this—literally disappear, in death as in life. And yet the common misperception of an immaterial Internet might teach us something about our own reluctance to imagine a world without borders or nation-states or polities that begin and end in citizenship, which is its own disappearance.

How does the Internet foster activism and how does the Internet prevent its realization? Far too often, political struggle or the potential for it moves from a call to action to an object of enjoyment, a leisure activity whereby measures are contemplated and commented upon a great deal and hardly ever engaged with. I would only ask us to orient our activity toward reflecting on our position within these processes of production.

And to disrupt it. *11.11.15-*
8.27.18

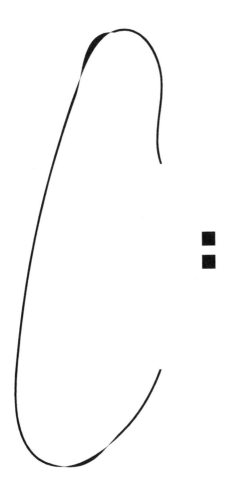

imagine to be looked at from the other side of the screen with one thumb close to almost an hour

In this way seeing and not seeing can coincide. Nothing happens in these films except everything

*"Did we act it are we dead ...
do we feel funny, are we dead"*

Someone has a foot fetish
& it isn't me

(Which is both
Tangential reaction &
Title of this poem)

I swear   I learn more about
Myself the more
I encounter

Myself in the most
Unpredictable places
Someone's floating

Background for instance
In an image on the Internet
Or an image of the Internet

My torso unfurls into slates
Of desktopped wallpaper
Against another's home

& so it is too
Easy to imagine
Myself containing multitudes

Sexuality as hypothesis
Sexuality as hypnosis

Gaining entry to the inner sanctums
Of one's machine with a literal face-lift
(In this scenario I am lifting my own face)

Television as global
Non-event   Every message
I receive between now & when

I began writing this as a global
Non-encounter   Promiscuity
As screen-grab   Cum shot

As severance package   The pull
Of tradition, to remake
My own mythology   A deep deep longing

To watch the Spanish language
Variety series of my youth
Rocking periodically periodically rocking

On the lap of A, or in A's arms
(The trouble or the true pleasure
Of memory & dreams & memory of dreams is always

In doubling one's experience)
I swear sometimes I can be
Baudrillard's imagination

Of someone laughing on the back
Of the set
Of the reality show

When the orgy is replaced
By Instagram   When Instagram is
Replaced by parts

Of bodies without a body
Part of any story
Of natural selection

Hashtag meatyfeet
Hashtag mensfootfetish
Hashtag soleworship

Knowing that
When technology eliminates any one
Thing in culture it comes back

As an experience
Of entertainment
& so it is not hard

To break open upon the cross-
Section of my feet, cropped & zoomed
To heighten the veins

Below the toes & before
The ankles, the faint cusp
Of fleshy calves grounded in place

In the photo below it, to the right
A tease of actual mannequin, to the left
My bandaged smile at a bar in Lourdes

Hawking my own copy
Of a book I by
Now know by heart

Still waiting to be cured, or to bathe
In the sacred grotto of my own
Lofty extinction

Server Leak

I tell students I know their writing is good if you're embarrassed to read it. A successful notebook, I say, produces shame

•

(After having achieved some notoriety as "the well-known Brooklyn autograph collector," B decides to take a trip to New England to collect the signatures of famous US literary & political figures ...)

•

What B is after, or was after, or is still after is the physical before
Or underneath the copy   Not the handwriting but the hand that writes

•

Karameh! Karameh! Karameh!

In the spring of 2011, staged mass demonstrations & protests in Syria centered around this cry for dignity

•

Meanwhile, a mother & a baby brown bear are taking up residence in someone's home in California. They have been granted asylum, the news anchor says, as I look up from the treadmill, & toward the faces of the brown bears

•

There is something I want to say about hospitality but I'm not sure what, or how to situate a feeling into fact, I mean words, I mean the way they move in a long straight line down the page or do they

•

In the 2004 film *Private*, the Israeli army occupies a Palestinian family's home, confining the family to a few rooms downstairs in the daytime & a single room at night. The Israeli soldiers become more than just a guest, & certainly not one who liberates their host from their host's own captivity, as D would have wanted, or said he wanted, or wanted without saying

•

What would it mean to take up meaning in a system without ow(n)ing residency to it?

•

The host becomes the hostage, the guest becomes the host, a reversibility revealed by the word's roots from Late Latin *hostis*, from stranger, enemy—more at *guest*. I can remember—if I try, if I close my eyes, if I stay still, which is not the same as staying silent—the sacrificial rite of the Eucharist, & how the host is one that receives but also one that is received. A host can also be a network, the manager that administers a database or a computer that controls communications within a server. To be a host means to manage or negotiate an inevitable power dynamic. & then again—the host becomes something ingested, taken in, turned into something else. This transubstantiation is the answer—the flesh made word—turned into a question: the refugee as *calling into question* the relationship of the individual to the state

•

Is the secret something that shouldn't be shared or something that *can't*? Is the secret something which remains unspoken or ineffable? & if the secret is something that can only be felt, what's the point of holding it in?

•

Everything that can be felt should be felt by another, I always think, or feel, or know without having to say

•

Unlike freedom, A says, dignity isn't sexy. Dignity can't be packaged & marketed; dignity can't be used to legitimate mass murder or debilitation on a global scale, the way freedom is; the way freedom does. & it was true, too, for the ancients, who believed that dignity had no place in the bedroom; the ancients for whom dignity meant self-defense—the protection or preservation of an external image that can't be maintained in extreme situations, like the act of love, or fucking. *Dignity isn't sexy*

•

The real person leaks out from the model, along with so much else

•

Law of probability, or permeability: nothing is wasted, not even waste. Acting by any other name is writing, except when you're only acting, which is the fakest form of non-fiction. What a sublime feeling to reach out & feel nothing, except for the knowledge of the framing; the actuality or inevitability of the mask as it's being fit to form

•

It took me all these years to realize a photograph of death does not present its aftermath but is in fact its precursor

•

A, who remains anonymous, produces disruptive-documentary films which respond to the challenge of representing dignity for the Syrian person, providing alternatives to a cycle of dehumanization; the representations of the refugee that focus on dead & disfigured bodies, & which present audiences an economy of desire that translates, always, into a desiring economy

•

I like pop better than anything because it doesn't pretend to represent anything outside of itself. What I want is not the permanence inside naming but to disappear across the temporary

•

But I don't want to be a refugee, M screams, about ten minutes into *Private*, as his wife begs him to abandon their home. Being a refugee, M wails, means not being

•

A few months after the brown bear encounter or incident or episode— everything that exists exists a second time on television—it was revealed that during the last three months of 2017, the US government lost 1,500 immigrant children. Lost or disappeared—what's the difference or is there any between being here & being nowhere, or having nothing, or becoming nobody if one can become anything in this life other than death

•

Representations of atrocity do not remain in the confines of our screens or the border of a frame but rematerialize in real, physical, bodily violence

•

The only human right, according to my student, is the right to experience

•

Everything I forgot I'll remember in another book

•

The moment I forget myself is the moment you can remember me

•

The first one
To Adorno
Always wins   Says

A professor
I've never pictured
Naked   Waiting

For global warming
Is like waiting for everyone
To become a refugee

That is to say
To become
What we were

Born to be   Looking
Into the sky isn't a yearning
To be somewhere else but to be someone

You aren't   The person
You can only imagine
On the other side

•

F thought that every intellectual gain requires a loss in sexual potential, not thinking that thinking & feeling or intellect & sex are two sides of the same coin I am holding or being held by as I write this; as I leak out & allow you to think of me or think for me. It is past time we switched places

The author thanks the editors and readers of the following publications, in which portions of this book, sometimes in different versions, appeared:

3:AM Magazine: "Ghost in the Machine" and "Art Is For Necrophiliacs"

A VOID, volume 1: "Body Swap At the Airport" and "Transformation Tuesday"

Abridged, 0-45: Why Is It Always December?: "Sex for trash"

Ambit, issue 225: "Ash Wednesday"

At Large Magazine, volume 8: "You and 753 other people" and "How Do I Look?"

Civil Coping Mechanism's #finalpoems (May 31, 2016): "Send Help" and "Installation in progress"

Connotation Press, September 2016: "the world is flat," "On Permanent Display," "This body's long (& I'm still loading)," "shutter/speed," and "A handclap at the base of the temple"

Corium Magazine, issue 20: "Let's hope there's a way to do this"

Cosmonauts Avenue, January 2018: "Manufactured Pleasures"

DIAGRAM, issue 16.5: "ai," "Love You," "esp," "am," and "Blue van"

Dostoyevsky Wannabe's *Brooklyn* anthology: "I call it post Internet," "exit theme" and parts of "Time Piles Up, Presses In & Flattens" (as "the Zero Years")

Entropy (August 25, 2016): "Hot Tips For Healthy Living"

Five2One, no. 16: "Intruder Gets Within Steps Of White House," "Innocent Teen Tricked & Used," "#bts (The Ten Things You Need To See In NYC Before You Die)," "The Ghost in the Mirror (The Beast in the Jungle)," and "#RelationshipGoals (Watch Taylor Swift's 'Wildest Dreams' Music Video)"

fluland (July 27, 2017): "final fantasy (body double)," "& also something that has nothing," and "My Fair Lady (1993)"

Funhouse Magazine (October 19, 2016): "Casual Encounters" and "I sit at the broken off"

Glass: A Journal of Poetry, November 16, 2016: "donald trump shakes"

Glittermob, issue 10: "Truckstop Fantasy Number One"

gorse, no. 7: "the Internet is for real" and "please rewind tape & place in protective sleeve"

Hartskill Review, volume 2, issue 3: "island kingdom" and "Book of Genesis"

Hobart: "Instructions in the event of an emergency" and "give us the runway & we will lift the world"

HVTN, issue 3.1: "I never see you before or after," "the only thing," and "Scheduled To Appear"

IC: Revista Científica de Información y Comunicación, volume 15: "Letters From Santiago"

London Journal of Fiction, volume 2: "Buffering"

Palimpsest, no. 8: "Missing Letters"

Paris Lit Up Magazine, no. 5: "See What Happens When These Naughty School Girls Stay After Class For Detention"

Petrichor, issue 3: "Proximity to the victim," "ways," "met," and "pass words"

Pithead Chapel, volume 5, issue 3: "We rented Roman Holiday"

Public Pool: "Send Help" and "Opening Shot"

Queen's Mob Teahouse (June 17, 2016): "drinking five dollar tap water at a club"

Quiet Lunch, book 4: "in the beginning was the word, & the word"

Reality Beach, issue 3: "I arrive as I always do"

Redivider, issue 16.1: "Time Piles Up, Presses In & Flattens"

RHINO, 2017: "To be named"

Routledge's *Revisiting the Elegy in the Black Lives Matter Era*: "#IWokeUp-LikeThis or: The Latest In Space-Age #PostInternet Pajamas"

Stat®Rec (November 22, 2017): "I once had a dream so I packed up & split," "Private Moments in Moving Cars," and "this party's crowded (I want meat)"

Supernatural Studies, issue 4.2: Parts of "Art Is For Necrophiliacs," "Ghost in the Machine," and "How Do I Look?"

The Normal School, volume 10, issue 2: "Feed Me Diamonds" and "scores"

The Operating System's ExSpecPo Series: "Attempts to climb," "Transformation Tuesday (#SoFreshSoClean)," and "Wanna see all (I've covered up almost everything)"

The Opiate, volume 7: "We Hope You Enjoy the Selection"

Whitehot Magazine, "The Right To Carry" and "I went to the Whitney Biennial & all I got was this poem"

Yemassee, issue 23.2: "Privileged/Witness"

ARCHIVALS // PLAYLIST

"Be Right Back." *Black Mirror*, season 2, episode 1. Written by Charlie Brooker, directed by Owen Harris. Netflix, February 11, 2013. TV.

"Marilyn reading *Leaves of Grass* by Walt Whitman." Photograph, 1951. *Pinterest*. Web.

"San Junipero." *Black Mirror*, season 3, episode 4. Written by Charlie Brooker, directed by Owen Harris. Netflix, October 21, 2016. TV.

"Search." *Halt & Catch Fire*, season 4, episode 9. Written by Mark Lafferty, directed by Daisy von Scherler Mayer. AMC, October 14, 2017. TV.

Abounaddara, "Dignity has never been photographed." March, 24, 2017. Web.

À bout de souffle. Directed by Jean-Luc Godard, UGC, March 16, 1960. Film.

Agamben, Giorgio. *Remnants of Auschwitz: The Witness and the Archive.* Trans. Daniel Heller-Roazen. Zone Books, 1999. Print.

Alphaville. Directed by Jean-Luc Godard, Athos Films, May 6, 1965. Film.

Aristotle. "On Prophesying by Dreams." The Internet Classics Archive, 350 BCE. Web.

Baudrillard, Jean. *America*. Verso, 1988. Print.

Baudrillard, Jean. *Simulations*. Trans. Phil Beitchman, Paul Foss, and Paul Patton. Semiotext(e), 1983. Print.

Ball, Hugo. *Flight Out of Time*. Trans. Ann Raimes. University of California Press, 1996. Print.

Berger, John. *Ways of Seeing.* Penguin, 1973. Print.

Biddle, Sam. "Privacy Scandal Haunts Pokemon Go's CEO." *The Intercept,* August 9, 2016. Web.

Bieber, Justin. *Purpose.* RMBG and Def Jam, 2015. Album.

Boccaccio, Giovanni. *The Corbaccio.* Trans. Anthony K. Cassell. University of Illinois Press, 1975. Print.

Brainard, Joe. *I Remember.* Ed. Ron Padgett. Granary Books, 2001. Print.

Broken Social Scene. "The Sweetest Kill." *Forgiveness Rock Record,* Arts & Crafts, 2010. Song.

Burroughs, William S. *The Ticket that Exploded.* Grove Press, 1967. Print.

Caruth, Cathy. *Unclaimed Experience: Trauma, Narrative, and History.* The Johns Hopkins University Press, 1996. Print.

Chaucer, Geoffrey. *Dream Visions and Other Poems.* Ed. Kathryn L. Lynch. Norton Critical Editions, 2006. Print.

Christain, Annie. *Tall As You Are Tall Between Them.* C&R Press, 2016. Print.

Dadaglobe Reconstructed. June 12-September 18, 2016. The Museum of Modern Art, New York. Exhibition.

Derrida, Jacques and Dufourmantelle, Anne. *Of Hospitality.* Trans. Rachel Bowlby. Stanford University Press, 2000. Print.

Fanon, Frantz. *Black Skin, White Masks.* Trans. Charles Lam Markmann. Pluto Press, 1986. Print.

Foucault, Michel. "Dream, Imagination and Existence." *Dream and Existence.* Ed. Keith Hoeller. Review of Existential Psychology & Psychiatry, 1986. Print.

Freud, Sigmund. *The Interpretation of Dreams*. Trans. A. A. Brill. MacMillan, 1913. Print.

Glissant, Édouard. *Poetics of Relation*. Trans. Betsy Wing. University of Michigan, 1997. Print.

Hartmann, Ernest. *Dreams and Nightmares*. Perseus Publishing, 1998. Print.

Hobson, J. Allan. *The Dream Drugstore: Chemically Altered State of Consciousness*. MIT Press, 2001. Print.

HTRK. "Wet Dream." *Psychic 9-5 Club*, Ghostly International, 2014. Song.

Huet, Ellen. "Pushing the Boundaries of AI to Talk to the Dead." *Bloomberg*, October 20, 2016. Web.

INXS, "Need You Tonight." *Kick*, Atlantic and Mercury, 1987. Song.

James, Henry. *A Small Boy and Others*. Turtle Point Press, 2001. Print.

James, Henry. *The Ambassadors*. Penguin Classics, 2008. Print.

James, Henry. *The Portrait of a Lady*. Penguin Classics, 1986. Print.

James, Henry. *The Sacred Fount*. Grove Press, 1953. Print.

Joy Division. "Love Will Tear Us Apart." *Substance*, Factory, 1988. Song.

Jung, Carl. *Dreams*. Trans. R.F.C. Hull. Princeton University Press, 1974. Print.

Kabir, Ananya Jahanara. "Affect, Body, Place." *The Future of Trauma Theory: Contemporary Literary and Cultural Criticism*. Ed. Gert Buelens, Samuel Durrant, Robert Eaglestone. Routledge, 2013. Print.

Keats, John. *Complete Poems and Selected Letters*. Ed. Clarence DeWitt Thorpe. The Odyssey Press, 1935. Print.

Kruger, Steven F. *Dreaming in the Middle Ages*. Cambridge University Press, 1992. Print.

Lacan, Jacques. *Transference: The Seminar of Jacques Lacan, Book VIII*. Trans. Bruce Fink. Ed. Jacques-Alain Miller. Polity, 2001. Print.

Lauper, Cyndi. "The Goonies 'r' Good Enough." 1985. Music video.

Le Mépris. Directed by Jean-Luc Godard, Embassy Pictures, December 20, 1963. Film.

Lévinas, Emmanuel. *On Escape: De l'évasion (Cultural Memory in the Present)*. Trans. Jacques Rolland. Stanford University Press, 2003. Print.

Lynch, David (creator). *Twin Peaks*. ABC and Showtime, April 8, 1990-September 3, 2017. TV.

Masculin Féminin. Directed by Jean-Luc Godard, Columbia Films, March 22, 1966. Film.

MiBBs. "Freebass." *The Program*, RBC Records, 2014. Song.

Miller, Greg and Mekhennet, Souad. "Inside the surreal world of the Islamic State's propaganda machine." *The Washington Post*, November 20, 2015. Web.

New Order. "Touched by the Hand of God." *Brotherhood*, Factory, 1986. Song.

Palmer, Robert. "Simply Irresistible." 1988. Music video.

Phantogram. "Mouthful of Diamonds." *Eyelid Movies*, Barsuk, 2010. Song.

Plato. *Republic.* Trans. Benjamin Jowett. The Internet Classics Archive, 381 BCE. Web.

Prayer of the Rollerboys. Directed by Rick King, Academy Entertainment Inc., November 1990. Film.

Private. Directed by Saverio Costanzo, Typecast Releasing, September 10, 2004. Film.

Rihanna. "Kiss It Better." *Anti*, Westbury Road and Roc Nation, 2016. Song.

Rihanna. "Work" ft. Drake. 2016. Music video.

Rist, Pipilotti. *Pixel Forest.* October 26, 2016-January 15, 2017. New Museum, New York. Exhibition.

Rochant, Éric (creator). *Le Bureau des Légendes.* Canal+, April 25, 2015-present (July 11, 2018). TV.

Roman Holiday. Directed by William Wyler, Paramount Pictures, August 27, 1953. Film.

Sheindlin, Judy and Douthit, Randy (creators). *Hot Bench.* CBS, September 15, 2014-present (July 11, 2018). TV.

Solveig, Martin and GTA. "Intoxicated." 2015. Song.

Sontag, Susan. *As Consciousness Is Harnessed to Flesh: Journals and Notebooks, 1964-1980.* Ed. David Rieff. FSG, 2012. Print.

Star, Darren (creator). *Beverly Hills, 90210.* Fox, October 4, 1990-May 17, 2000. TV.

States, Bert O. "Bizarreness in Dreams and other Fictions." *The Dream and the Text: Essays on Literature and Language.* Ed. Carol Schreier Rupprecht. State University of New York Press, 1993. Print.

Stein, Gertrude. *Writings 1903-1932*. Ed. Catharine R. Stimpson and Harriet Chessman. The Library of America, 1998. Print.

Tears for Fears. "Everybody Wants to Rule the World." 1985. Music video.

The 2017 Whitney Biennial. March 17-June 11, 2017. Whitney Museum of American Art, New York. Exhibition.

The Glass Room. November 29-December 18, 2016. 201 Mulberry Street, New York. Exhibition.

The Goonies. Directed by Richard Donner, Warner Bros., June 7, 1985. Film.

Wale. "My PYT." *Shine*, Atlantic, 2016. Song.

Wamsley, Erin J. "Dreaming and Offline Memory Consolidation." *Current neurology and neuroscience reports*. Springer Science. 2014. Web.

Warpaint. "Disco//Very." *Warpaint*, Rough Trade, 2014. Song.

Weil, Simone. *Gravity and Grace*. Routledge & Kegan Paul, 1952. Print.

Wieland, Valerie. "Death of Art: Nonfiction by Chris Campanioni." *New Pages*, October 5, 2016. Web.

Wittgenstein, Ludwig. *Philosophical Investigations*. Trans. G.E.M. Anscombe. Basil Blackwell, 1958. Print.

Wittgenstein, Ludwig. *Tractatus Logico-Philosophicus*. Trans. D.F. Pears and B.F. McGuinness. Routledge, 2001. Print.

Yaz. *You and Me Both*, Mute, 1983. Album.

Yellow Claw. "Till It Hurts" ft. Ayden. 2016. Song.

Chris Campanioni is a first-generation American and the son of immigrants from Cuba and Poland. He lives in Brooklyn, where he runs PANK and PANK Books and edits At Large Magazine and Tupelo Quarterly.

www.chriscampanioni.com

C&R PRESS TITLES

NONFICTION

Women in the Literary Landscape by Doris Weatherford, et al
Credo: An Anthology of Manifestos & Sourcebook for Creative
Writing by Rita Banerjee and Diana Norma Szokolyai

FICTION

Last Tower to Heaven by Jacob Paul
No Good, Very Bad Asian by Lelund Cheuk
Surrendering Appomattox by Jacob M. Appel
Made by Mary by Laura Catherine Brown
Ivy vs. Dogg by Brian Leung
While You Were Gone by Sybil Baker
Cloud Diary by Steve Mitchell
Spectrum by Martin Ott
That Man in Our Lives by Xu Xi

SHORT FICTION

Notes From the Mother Tongue by An Tran
The Protester Has Been Released by Janet Sarbanes

ESSAY AND CREATIVE NONFICTION

In the Room of Persistent Sorry by Kristina Marie Darling
the Internet is for real by Chris Campanioni
Immigration Essays by Sybil Baker
Je suis l'autre: Essays and Interrogations
by Kristina Marie Darling
Death of Art by Chris Campanioni

POETRY

A Family Is a House by Dustin Pearson
The Miracles by Amy Lemmon
Banjo's Inside Coyote by Kelli Allen
Objects in Motion by Jonathan Katz
My Stunt Double by Travis Denton
Lessons in Camoflauge by Martin Ott
Millennial Roost by Dustin Pearson
Dark Horse by Kristina Marie Darling
All My Heroes are Broke by Ariel Francisco
Holdfast by Christian Anton Gerard
Ex Domestica by E.G. Cunningham
Like Lesser Gods by Bruce McEver
Notes from the Negro Side of the Moon by Earl Braggs
Imagine Not Drowning by Kelli Allen
Notes to the Beloved by Michelle Bitting
Free Boat: Collected Lies and Love Poems by John Reed
Les Fauves by Barbara Crooker
Tall as You are Tall Between Them by Annie Christain
The Couple Who Fell to Earth by Michelle Bitting

CPSIA information can be obtained
at www.ICGtesting.com
Printed in the USA
FSHW010851180319
56389FS